he last da

AUTOMATION IN THE TEXTILE INDUSTRY

FROM FIBERS TO APPAREL

Edited by

G. A. Berkstresser III

D. R. Buchanan

P. L. Grady

The Textile Institute

This book is dedicated to all the textile and apparel faculty, researchers and practitioners who are involved in introducing automation into this industrial complex.

G. A. Berkstresser III
D. R. Buchanan
P. L. Grady

© The authors and The Textile Institute 1995

The Textile Institute
International Headquarters
10 Blackfriars Street
Manchester, M3 5DR, UK

ISBN 1 870812 68 9

Printed in the UK by Latimer Trend

PREFACE

Nine years ago two of the editors of this work created the first major book covering automation and robotics in textiles and apparel. Although this first book is now out of print, the continuing demand we have received for it convinced us that a new book would be a real service to the industry.

Many of the authors of the papers contained in this volume have presented results of their work at seminars at N C State University College of Textiles or other conferences, and some have published papers in journals germane to the field. All of the authors continue to be active in research, and all of us feel that this book is merely the second organized collection of knowledge about this admittedly specialized subject matter.

A good part of the credit for the continued support of research in the subject must be given to large publicly-funded projects such as BRITE in the European Community and the National Textile Center in the USA. These mega-programs have allowed researchers to allocate far more resources to the study than had previously been available, and the resulting progress has been documented in the many research papers which have been published.

It is interesting to contemplate the changes in ambitions and reality since our first compilation of this scene was published. Certainly one important change is from an emphasis on automation as a replacement for people to a greater understanding of automation as an integral part, on its own merits, of the manufacturing system.

Another major change is to recognize that automation can have many faces. An emphasis of our first book was on classical robotics, with an implicitly stated view that highly flexible and capable robots could provide answers to most automation issues. This view was confirmed in machinery shows of that era, namely ITMA 83 and ITMA 87. However, we all learned that, for all too many applications, six-axis robots were too expensive, too slow, or too sophisticated for many automation programs. Today, the emphasis has definitely shifted from a view of robots as an off-the-shelf solution to a much more integrated view of intelligent automation, intelligently designed and intelligently applied for specific applications.

Although much of the material is still in a formative stage, the age of automation and robotics in the fiber/textile/apparel industrial complex has clearly dawned and morning is upon us. We are not yet certain just how the move from labor intensive to more capital intensive manufacturing will affect us. Just how many jobs will be lost in manufacturing is not known, nor can we predict the number of jobs that may be created by the increased opportunities for new products which the new types of capital intensive organizations will permit. What is known, however, is that existing firms that are aware of and ready to respond to the changes will have the opportunity to survive. Those who believe in business-as-usual will surely perish.

The editors are in debt to the contributors for their willingness to share their work; to Professor John Hearle for encouragement; to Paul Daniels, Vanessa Knowles, and Freya Rodger for detailed guidance; to Mrs Joann Fish for prompt and accurate typing of the manuscript; and to their families for the understanding support they have given.

G. A. Berkstresser III
D. R. Buchanan
P. L. Grady

Raleigh, North Carolina
February 1995

Contents

INTRODUCTION

**Manufacturing Innovation, Automation and Robotics in the
Textile Industries** 3
D. R. Buchanan
Introduction 3
   Issues of International Competitiveness 3
The Nature of Manufacturing Innovation 4
   Traditional Measures of Manufacturing Efficiency 4
   New Requirements for Manufacturing Efficiency 6
   New Measures of Efficiency 7
   New Measures of Quality 8
   New Measures of Flexibility 9
The Role of Automation in Innovation 9
   The Proper Purposes of Automation 9
   Characteristics of Proper Automation 10
   Automation in the Fiber Industry 12
   Automation in the Textile Industry 12
   Automation in the Apparel Industry 13
   Automation in the Retail Industry 14
   The Role of Information Transfer in Innovation 14
Conclusions 15

TECHNOLOGY OF AUTOMATION

Computer Integrated Manufacturing in the Textile Industries 19
P. L. Grady, G. N. Mock, T. G. Clapp, and H. Hamouda
Introduction 19
Computer Aided Design Systems 23
Yarn Manufacturing 23
Fabric Manufacturing 24
Dyeing 27
Automated Material Handling 29
Robotics 30
Conclusion 31

**Requirements for Process Integration and Automation in
Textile Manufacturing** 34
J. Eapen
Overcoming the Barriers to Process Integration and Automation 34
Management Commitment 36
Justification of Process Control Systems and Automation Projects 36
Vendor Selection 36
Vendor-user Partnership 37

The Requirements for Automation in Today's Textile
   Manufacturing Environment 38
J. L. Eckert

Electronic Data Interchange: the Business Tool of Quick Response 40
T. J. Little
Introduction 40
Linkage Background 41
The Need for Other Linkages 42
The Formation of Trading Partnerships 43
Linkage Between Trading Partners 43
Electronic Data Interchange 44
Definitions, Hardware and Software 46
Public Data Networks 46
Size of the Electronic Commerce Market 47
Benefits Resulting from EDI 47
American National Standards Institute (ANSI) 48
Transaction Sets and Transmission Structures 48
Implementation of Electronic Data Interchange 50
EDI Directions 52
Summary 53

Quick Response and Technology 54
A. Hunter
Quality 56
Electronic Data Interchange and Linkage 58
Non-traditional Methods of Assessing Capital Expenditures 63
A Technology Model 64

MANAGING OF AUTOMATION
Making Investment Decisions — The Age of Discontinuity Revisited 69
R. A. Barnhardt, G. A. Berkstresser, and G. L. Hodge

Multiple Attributes/Criteria for Evaluating Manufacturing Systems 75
G. L. Hodge and J. R. Canada

Low Cost Microcomputer Software for Non-traditional Economic
   Decision Analysis 79
G. L. Hodge and J. R. Canada

Persistent Pitfalls and Applicable Approaches for Justification of Advanced Manufacturing Systems 85
J. R. Canada and W. G. Sullivan
Introduction 85
    Hurdle Rates 85
    Comparison with the Status Quo 86
    Incomplete Benefits Analysis 86
Justification Studies 86
    Quantifying Tangible Benefits 87
    Examples of Breakeven Approach to Intangible Benefits 87
    Other Economic Analysis Impediments 88
Cost Accounting Anachronisms... 89
    Cost Assignment for AMS 89
    Equipment Rental 90
    AMS Mortgage Model 91
Conclusions 92

Evaluation of Computer-integrated Manufacturing Systems 93
J. R. Canada
Introduction and Need 93
Methodology and Examples 94
    Opportunity Selection 96
    Alternative Selection 97
    Mutually Exclusive Combinations and Interdependent Effects 102
Summary 104

Is Investment in Technology a Winning Strategy? 105
J. M. Childress II
Global Competition 105
Technological Revolution 105
Mergers and Acquisitions 106
Why Does the US Lag in Reinvesting in New Technology? 108
Applying Decision Methodologies.. 108
    Quantifying Today's Key Business Issues 108
    Internal Hurdle Rates 110
    Inflation 110
    The No-investment Alternative 110
    Incremental Investing 111
International Structural Differences 111
    Examples 111
    Europe 111
    Pacific Basin 112
    Government Influence 112
Is Investment in Technology a Winning Business Strategy? 113
A Lesson from History 113
Textile Winners and Losers 114

ECONOMIC AND HUMAN FACTORS

Factor Input and Output in the German Textile Industry –
An Econometric Approach 117

F. W. Peren

Introduction 117
Econometric Models 118
Empirical Results 125
Conclusion 139

Technology, Trade, and the Future of the US Textile and Apparel Industry . 143

H. C. Kelley

The Argument 143
How to Think about Technology 144
Some Recent History 147
Emerging Technologies and the Nature of Trade 150
Where do We Go from Here? 153

Human Resource Management in the Modern Textile and
Apparel Industries 154

T. Bailey

Introduction 154
The Traditional Production System 155
The Traditional Human Resource Strategy 156
Pressures on the Traditional Production System 157
The Emerging System of Production 158
Technology 159
Organizational Change within the Firm 160
Industry Structure 160
Human Resource Implications 162
Technology and the Traditional Human Resource System 162
Industry Transformation and the Decline of the Traditional Human
Resource System 163
Elements of a New Human Resources Strategy 165

Educating Managers for Advanced Manufacturing Environments 169

R. A. Barnhardt

Attributes of an Ideal Employee 172
Preparing Better Graduates 174
Characteristics of Textile Education 175

Training for an Automated Textile Industry 179

G. A. Berkstresser and K. Takeuchi

INTRODUCTION

Manufacturing Innovation, Automation and Robotics in the Fiber, Textile, and Apparel Industries

D. R. Buchanan

College of Textiles, North Carolina State University

INTRODUCTION

Issues of International Competitiveness

The competitiveness of American manufacturing industries is facing a severe challenge. Indeed, the United States faces the real prospect of a major decline both in influence and in wealth if steps are not taken to regain the ability to compete strongly in the international practice of manufacturing. While there are a number of issues that seem peculiar to the fiber-textile-apparel manufacturing complex, the general issues apply equally to all industry — both high-tech and low-tech, consumer goods and speciality products, new and traditional. The answers are not easy, but at this time, it is not even evident that many of the questions are understood.

A number of questionable strategies have been proposed for regaining economic competitiveness. Among these are the following:
 (i)   The United States should accept its decline in manufacturing superiority, since economic evolution requires that a country progress from agriculture to manufacturing industry to service industry. Service industries, particularly those involving intellectual and information services, are the highest and most respectable form of economic endeavor, and we should welcome the transition.
 (ii) US manufacturing industries should be protected from unfair foreign competition — caused by low labor rates, unfair foreign government intervention, or other factors — by imposing substantial trade restrictions on imports.
 (iii) Adopting the new technology that will allow an industry to compete effectively is easy. All that prevents affected industries from doing so is their own conservatism and reluctance to invest (applied often to the traditional industries, and particularly to the textile and apparel industries).
 (iv) There is a new technology out there that, if invented or discovered, would completely transform an industry from non-competitiveness to competitiveness. All that is lacking is the will to innovate.
These are all simplistic solutions, however. The true key to any country's

manufacturing competitiveness lies in its understanding of the uses of manufacturing innovation as a strategic policy for enhancing the demand of both the domestic and the international marketplace for that country's products. Other countries have understood this better than the United States. Manufacturing innovation, in contrast to other kinds of innovation, is poorly appreciated. Its essential elements are just beginning to be understood. As we will see, it has elements of production efficiency and product quality, concepts that have been understood and practiced by American manufacturers. However, it is dominated by the concepts of manufacturing flexibility in response to the demands of the marketplace. These concepts are not yet well understood, particularly in a culture whose manufacturing tradition embodies the precepts of mass production and production efficiencies through production volume.

THE NATURE OF MANUFACTURING INNOVATION

Traditional Measures of Manufacturing Efficiency

For most Americans, our understanding of innovation is based in what we were taught about the Industrial Revolution as schoolchildren. Typically, we learned that the Industrial Revolution represented the invention and widespread adoption of machines that replaced human muscles with machine power. The primary example is the steam engine. Rarely is it mentioned in grade school texts that English textile manufacturing was the primary motivator and the main immediate beneficiary of these inventions. Nor is it mentioned that arguably the most important invention of all was a system — the factory system — in which textile manufacturing endeavors located in homes were consolidated under one roof and powered by a common source-falling water.

The result, both of the introduction of the factory system and the invention of individual machines, such as the fly-shuttle loom and the spinning jenny, was that the manufacture of textile products started a long process of ever-improving worker productivity that continues to the present day. Some 25 years ago, Hans Krause of the Swiss Federal Institute of Technology gave a Textile Institute Mather Lecture, in which he first presented the famous graph that shows this continuing productivity improvement very convincingly. Krause's graph shows that discrete machinery inventions have increased worker productivity in both the yarn and fabric manufacturing areas by a factor of 10 every 50–60 years since the Industrial Revolution. The total productivity increase over the 250 years since the Industrial Revolution is a factor of between 10,000 and 100,000 (Figure 1).

As important as these inventions were to manufacturing productivity, the new factory system, which had to be developed in response to the capabilities of the new machines, had the most long-lasting effect. Because of the factory system, mass production became possible, with a consequent lowering of prices for textile goods and increasing demand for them. Just as important for England, the factory system, together with the new production machinery, gave English textile companies dominance in world markets for several hundred years. As a result, the factory system and mass production became the world's model of how manufacturing systems should be operated, and this influence

4

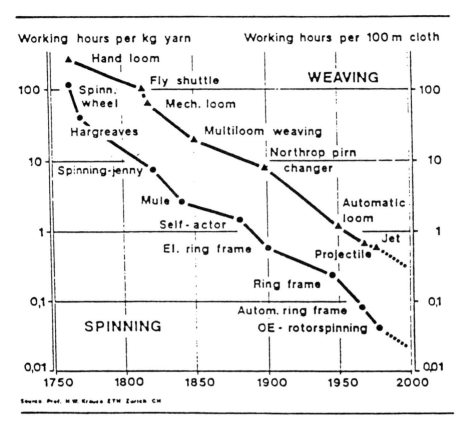

Fig. 1   Changes in Worker Productivity since 1750 Spinning and Weaving (Source: H. Krause, ETH Zurich)

was brought to the American colonies (by Samuel Slater, who had to disguise himself and memorize every detail of the technology to escape the British embargo on exporting that technology).

The mass production model of manufacturing was refined and improved by a succession of American entrepreneurs, including Henry Ford, until the United States led the world in manufacturing ability from about 100 years ago up until only recently. The American textile industry enjoyed its share of this dominance. Starting with the early 1970s however, American manufacturing firms started to undergo increasing pressure from products imported, for the most part, from countries that had rebuilt from the devastation of World War II. These countries had the benefit of being forced to start with relatively new technology, their old capabilities having been destroyed, and the opportunity to rethink the old ways of managing manufacturing enterprises. One of the leaders in this innovation was Japan, which introduced a new concept of manufacturing efficiency.

New Requirements for Manufacturing Efficiency

Traditional measures of manufacturing efficiency have been calculated in terms of the output per worker hour for the manufacture of a specific product. This is the concept shown in the Krause diagram (Figure 1). It is important to note that worker productivity, hence manufacturing efficiency, has historically been dependent on the invention of machines (that is, automation) to allow a single worker to produce more and more product over the decades. For Krause's examples of woven fabric production and spun yarn production, the increase in worker efficiency in the industrialized West has been 10 times every 50 or 60 years for the last 200+ years.

But the advent of competition from 'threshold' countries and 'developing' countries has changed the effect of this systematic improvement of manufacturing efficiency for the textile industries of the 'industrialized West'. These terms were introduced by H.H. Kaup, in a speech delivered at the 1987 Man-Made Fibers Conference in Dornbirn, Austria. In Kaup's terms the 'industrialized West' includes the United States, Canada, Australia, New Zealand, Israel, South Africa, Western Europe, and Japan. 'Threshold' countries include Turkey, Mexico, South Korea, Taiwan, Hong Kong, Malaysia, and Singapore. 'Developing' countries include China, India, the near East, developing African countries, and Central and South American countries. Even though this speech was delivered seven years ago, the definitions still seem appropriate today.

Figure 2 shows that each of these three groups of countries is on a different point of the industry life-cycle curve, which was constructed from data for industry growth rates in the period 1960–1985. From their position on this life-cycle curve, the textile industries of the industrialized West can be classified as mature industries, while those of eastern

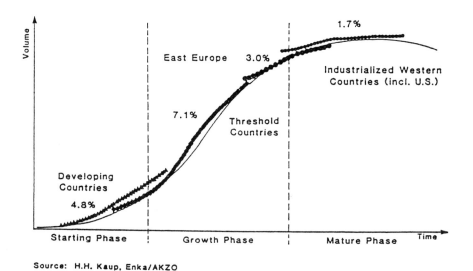

Source: H.H. Kaup, Enka/AKZO

Fig. 2   Life Cycle Curves for the World's Textile Industries (1960–1985)

6

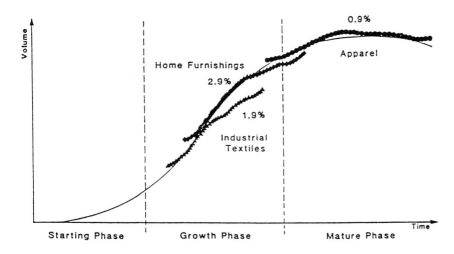

Source: H.H. Kaup, Enka/AKZO

Fig. 3   *Product Life Cycle Curves for the Textile Industries of the Industrialized Western Countries (1960–1985)*

Europe and the threshold countries are in the growth phase of their life cycles. On the horizon is competition for all from the developing countries, which currently are only in the start-up phase of the life cycle curve.

However, to consider the textile industries of the United States and western Europe as simple mature industries is somewhat misleading, as Figure 3 shows. Only the apparel portion of these industries is in a mature phase, if mature is defined by an essentially flat growth. The home furnishings and the industrial portions of these industries clearly are in the growth region of this product life-cycle curve. Thus the 'mature industry' problems of the western textile complex are essentially those of the apparel-related segment. These problems affect, however, all parts of the textile industrial complex — from fiber production through yarn and fabric manufacture to the manufacture of apparel goods. In the United States, at least, it finally is being realized that solutions to problems in one portion of the complex bring benefits to all of the members of the complex.

The increasingly held view that all parts of the textile complex are interrelated is accompanied by a necessary corollary: new measures of production efficiency are necessary, since it is the production efficiency of the complex that is important, as well as the production efficiency of the individual members of that complex.

New Measures of Efficiency

This alternate manufacturing system is characterized by the fact that productivity, quality, and flexibility are equally the goals sought by a particular firm. Furthermore, the firm's

7

inputs and outputs of material, products, and information depend greatly on the ability of its suppliers and customers to also operate with high productivity, high quality, and high flexibility.

In this model of manufacturing, which has been used by many Japanese manufacturing firms with great success, a general reorganization of manufacturing strategies has been accomplished that leads to:

(i)   reduced inventories,
(ii) improved material flows,
(iii) altered quality control processes, and
(iv) reduced labor content.

More important, the relation between production and corporate strategy has been altered.

The new corporate strategy is characterized by the view that manufacturing is a competitive weapon to be used to capture markets. This strategy is based on the view that low cost is not the most important characteristic of the system. Instead, production systems should be evaluated in terms of their yields of products suitable for the marketplace at a particular instant. The organization of production should allow the rapid and timely introduction of new products as they are demanded by the marketplace. Such a production system must be organized to allow its continual modification, so that it can be improved and adapted quickly to new circumstances.

In this system, advanced production techniques are not an alternative to skilled workers. These manufacturing systems derive their flexibility from continuous production innovation and they require both an in-house equipment design capability and a work force skilled enough to adapt to continual change.

New Measures of Quality

In the old manufacturing philosophy, quality was important, but it was the quality characteristic of the manufacturing process that was meant. In this philosophy, quality was judged by manual inspection methods whose goals were:

(i)   to assess the price to be charged for each product based on its quality level;
(ii) to provide statistical information for management from which worker pay and the overall efficiency of the process could be determined; and
(iii) to detect, after the fact, faults in the manufacturing process.

In this system, there was no real-time process feedback; what information was obtained was applied hours or days later.

An innovative manufacturing system uses quality as a measure of how well the manufacturing process meets customer quality requirements, and it also provides real-time feedback and (ideally) control to correct quality problems as they occur. Because of the emphases on real-time activities, manual inspection at separate stations out of the manufacturing sequence is usually not adequate. Manual inspection stations must be replaced by automated inspection systems, located within the manufacturing sequence. A significant feature of these systems is their ability to transmit quality information directly to the customer for his use, as well as to the process for its control.

New Measures of Flexibility

One of the dangers of conventional automation of textile mills is that the completely modernized, automated mill lacks flexibility and the ability to turn around quickly. High throughput production and large-scale dedicated operations perform poorly when the situation calls for production flexibility and fast turnarounds.

The new flexibility must be characterized by decreased emphasis on both 'volume production' and on 'standard product', and increased emphasis on production and products suitable for a market demand that is continually changing. It requires both more flexible, less specialized machinery, and, most of all, new thinking about the organization of manufacturing activity. There are two kinds of flexibility.

A firm capable of static flexibility has the ability to adjust operations at any moment to changes in the mix of products the market is demanding. If one of the firm's products is not selling, another can be produced instantaneously. For a firm to be able to utilize this kind of flexibility, it must appreciate the difference between economies of scale and economies of scope. Economies of scale are based on the traditional mass production principle that the cost of producing a single unit decreases as the volume of that unit increases. On the other hand, economies of scope are gained in the overall volume production of an array of goods, not in the volume production of a single product. Both scope and scale may be present in a real manufacturing system.

A firm capable of dynamic flexibility has the ability to increase productivity by the improvement of production processes and through product innovation. It has the ability to put new ideas and technologies into use quickly, and is particularly adept at assessing and implementing new automation technologies, as they become available. However, in order that the introduction of new automation technologies will result in improved manufacturing flexibility, and not just in greater production efficiency or in decreased dependence on human labor, it is necessary to understand what ought to be expected from automation.

THE ROLE OF AUTOMATION IN INNOVATION

The Proper Purposes of Automation

In a little-noticed speech delivered in 1984, David Pearl, then the President of Gerber Garment Technology Inc., suggested that the proper purpose of automation in the apparel industry is not the mere replacement of human labor, but rather the accomplishing of three things:
  (i)   improvement of the marketability of the product to ensure the selling of more units, and thus the generation of more income;
  (ii) improvement of the efficiency of production, thus reducing unit costs while supplying the increased demand; and
  (iii) allowing optimal management control of both marketing and manufacturing, thereby balancing income and expense to allow maximum profitability.

Characteristics of Proper Automation

On this view, proper automation ought to possess one or more of the following characteristics:

(i) It should improve manufacturing efficiency, either in terms of output, quality, or the ability to use new processes that, themselves, will enhance output and/or quality.

(ii) It should improve product quality, both in terms of the customer's quality requirement and in terms of providing ways of controlling the production process to ensure consistent and reproducible quality.

(iii) It should provide a firm with the capability to practice either static flexibility — the ability to move easily within a product mix in response to changing market conditions — or, better, dynamic flexibility — the continuing ability to bring new products to market in a timely and effective manner.

(iv) It should contribute to the ability of management to exert control on the entire range of the firm's activities, encompassing product design, manufacturing, and marketing, in a timely and effective manner.

Historically, technological change in the textile industry could be classified by the effect it had on the industry. Evolutionary change had the effect of replacing humans with machines, or human power with machine power, so that production efficiency was improved. The new technology often performed better, sometimes produced a better quality product, and even eliminated some process steps. However, the key concept is that the task being performed is little different than was being performed before. Two of many examples are the invention, 250 years ago, of the fly-shuttle loom, which allowed the manufacture of wider, better quality woven fabrics than was possible when human power threw the shuttle through the shed; and the invention of open-end spinning just 30 years ago, in which an entirely new process was capable of making high-quality yarns in some counts and eliminating several traditional processes as well. It should be noted, however, that in both of these examples the product being made had, and has, some significant differences compared with the old way.

Interestingly, these kinds of inventions are often associated with measures of automation and/or modernization. Tables I and II show assessments of these concepts for several countries in weaving (use of shuttleless looms) and in yarn making (use of open-end spinning). However, the concepts shown in Tables I and II tend to ignore the rules for 'proper automation' stated earlier. Both shuttleless looms and open-end spinning frames are good examples of automation only if the products they can make are suitable for the market being targeted.

Revolutionary change ought to be recognized by the major changes that it forces on entire industries. The invention of the factory system at the Industrial Revolution is a fine example. Likewise, the invention of the computer has revolutionized entire industries, including the textile industry, in recent years. These examples suggest that most single inventions, such as those displayed at the international machinery shows, do not themselves qualify for revolutionary change agents; however, systems of such inventions are exactly what bring about revolutionary change in manufacturing. The factory system was made possible only after the invention of the fly-shuttle loom, the spinning jenny, and power

10

Table I
Rate of Modernization and Level of Technology in Weaving
by Selected Countries (%) — 1980–85

Country	Rate of Modernization (%)[1]	Level of Technology (%)[2]
USA	17.7	39.4
Hong Kong	19.0	26.7
Taiwan	22.7	24.9
South Korea	19.8	8.4
China	0.9	1.0
Japan	11.3	11.8
Italy	25.1	47.7

[1] Ratio of deliveries of new looms during 1980–1985 to installed capacity at the end of 1985.
[2] Ratio of installed capacity of shuttleless looms to total installed loom capacity operating on the cotton system at the end of 1985.
Source: Compiled by the staff of the US International Trade Commission based on data published by the International Textile Manufacturers Federation in International Textile Machinery Shipment Statistics, 1981 and 1986.

Table II
Rate of Modernization and Level of Technology in Spinning in Selected Countries (%)

Country	Rate of Modernization[1]			Level of Technology[2]
	Short staple sector	Long staple sector	Open end rotors	Short staple sector
USA	2.7	10.4	77.7	6.1
Hong Kong	14.4	3.6	86.5	30.8
Taiwan	19.7	N.A.	49.0	5.9
South Korea	9.2	10.6	41.0	2.4
China	0.7	6.3	46.0	1.4
Japan	6.8	2.5	14.0	5.3
Italy	21.3	14.8	98.4	7.6

[1] Ratio of deliveries of new equipment during 1980–1985 to installed capacity at the end of 1985.
[2] Ratio of stocks of open end spinning rotors to total installed spindle capacity as of 31 December 1985 (one open end spinning rotor is equivalent to 2.5 spindles).
Source: Compiled by the staff of the US International Trade Commission based on data published by the International Textile Manufacturers Federation.

transmission devices necessary to operate them. It is not really the computer that has revolutionized industry, but rather it is the ability through software to apply the computer's skills to an entire spectrum of technical and managerial problems, with a response time that could not be imagined 50 years ago, that has completely transformed the way we operate an industry.

Since it is the accumulation of manufacturing process inventions, each of them probably evolutionary, that lead to the major revolutionary changes necessary for the new textile manufacturing industry, we should monitor quite closely those inventions or applications that seem to be leading us in that direction. Important examples of technological change, that nearly always have an automation component, can be seen at every major fiber, textile, or apparel machinery exhibition.

Automation in the Fiber Industry

A major direction for evolutionary change in extrusion technology is the continuing integration of extrusion with downstream processes. Today it is possible to find commercial examples for spin-draw-wind, spin-draw-warp, and spin-draw-texture processes. These technologies place a different emphasis on material handling requirements; robotic technologies for package doffing and transport are increasingly available and yet, because of the linking of processes, need be placed only at critical points in the overall process.

The emphasis on flexible manufacturing, even in the fiber industry, has led to the development by some fiber producers of robotic techniques for the rapid change and replacement of spin packs and spinnerettes. In these examples, robots are called upon to do what humans cannot do — change hot parts before they have cooled.

Automated inspection of yarn packages for broken ends, poor package building, improper tensions, and misidentified packages is a goal being pursued by a number of fiber producers. At least one system is available commercially. Speed and cost remain problems in this area — accuracy usually is not a problem.

The history of the man-made fiber industry has emphasized process control more than any other segment of the textile complex. Increasing emphasis on product uniformity and adherence to quality standards continues to require fiber diameter monitoring, temperature and tension control, and monitoring of the solution properties of the polymer. These requirements are especially critical in microdenier fiber extrusion, a process that produces fibers and eventually fabrics of truly different properties, and therefore a possible example of revolutionary change.

Automation in the Textile Industry

In the primary textile industry, tentative applications of robotics have now a fairly long history, although with relatively few commercial successes. Starting with the 1983 ITMA in Milan, a number of robots have been shown, at first doing only very simple jobs. However, vendors have learned that robotics are more applicable to textile processes when they are combined with other forms of automation to form a system.

Typical uses of robots are in the material handling areas. Just as with extrusion, the trend toward the linking of processes actually simplifies material handling issues. Thus, systems for handling yarn packages at the output of spinning systems, or at the input to dyeing systems are quite commonly available. Other notable uses of robotic automation are the class of automatic guided vehicles (AGV's) in use in some US textile mills. When coupled with appropriate trailers, these systems move yarn, fabrics, and other materials throughout a plant on a Just In Time basis. Since the entire system is computer-controlled, integration of a plant's processes becomes much easier.

Process linkage is an extremely important form of automation. It can be observed in the offerings of most spinning system manufacturers, in most nonwovens lines, and in many dyeing and finishing systems. In spinning systems, the typical system features automated material transfer from point to point in the system — with appropriate provision for balancing the system as yarn counts change. Computer monitoring of the system allows tracking of material throughout the entire process, and the early warning of problems in operation.

Process linkage in nonwovens systems takes a somewhat different form. Computerized process control is combined with the computerized setting and/or adjustment of machine mechanisms through the use of servo-mechanisms. Thus, to change a style, the operator simply enters the style number into a console. In response, card settings, cross-lapper settings, and thermo-bonding settings, for example, are all changed automatically.

Process linkage in dyeing and finishing systems depends heavily on computer monitoring and control of each process. It also uses some sophisticated material handling automation to aid the transfer of material between process steps.

Automated inspection of yarn packages and of fabrics was shown for the first time at the 1987 ITMA. These systems depended on highly sophisticated machine vision techniques, and elegant computer hardware, and were, it turns out, premature for the market. They were costly and limited in the numbers and types of defects that they could detect reliably. Today's commercially available systems make use of imaging technology developed for satellite reconnaissance. Even so, the problem is not considered solved in terms of cost effectiveness.

Automation in the Apparel Industry

In no segment of the textile manufacturing complex have more dramatic changes taken place than in the apparel industry. Two major technologies — computers and robotics — have made a major impact on the possibilities, if not the actual practice, of technology change in this industry.

Today it is possible to integrate totally the fabric design, apparel design, marker (pattern) making, spreading, and cutting processes. This integration is a prime example of the result of integrating information throughout a series of linked processes. As the designer specifies fabric pattern and then the shapes of parts necessary to produce a garment, this information is used to guide the packing of pieces on the fabric to be cut, and eventually a robotic cutter uses the same data to physically cut the fabric plies.

It is at this point that difficulties arise. The manipulation and handling of fabric parts is not nearly so far advanced as the computer technology used to prepare them. Considerable research throughout the world is devoted to the issue of moving fabric pieces through the assembly system in a semiautomatic way.

One of the best ways to move material efficiently and reduce in-process time in the assembly process is to replace the bundle system of fabric handling with the 'unit production system'. This represents an excellent example of automation that affects the philosophy of the manufacturing processes. The unit production system requires that assembly operations treat a shirt, for example, as a unit that is to be assembled as a unit in the shortest possible time, rather than, as in the case of the older bundle system, as a series of partially-complete assemblies that are completed together at some future time.

Automated devices for apparel assembly are being shown at machinery shows on a continuing basis. Many of them combine robotic principles with hard automation modules, to completely automate a portion of the assembly process. Unfortunately, the flexibility of these devices, with respect to their ability to operate on widely different fabric types, is not yet as good as it should be. Research on the relation between fabric properties and the requirements for automation is needed, and is currently underway.

Automation in the Retail Industry

The new flexibility required of manufacturing processes in the textile complex implies that information about market needs can be obtained in an accurate and timely fashion. For many textile products, this translates to the requirement that retailers must have accurate information about which items sell and which do not. The situation is complicated by the fact that the number of stock units to be tracked is very large — including information on style, color, and size. For a standard item such as a woman's blouse, over 100 categories may apply to one blouse alone.

Point-of-sale tracking, applied routinely in the US to supermarket sales, is starting to be introduced into apparel sales. Readily available computer hardware and software are an essential element for the success of this initiative, but ways of uniquely identifying each garment are also necessary. This requirement is met by the widespread adoption of bar-coding technology. Interestingly, one of the principle barriers has been the lack, until recently, of a uniform coding system. However, industry voluntary standards groups have made great progress toward specifying a uniform coding system in the last few years.

The Role of Information Transfer in Innovation

Automation of an entire complex industry requires considerable attention to the structure of that complex and the ways in which members of that complex may interact. Activities in the United States that promise to promote integration in the textile complex are centered around the theme of 'Quick Response'. Quick Response philosophy requires modification of production processes and fundamental changes in manufacturing logistics, as well as improved communications between buyer and supplier. The success of this philosophy, even in a primitive version, is demonstrated by the success of initial retailer-apparel manufacturer-textile supplier collaborations in combining to deliver products to the consumer in a timely manner.

Communication is one of the keys to a successful Quick Response strategy. In an industry as fragmented as the textile complex, uniform protocols and descriptions of communication processes are essential. In the US, this is being accomplished by industry standards groups, which have been successful in enlisting large numbers of members from the industry.

The linking of processes within different firms is another issue of great interest. Process linkage in this sense means something different from process linkage of machines. Rather, finding ways to integrate material and information flow between firms as well as within a manufacturing operation is needed. Research is in progress to develop dynamic models, in the operations research sense, of the way in which information and/or material travels through the industry complex. Successful models will also provide ways of assessing the effect of adopting new technologies not only on the operation of an individual firm, but on the operation of the entire complex.

14

CONCLUSIONS

(i)   Weakness in production innovation leads to competitiveness and trade problems.

(ii)   The definition of manufacturing innovation has changed. It no longer refers exclusively to the invention and application of new production machinery and technology. Instead, it must include, and indeed is driven by, the need for the invention of new manufacturing systems.

(iii)   These new manufacturing systems must be characterized by the ability to alter the product manufactured depending on the needs of the market. This flexibility may be static — allowing easy changes in product mix from a well-defined manufacturing capability at the very least. But these systems should also have elements of dynamic flexibility — the ability to alter the very nature and output of a firm, through the rapid, efficient, and continuing introduction of new manufacturing technologies.

(iv)   The development of the new technologies must come from a variety of sources. They will include not only developments in automation and robotics, but also developments in information transfer. For most of these sources to be effective, substantial levels of inter-industry cooperation will be required.

BIBLIOGRAPHY

'Competing in the Global Economy', National Association of Manufacturers, 1987.

'IAMB: Bigger, Better', *App. Ind. Mag.*, August 1988, p.66.

'ITMA '87 Review', Raleigh, NC: North Carolina State University, 1987.

'ITMA '91' Review, Raleigh, NC: North Carolina State University, 1991.

'Technology and the Competitive Challenge', *Res. & Dev.*, July 1988, p.44.

D. R. Buchanan, 'Directions of Technological Change in the Fiber, Textile and Apparel Industries' in *'Automation and Robotics in the Textile and Apparel Industries'*, G.A. Berkstresser and D.R. Buchanan, ed., Park Ridge, NJ: Noyes Publications, 1986.

J. Carey, 'The Myth that American Can't Complete', *Bus. Week*, Innovation 1990.

Steven S. Cohen and John Zysman. 'Manufacturing Matters: The Myth of the Post-Industrial Economy', Basic Books Inc., New York, USA, 1987.

Steven S. Cohen and John Zysman. 'Manufacturing Innovation and American Industrial Competitiveness', *Science, 239*, 1988, 1110.

T. Finnie and J. Werner. 'The Changing Face of the US Textile Industry', *The Executive Letter 1* (9) June 1989.

George N. Hatsopoulos, Paul R. Krugman, and Lawrence H. Summers. 'US Competitiveness: Beyond the Trade Deficit', *Science, 241*, 1988, 299.

H.H. Kaup. 'Chemiefasern im Wettberwerb' (Man-made Fibers in Competition), International Fiber Producers Conference — Dornbirn, May 1987.

H. Krause in A. Heusser. 'The Shape of Weaving Machines to Come', *Tex. Ind.*, September 1983, p.109.

Edwin Mansfield. 'Industrial Innovation in Japan and the United States', *Science, 241*, 1988, 1769.

D. R. Pearl. 'Automating the Clothing Industry', *Tex. Asia*, September 1984, p.109.

TECHNOLOGY OF AUTOMATION

Computer Integrated Manufacturing in the Textile Industries

P. L. Grady, G. N. Mock, T. Clapp and
H. Hamouda
College of Textiles, North Carolina State University

INTRODUCTION

The era of applying computers to textile operations has evolved into the era of computer integrated textile manufacturing. This has taken place in certain segments to the point that yarn and fabric manufacturing can now be reasonably referred to as being computer integrated, and it is easy to see the possibility that the entire fiber, textile, and apparel pipeline can be integrated by computer networks in the next few years. In order for this integration to occur, many different things must happen. If certain events, such as setting standards for electronics, take place, all the computer applications will jell into efficient networks, but if care is not taken, all the computer systems being designed may create an information gridlock. This problem and a possible solution are discussed in an Institute of Textile Technology white paper [1].

For many years, we have seen the development of monitoring and control systems in textile manufacturing with most of the emphasis on monitoring in dry processing and with control applications being limited, for the most part, to wet processing. Recently, there have been many movements toward controlling dry processing machines as well, and true control of these machines appears to be coming of age. We have also witnessed the development of computer-aided design (CAD) and some islands of automation that we would legitimately call computer-aided manufacturing (CAM). Now several companies are claiming to have computer integrated textile manufacturing available on a plant-wide basis. In actual practice, this is still in the future but the technology to accomplish this is near reality.

This paper will concentrate on the overall use of instrumentation, process monitoring and control, and how they can be integrated by the use of computers. Each process area will be analyzed in more detail in later papers. First, a few general concepts will be discussed to set the stage for discussions of particular textile processes.

As automation increases in the textile and related industries, the need to integrate equipment from different sources will reach a point where a non-proprietary protocol will be essential to facilitate further progress. The automotive industry has already reached that point. General Motors has initiated the development of the Manufacturing Automation Protocol (MAP) for specifying standards to link computers and computer controlled devices. Automation in the textile industry is rapidly reaching the critical point where a similar non-proprietary communication standard is needed. The textile industry may already be past the critical point without realizing it. Some benefits that are expected from such a communication protocol are [2]:

(i)   Ability to integrate multi-vendor control and measurement systems;
(ii) Integrated information flow throughout the plant;
(iii) Reduction in integration costs and risks;
(iv) Faster new process implementation;
(v)   Increased flexibility for network modification and expansion; and
(vi) Improved quality of communication service.

Boeing Computer Services has initiated a related effort to MAP that has led to the Technical and Office Protocol (TOP) for office and engineering environments.

Electronic Data Interchange generally refers to transmitting data between computers, but in the textile industry, it has been used to specifically describe the sharing of product information between a vendor and client (e.g., fabric width measurements from a textile company to an apparel manufacturer) [3]. The Textile-Apparel Linkage Council (TALC) has promoted this type of interchange and developed standards for its implementation. The Voluntary Interindustry Communications Standards (VICS) [4] committee has been formed to develop voluntary standards for item identification, electronic data interchange and case coding for textile, apparel, and home furnishing manufacturing and the retail industries. In addition, the Fabric and Suppliers Linkage Council (FASLINC) promotes linkage between the natural and synthetic fiber, yarn, fabric, dye, chemicals, and supply manufacturers [5]. The Textile and Apparel Machinery Modernization Foundation (TAMMF) funded a project to study factory communications standards and CIM/LINC has been formed to address the need for an implementation of voluntary CIM standards in the apparel industry [6].

Everyone is familiar with the use of bar coding in grocery stores. It is beginning to be used more widely in the textile industry, and groups like TALC, VICS, and FASLINC are working to set standards that will facilitate its use. Soon, it will probably be an unusual textile manufacturing plant that does not use bar coding in some form.

Bidirectional communication refers to the ability to transmit, as well as receive, information to and from production machines [7]. Machines, such as looms, can now be adjusted and controlled by a computer in addition to being monitored.

Just In Time (JIT) and Quick Response (QR) [4,8] are terms that refer to manufacturing plant operating philosophies intended to reduce inventories, improve flexibility, and allow the textile and related industries to respond quickly to customers' needs. Having the advantage of location near the customer, combined with quick response, should give US industries a 'home team' advantage in competition with imports. Implementation of JIT and QR is moving rapidly and creating many new demands for computers and electronics in textiles.

Automation has a number of benefits that enhance quick response and facilitates implementation of the 'Just In Time' management philosophy. A partial list of these benefits is given as follows:

• Reduction of work-in-process time,
• Reduction of work-in-process inventory,

- Enhanced flexibility,
- Improved scheduling, and
- Improved production control.

The 'Quick Response' management philosophy requires a never ending quest to reduce work-in-process (WIP) time. As the WIP time decreases, the time required to complete an order decreases. Technological developments for automation will reduce WIP time.

The majority of automated devices and processes are computer controlled. As the industry moves in the direction of computer integrated manufacturing (CIM), information will be available to automatically modify machine parameters for different products.

Computer-generated weave patterns can now be used to instantly control a new automated draw-in-frame. In the nonwovens area, many machines can automatically set cards, cross-lappers, needle looms, and calenders using a computer. These examples illustrate a reduction in time to receive and process information and a reduction in change-over or set-up time between product lots. Flexibility is also greatly enhanced by the versatility of machines that can automatically change operating parameters.

Other benefits of automation are a reduction in WIP inventory, improved scheduling, and production control. WIP inventory is reduced as automated handling systems link processes and are able to automatically feed subsequent processes on demand. Yarn manufacturing highlighted automated material handling and linking of processes, which will be discussed later in this paper.

Automated systems generally perform at higher efficiencies and speeds on a continuous basis. These improvements result in increased production, more accurate forecasting of job completion times, and improved scheduling of material flow through the plant.

Automation will improve efforts to achieve 'Quick Response' management strategies. Past 'hard' automation is being replaced by computer-controlled automated systems that enhance flexibility and overall manufacturing response. Look for machinery that can be automatically set-up and controlled electronically. Capital investment decisions should include flexibility when automation is being considered. Also, the capability of the automated system to be set-up and controlled by a central computer will be important as mills become more integrated.

Artificial Intelligence (AI) implies that a machine makes 'reasoned judgments' [9] and an Expert System is theoretically created by assembling the knowledge of an expert into a computer program enabling the computer to act somewhat like a human expert. This is, of course, very difficult to accomplish in practice, but the application of these concepts to textiles can increase our ability to deal with very complex problems. Exactly what constitutes artificial intelligence and expert systems is still being debated, but software of this type is being created for use in the textile industry [10,11].

Robotic Vision and Tactile Sensing can allow robots to perform functions far beyond just simply moving packages from one place to another. These types of systems can be designed to improve quality, manufacturing flexibility, and response time to orders.

On-Line Quality Control is a new approach to controlling quality for the textile industry that is long overdue. This should improve quality by cutting out most of the second quality merchandise produced.

Simply stated, 'Quality permits automation'. Quality is a prerequisite for automation.

The old saying 'garbage in, garbage out' can be restated for an automated process as 'garbage in, nothing out'. An automated process must receive materials with consistent quality to efficiently perform a desired task. Successful operation of an automated process will often result in tighter quality specifications. To achieve this level of quality, processes must be continuously monitored and automatically controlled at every stage of production. Improved quality creates an added benefit by increasing production efficiency and increasing overall productivity of the process.

Continuous monitoring of processes at every stage of manufacturing will be necessary to maintain consistent quality levels. Continuous monitoring systems were shown by a variety of companies. Examples of these systems already in use are autolevelers on carding machines, yarn clearers on winding machines, and loom efficiency systems. Continuous monitoring systems are standard features on many new machines and will be necessary on existing machines to achieve consistent product quality for a subsequent automated process. When making capital investment decisions, considering the consequences of automation on quality monitoring is a must.

Machinery manufacturers are seeing the next necessary step beyond continuous monitoring, which is control. A totally automated process must react to the monitoring system in real time to maintain consistent quality. Automation will improve the overall level of quality in manufacturing. A necessary step toward automation is the investment in continuous monitoring and control systems. Monitoring systems currently are available for many processes. Look for future developments in continuous monitoring systems with real-time process control.

Computer Integrated Manufacturing (CIM) regards manufacturing as a continuous flow process and implies the tying together of adjacent operations and overall control systems with a central computer system [12]. Obviously, this is the direction of the development of automation and the use of electronics in textiles. In order to develop JIT and QR, it is inevitable that we treat the total textile and related industries manufacturing pipeline as well as individual processes as a manufacturing system that must be integrated by the use of computers.

Computer integrated manufacturing is the technology that allows just-in-time to be efficiently implemented and a quick response to customers' needs to take place. CIM is the computer technology that allows us to integrate monitoring and control systems and islands of automation along with all of the concepts discussed above into one integrated system. CIM offers the promise of automation that does not limit flexibility of the product line, and it can enhance flexible manufacturing systems (FMS).

We will now discuss CIM in detail and see how it applies to textile manufacturing. A diagram of a typical CIM system, as it applies to a textile manufacturing plant, is shown in Figure 1. All production units are managed by the computer according to management's desires by input from the CAD system and production planning all in real time [13]. Information can be taken from any part of the system at any time without disturbing its operation. Systems can be designed for one area, such as spinning or weaving, or for a vertically integrated operation. While most of the actual installations still consist of monitoring only, the move is toward control with the ultimate goal being some form of CIM.

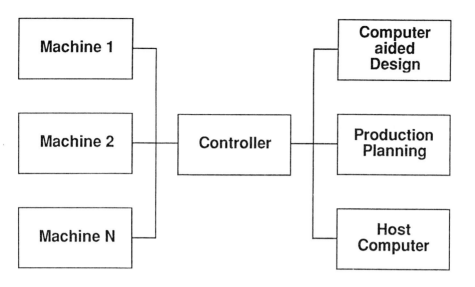

Fig. 1   *Typical Computer Integrated Manufacturing System (Source: Dinema)*

COMPUTER AIDED DESIGN SYSTEMS

Perhaps the best indication of the use of computers in the textile industry is the remarkable ability of CAD systems to produce fabric designs on paper that are visually indistinguishable from fabric. This can be demonstrated by placing a sample of fabric over part of a paper design so that the difference can be detected only by touching the two samples. This probably cannot be accomplished with all types of fabrics, but the capability of the systems is truly remarkable. Most of these systems are based on inexpensive personal computers and, therefore, are relatively inexpensive and user friendly.

YARN MANUFACTURING

Computer Integrated Manufacturing systems are available that monitor and/or control practically all yarn production processes from opening and blending to spinning, winding, and twisting. Applications include production monitoring, quality control, testing, inventory control, order tracking, maintenance control, budgeting, mill management and many others. Most companies now offer advanced controls on opening, blending, carding, and other fiber preparation equipment which are compatible with CIM. Ring spinning machines with individual spindle drives are available, and these offer great flexibility and will readily fit into the CIM concept. Sliver weights can be controlled and the levels changed by on-machine electronics that can readily be connected to a computer network.

23

On-line quality control in carding and drawing can perform spectral analysis and determine the cause of problems based on the frequency analysis of the defects. Passive acoustic detection systems to measure the evenness of sliver passing from both carding and drawing machinery are available that are easily adapted for all types of cards and draw frames. They use a large number of acoustic sensors serviced by a few local monitors that, in turn, feed a single central analyzer. Yarn spinning is now so automated that a large spinning mill can be operated by a very small number of people since automatic end piecing and automatic doffing is performed by robotic mechanisms. Although direct control of many operations in yarn spinning still is not possible, great advances have been made and CIM in yarn spinning seems to be on its way to being a reality

FABRIC MANUFACTURING

Weaving and knitting machine builders have been leading the way in utilizing computer technology in textile manufacturing for many years with their use of CAD, bidirectional communication and artificial intelligence. With the availability of electronic dobby and Jacquard heads, automatic pick finding, and needle selection, etc., these machines are the most easily integrated into computer networks of any textile production machines. Figure 2 shows how bidirectional communication systems can be used to control many functions on a weaving machine. As Figure 3 shows, a CAD system can be used to develop the fabric to be produced and the design can then be transmitted over the

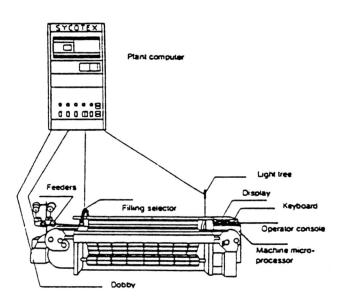

Fig. 2   Bi-Directional Communication System (Source: Barco Industries)

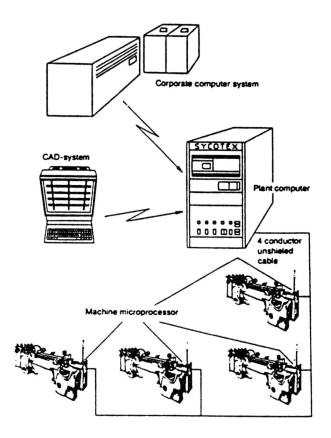

Fig. 3   CAD System Connected to CIM Network (Source: Barco Industries)

network to the production machines to produce the desired fabric. These technologies can greatly reduce the time needed to produce a fabric and give true meaning to the term 'quick response'. These systems, combined with the techniques being developed by loom manufacturers that allow faulty picks to be removed, may result in almost defect-free fabric that can be produced with very little labor.

Weaving also is the area where artificial intelligence is progressing the fastest with developments such as expert systems to assist in troubleshooting looms as described in Figure 4. As AI systems are combined with on-line data collecting systems in a CIM network, the possibilities for full automation in weaving are greatly enhanced.

Sizing machine control systems provide a tool for management to insure that all warps are sized identically under standard operating conditions. Figure 5 is a typical computer generated sizing machine report that illustrates these capabilities. Obviously, these monitoring and control capabilities can be included in a computer network.

For years knitting machine manufacturers have been making excellent use of

25

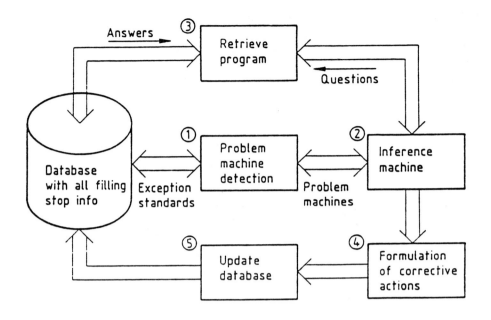

Fig. 4   *Expert System for Weaving (Source: Barco Industries)*

```
OPERATING PARAMETERS
CYLINDER GROUP 1 TEMP              140
CYLINDER GROUP 2 TEMP              140
CYLINDER GROUP 3 TEMP              140
CYLINDER GROUP 4 TEMP              140
CYLINDER GROUP 5 TEMP              140
SIZE BOX 1 TEMP                     88
SIZE BOX 2 TEMP                     89
BEAM TENSION                       420
LEASING TENSION                    260
CREEL TENSION                       40
SQUEEZE ROLL 1 PRESSURE            2.5
SQUEEZE ROLL 2 PRESSURE            2.5
PACK ROLL PRESSURE                 2.0
STRETCH 1                         1.5%
STRETCH 2                         1.5%
MOISTURE                          6.5%

WEST POINT FOUNDRY AND MACHINE COMPANY
PACESETTER
SIZING MACHINE
CONTROL SYSTEM
```

Fig. 5   *Computer Printout of Sizing Machine Control System (Source: West Point Foundry and Machine Company)*

electronics to provide machines that are more automatic and versatile, and many refinements of these advances have been made. These automatic machines are already 'islands of automation' that can be incorporated into a CIM network.

Machines that produce nonwovens lend themselves very well to electronic control and automated materials handling techniques that lend themselves to a CIM environment

DYEING

The automatic control of dyeing machines dates well back into the 1960s, and each succeeding year has shown miniaturization and enhancement in the management of information on a more timely basis. A typical system is described in Figure 6. The monitor displays scheduling for any machine and allows the operator to arrange the next lot. Manpower scheduling can be an integral part of the system. Batch weighing updates inventory each minute and gives inventory of each dye by bulk and container. Any errors later in the process can be traced to a particular container if it should become necessary.

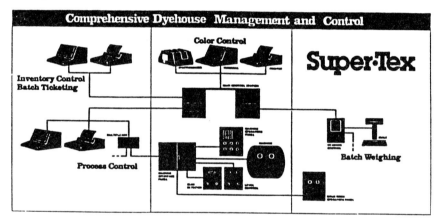

Fig. 6   Typical Dyehouse Management and Control System (Source: Gaston County Dyeing Machine Company)

A 'Data Concentrator' accepts inputs and downloads to the central CPU. Forecasts of end-of-cycle with one keystroke, procedure display and step highlight are standard features. A parameter table allows each machine to be set-up independently and sets, for example, fill times which can easily depend on the proximity of the machine to the header supply line. Exceptions are sent: (a) to file; (b) to printer; and (c) to area exception files. There is no limit to the lot scheduling ability. The computer has the latest information on each machine and can take over within one minute.

Automation of batch dyeing and finishing operations using state-of-the-art electronic technology generally includes:
*   Microprocessor Dye Machine Controllers;
*   Management Information Host Systems;
*   Drug Room Check Weighing Systems;

27

- Automated Liquid Dispensing Systems;
- Dye and Chemical Inventory Control Systems;
- Computer Color Matching and Control;
- Color Display — Color Simulation;
- Energy Management Systems;
- Bar Code-Based Lot Tracking Systems; and
- Linkage of Mainframe and Dyehouse Host Computers for real-time/ manufacturing information and production planning.

Automated color lab dispensing systems allows dispensing from up to 80 or more liquid components. Once swatches are weighed, the amount of colorant is automatically adjusted and dispensed for the lab technician.

A tenter frame automation system with touch-screen color-graphics and real-time voice alarms to operators when zones overheat or motors overload is described in Figure 7. Software control strategies include:

- Infrared fabric temperature, chain speed and zone temperature control;
- Circulation fan control;
- Width monitoring and track control;
- Pad temperature, level, flow and pressure control;
- Seam detection, lot start/stop, SOP loading, shut-down and lot changeover provisions; and
- Differential pressure-based exhaust control, and Yield monitoring and control.

Mathematical modeling has been used to develop an optimization procedure for continuous washing operations via a process simulation which allows the operator to determine whether a desired final concentration of impurities can be obtained with a given set of operating conditions. For different speeds, fresh water consumption and final water content, the computer determines, in real-time, whether these parameters will work. Mathematical models of package dyeing can be used to assist a dyer in choosing the optimum operating conditions for the particular package parameters.

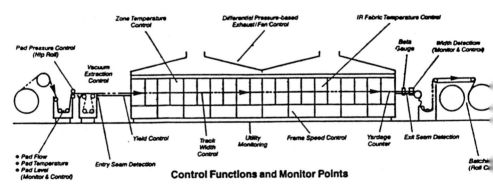

Fig. 7   Tenter Frame Automation System (Source: Keiltronix)

Laser engraving can provide an improvement in the quality of an engraved design and the ability of the print plant to respond to market conditions and give the quickest of quick response. In this development, designs digitized by a scanner and a small CAD computer are rapidly and very accurately engraved directly onto coated screens by a laser. No intermediate acetate films are needed to block the light in the traditional photo process. The most important advantage is to reduce the time necessary for the production of a ready-to-use screen to 15–30 minutes. Prudent printers in the past have made three back-up copies of every screen so that print runs would not have to be taken off the print machine when a hole developed in a screen. The number of back-up screens will probably now be reduced to two sets.

AUTOMATED MATERIAL HANDLING

Material handling is an obvious target for automation. Material handling contains a high component of low value-added labor. The labor is often tedious and strenuous, resulting in hard-to-fill positions and potential health hazards. Both conditions adversely affect the manufacturing process. Automated material handling can be justified based on elimination of this labor component and the indirect benefits such as lower health insurance costs and continuous operation.

The area of yarn formation is the most advanced toward total mill automation. Past and present developments in automatic doffing, splicing, and feeding have made automated material handling concepts a reality. All forms of automated material handling systems are available from opening to yarn package handling.

Material handling systems have been developed that can result in a highly automated, flexible mill for the complete processing short staple fiber from bale to cone using either ring or open-spinning. An automatic sliver transport system using an automatically guided vehicle (AGV) can move sliver cans from carding to drawing frames. A similarly designed vehicle can move sliver cans from drawing frames to roving frames or rotor spinning machines. This system eliminates tedious manual labor and automatically responds to the machines it serves. Other benefits include clearly arranged material flow, inventory reduction, and shortening of lot run times.

Other material handling systems that are available include an automatic box loader for rotor spinning frames, an automatic loader for palletizing, and an automatic loader for pin trucks. Systems for automatically handling large lap rolls for combing machinery are available.

The concept of automation of textile processing through linking of consecutive processes was demonstrated in 1983. This concept has evolved into standard manufacturing practice between ring spinning and winding.

Linking of processes is expanding to include roving and two-for-one twisting. As an example, systems are available that take automatically doffed roving bobbins via an overhead transport system and feeds them to ring spinning frames. Empty tubes are automatically cleaned and returned to roving. Advantages of linking are realized in a WIP inventory reduction, smooth product flow, labor savings, and a reduction in floor space. Direct linking of machines can limit flexibility and productivity if product flow is not managed properly. Multiple machine linking is a desirable goal. Complete roving and spinning departments can be served by a common overhead transport system with limited product storage.

Many future developments in linking with flexibility are expected. Companies such are developing link systems that can distinguish between production lots and at the same time run two different lots on the same spinning frame. Systems can transport full packages from winders to any one of three stations: inspection, creeling, or boxing. Several companies produce material transport systems for the purpose of linking processes in which equipment is already in operation as ring spinning frames with automatic winders. Automated material handling in yarn formation is a practical step for textile manufacturers that have automated machines such as autodoffers and autowinders. Automated material handling systems are available to textile companies that have existing equipment and want to automate portions of their manufacturing process. Investment in modern handling systems can be justified primarily by a reduction in labor and improved production performance

ROBOTICS

At ITMA '83, robots were new components for automating material handling. Many companies exhibited complex, expensive robots designed for a high degree of flexibility and accuracy that is not required in most textile applications. By 1987, 'specialized' was the term most widely used to describe the large number of robots exhibited. Most robotic systems were designed for a specific operation, such as yarn package boxing. This specialization reduces system cost and mechanical complexity without sacrificing performance or flexibility within the specific operation. These robotic systems are concentrated primarily in package dyeing and yarn formation.

Loading and unloading of yarn packages for dyeing is labor intensive, tedious, and strenuous. It is an excellent application for robotics. Most automated systems use a robot to load and unload packages. The robots are designed specifically for package handling, and only the necessary degrees of freedom are included. Companies such as Camel Robot, Gualchierani, and Galvanin produce large three degrees-of-freedom robots specially designed to handle stacked packages for full spindle loading and unloading. Manufacturers claim labor reductions as high as 6 or 7 people with an automated system.

Officine Minnetti and Galvanin also produce robotic systems for loading and unloading hank-dyed yarn.

In yarn formation, robots are available for handling sliver and full yarn packages. Automatic guided vehicles (AGV) are used to transport sliver cans, transport spindle boxes, move autodoffing systems, and even sweep the floor. Typical AGVs are battery-powered and follow an inductive signal emitted from copper wires embedded in the floor. The AGVs can be controlled by a central computer or by local inputs from operators or machines requesting service. Large AGVs are currently being used in automated weaving plants to transport warp beams and fabric rolls.

A typical robotic system removes yarn packages from spinning or winding machines, fills a pallet layer in a programmed sequence, adds a pallet spacer, and repeats the process. These units have special end effectors for handling packages and pallet spacers. Depending on the process, one robotic system can be designed to serve one or more machines.

Some robotic systems that are specialized for linking two-for-one twisting perform tasks beyond material handling. These systems-may check package weight and geometrical dimensions. Packages out of specification are rejected. This illustrates a more representative use of the robot than just a programmable pick and place device. Automated inspection by the robotic packaging system is a logical future development.

We expect robots to be an integral component of automated material handling. These robotic systems are available now. The cost of the systems has been reduced by specializing the robot systems and incorporating technology familiar to the textile industry. Future developments of specialized systems will continue. We look for inspection to be an integral function of these systems

CONCLUSION

Although the textile industry seems to be moving toward the use of CIM and total mill automation as a means of becoming more flexible and competitive, there are many roadblocks to its successful implementation. CIM should not be viewed as an end in itself but as a means of achieving management goals. Integration of the many subsystems into a network is a major problem in the absence of electronic protocol standards. The Europeans seem to be dealing with this, and the US textile and machinery companies will be affected by their decisions since much of our equipment is manufactured there. Although there are several groups working on data interchange standards in the US, no overall communication standard for the entire manufacturing pipeline has emerged.

Many companies have found that implementing a CIM system involves a lot of work over a period of years [15,16], and they may decide that it is not worth the effort. Most companies cannot afford to build new plants or completely renovate old ones just to automate, but many of the CIM concepts can be implemented as they update their machinery. This means that they must select production and auxiliary equipment that is amenable to networking, but they may need expert assistance to be successful. Fortunately, many textile machines are already highly automated and many of the advanced spinning frames and looms can be considered as 'islands of automation' that can be connected into computer networks with the proper electronics. However, the software needed may have to be written especially for that application.

Many companies are hesitant to spend even small amounts of money for CIM since it is often very difficult to justify with traditional cost accounting methods since they do not predict all the financial consequences. Improvement in quality and inventory control may be difficult to predict and quantify in terms of savings. If workers and production management do not support the changes, they may feel threatened and productivity may decline [15]. However, most companies recognize that they must automate or they simply won't be in business in a few years in our competitive environment.

It is obvious that most companies must move toward full flexible automation to compete domestically as well as internationally and that the machinery companies are providing the needed technology. The implications for the US textile industry are that we must take advantage of this by making the decisions that will insure that we will be the most efficient, innovative, and competitive textile industry in the world.

REFERENCES

[1]   R. C. Carson. 'Requirements for Factory Computer Network Communications', *Tex. World*, October 1987 p.93.

[2]   L. Van der Jagt. 'MAP - Is It Applicable to Textiles and Apparel', presented at conference on Automation for the Fiber, Textile, and Apparel Industries at NCSU, 13–14 January 1987.

[3]   H. E. Ashe, Jr. 'Milliken Electronic Data Access and Interchange - The Textile and Apparel Interface', presented at Electronics in Textiles Conference, Clemson, SC, 25-26 March 1986.

[4]   McAllister Isaacs. 'Special Report: Quick Response', *Tex. World*, February 1987 137, 2, 38.

[5]   'FASLINC to Provide Mill-Supplier QR Link', *Tex. World*, 1987, 137, 2, 27.

[6]   'TAMMF,' *Southern Tex. News*, 18 July 1988, p.14. 'The CIM Search', *App. Ind. Mag.*, May 1988, p.52, 'CIM/LINC Pursues the Ultimate LINK', *Bobbin*, April 1988, p.84.

[7]   J. F. Mallard. 'Bi-Directional Communications - What It Means to the Future of the Textile Industry', presented at Electronics in Textiles Conference, Clemson, SC, March 25-26, 1986.

[8]   R. E. Cotton. 'QR's Bottom Line,', *App. Ind. Mag.*, July 1986.

[9]   J. L. Dorrity. 'Fundamentals and Understanding of Artificial Intelligence', presented at Electronics in Textiles Conference, Clemson, SC, March 25-26, 1986.

[10]   K. W. Throneburg, P. L. Grady, and G. N. Mock. 'Cost Reduction in Textile Manufacturing through Energy Modeling - Bath Dyeing', Electronics in Textiles Conference, Clemson, SC, March 25-26, 1986.

[11]   C. Cahill and A. Demers. 'Using Knowledge Technology to Gain a Competitive Advantage through Predictive Control', Proceedings for the International Conference on Expert Systems and the Leading Edge in Production Planning and Control, Charleston, SC, May 10-13, 1987.

[12]   J. R. Canada. 'Evaluation on DS-Computer Integrated Manufacturing Systems', Automation for the Fiber, Textile and Apparel Industries Conference, NCSU, January 13-14, 1987.

[13]   Dinema CIM brochure.

[14]   B. Cruycke. 'Artificial Intelligence in Modern Weaving', presented at Electronics in Textiles Conference, Clemson, SC, March 24-25, 1987.

[15]   A. Klein. 'The Stumbling Blocks to CIM', *Mech. Eng.*, October 1987, 109, 10, 74.

[16]   J. F. Mallard. 'MAP . . . What It Means to the Future of the Textile Industry', Electronics in Textiles Conference, Clemson, SC, March 24-25, 1987.

Additional sources of information on CIM in the Fiber, Textile, and Apparel Industries.

J. W. Bernard, CIM in the Process Industries, Instrument Society of America, Research Triangle Park, NC, 1989.

A. Dockery. 'Greenwood Mills Cashes In On CIM,' America's Textiles International, Billian Publishing, Inc., Atlanta, GA, USA, 1991.

L. F. Fryer. Computer Integration of the Short-Staple Spinning Enterprise, MS Thesis, NCSU College of Textiles, Raleigh, NC, USA, 1992.

M. G. Rodd and F. Deravi. Communication Systems for Industrial Automation, Prentice Hall, New York, USA, 1989.

D. A. Turbide. 'Computers in Manufacturing', Industrial Press Inc., New York, USA, 1991.

North Carolina State University College of Textiles, ITMA'91 Review, Raleigh, NC, 1991.

'OshKosh B'Gosh Takes Command Of CIM,' *App. Ind. Mag.*, Shore Communications, Inc., Atlanta, GA, June 1991.

'Mountain City: OH, What a Yarn Mill!', *Tex. World*, Maclean Hunter Publishing Co., Chicago, IL, June 1991.

Computer Integrated Manufacturing, IBM Corporation.

R. S. Kaplan. 'Must CIM Be Justified By Faith Alone', *Harv. Bus. Rev.*, March-April, 1986.

Manufacturing Enterprise Handbook, Digital Equipment Corporation, Maynard, MA, 1990.

N. Cahill. 'CIM: Power to Differentiate Manufacturing', CIM In Textiles Executive Briefing, North Carolina State University College of Textiles, Raleigh, NC, September, 1992.

W. J. Jasper, E. T. Kovacs, and G. A. Berkstresser. 'Using Neural Networks to Predict Dye Concentrations in Multiple-Dye Mixtures', *Tex. Res. J.*, September 1993.

W. J. Jasper and E. T. Kovacs. 'Using Neural Networks and NIR Spectrophotometry To Identify Fibers', Submitted to the *Tex. Res. J.*.

Requirements for Process Integration and Automation in Textile Manufacturing

J. Eapen

Director, Process Engineering and Automation, Fieldcrest Cannon Inc.

Most of us will agree that technology is available now for the 'Factory of the Future,' but, before it can become a reality, Process Integration and Automation is a must.

There are five primary factors that contribute to the success of Process Integration and Automation. These factors are:

- Overcoming the Barriers to Process Integration and Automation;
- Management Commitment;
- Justification of Process Control Systems and Automation Projects;
- Vendor Selection;
- Vendor-User Partnership.

Let us examine these in closer detail as we discuss the requirements for Process Integration and Automation.

OVERCOMING THE BARRIERS TO PROCESS INTEGRATION AND AUTOMATION

Several barriers need to be overcome before integration can take place effectively. Integration is a very difficult area to address because of the history of manufacturing in our country. First, the existing infrastructure that was built to support specialization needs to be altered. The existing manufacturing base in a majority of the companies was built around specialization and the division of labor. Based on the culture of the company, performance measures and incentives need to be set up to facilitate cooperation.

Many companies may have mechanisms in place for dealing with increasing complexity. However, the problems posed by integration are new and unfamiliar. The challenge is to integrate various elements of the organization that do not have the management and organizational structure in place.

Secondly, in order to make the factory of the future a reality, manufacturing and industrial engineers must change their way of thinking and develop new skills. No longer can they think only in terms of optimizing individual processes. The engineers must think in terms of optimizing the entire process.

In the past, a manufacturing department consisted of several stand-alone units. The task of coordinating the machines to meet a specified production schedule was in the hands of a production supervisor. With a highly skilled production supervisor many of the inefficiencies in the process would not be apparent. In this environment, when problems would arise, management would take the attitude 'I don't want excuses; I just want results.' With this attitude, supervisors would find ways to cover the problems temporarily because the time and resources were not available to solve them.

To successfully implement automation, we must recognize that each machine no longer performs independently. Automated systems many times dictate that the process be performed in a synchronous fashion, with the output from one station providing the input to the subsequent operation. In this type of system inefficiencies such as downtime cannot be tolerated since problems in one stage of the process immediately affect the performance of the entire system. Understanding the system interactions is very important to implement the new technology successfully. Analysis tools such as computer simulation can be used to understand system interaction during the design phase.

Another major problem hindering the success of automated process controls and automated systems is the shortage of suitable engineers, technicians and craftsmen. We give low priority to manufacturing. Textile companies do not spend enough time and money on process innovation. Bright young engineers choose to go into high tech industries and we have not done enough to attract them into the textile manufacturing areas. In most of our organizations, the structure does not encourage long-term technical careers. After five to ten years, engineers peak out by reaching the top of the technical ladder. To progress further, an engineer must move into management. Some of these engineers move into management, perform poorly and hence stagnate or get frustrated and leave. If we are going to retain good technical personnel, we must establish rewarding careers in the technical areas. Several non-textile industries are beginning to do this.

Vendor liaison is another critical factor. The vendor-customer relationship can make or break a large project. Therefore, it is essential that the vendor liaison be someone who is inherently familiar with the process that is to be modified. But this is commonly violated in practice.

Many times problems arise when an inappropriate person is chosen to act as the vendor liaison. Companies often select a vendor liaison based on the power and clout that he or she carries within the organization-not on their knowledge of the process to be modified.

An improperly selected vendor liaison will have only an idealistic image of how the system will work. Then, when the system is implemented in a shop environment, field problems arise because actual needs turn out to be different from the projected requirements. It is very important to get personnel who work with the system every day involved in the initial stages of the project.

In the past, most of the control logic incorporated in an automated system was a function of the system hardware. Today, with the advancements in computer technology the control logic has been placed in the hands of a programmer. This has allowed total customization of complex systems. But, it is very important that the system programmer fully understands the process that he is trying to control. Poorly understanding the process can create major problems.

Finally, top management must determine and prioritize company objectives as they relate to manufacturing (cost, quality, delivery, Just In Time/Quick Response, flexibility, employee involvement, etc.). Management must continually emphasize these priorities through actions as well as words.

A few points must be remembered during the implementation phase. First, do not automate processes that are not consistent. Second, a system is only as strong as its weakest link. Third, if we leave bottlenecks, these hurt us even more after automation. Therefore, we can sometimes justify the elimination of bottlenecks even when they are not economically justifiable.

MANAGEMENT COMMITMENT

Management can show commitment in several ways. Personal interest can be shown by playing a role in establishing the real needs and setting the stage for change. Sufficient resources such as time, money and personnel should also be allocated to the projects. Corporate business plans should reflect the importance of these projects. A post audit is highly recommended.

JUSTIFICATION OF PROCESS CONTROL SYSTEMS AND AUTOMATION PROJECTS

Several cost saving items are used in the traditional justification process. Some of these items are:
- Increased Efficiency —
  Less Downtime
  Less Labor
- Quality Improvement
- Less Raw Materials
- Less Chemicals
- Less Energy
- Repeatability
- Helps the R & D Operations
- Return on Investment

It is extremely important to also consider other non-traditional items when process control and automation projects are justified. Most companies are still using a Return on Investment (ROI) calculation and, in most instances, no one knows where the figure originated. Hurdle rates and other factors are unrealistic and should be revised and updated to reflect the real cost of money to the particular company.

Synergistic benefits derived from a project should not be overlooked. Often downstream benefits from a process control or automation project alone can justify a major project, but very seldom does management allow engineers to include these savings as a part of the project.

VENDOR SELECTION

It is very important to choose the right vendor for the process and automation project. The system chosen should be a mainstream system for reliability, service needs and spare parts availability. A good project specification should be supplied to the vendor to avoid misunderstandings and problems later. Detailed specifications will convey the needs of the user to the vendor.

Vendor cooperation and allowing vendors total system responsibility are also factors that should be considered during the vendor selection phase.

VENDOR-USER PARTNERSHIP

Proper vendor-user partnership will play a major role in the success of a process integration and automation project. Factors that are vital to this relationship are trust building between the two parties, up-front education, system training, and providing the best people for the project from both sides.

Having discussed the requirements for process integration and automation, let us briefly discuss the reasons for process integration and automation.

The reasons can be numerous and should depend on the overall corporate strategy. These projects can be implemented to support one or several of the following items:

- JIT/QR, quality, CIM, etc.;
- Marketplace edge;
- Good payback;
- Accuracy;
- Overseas competition;
- Domestic competition;
- Survival.

In summary, I leave you with the following philosophy:

FUND STRATEGIES
NOT PROJECTS.

BIBLIOGRAPHY

K. R. Snyder and C. S. Elliott. 'Barriers to Factory Automation: What Are They, and How Can They Be Surmounted?', IE, April 1988, p.44.

The Requirements for Automation in Today's Textile Manufacturing Environment

J. L. Eckert

Manager Automation, Fieldcrest Cannon Inc.

Today's manufacturing environment is characterized by rapidly changing, fragmented markets with world-wide competition and high customer expectations in the areas of quality, reliability and responsiveness. This requires a more strategic approach to the business that emphasizes long range, broad based goals that will make the company responsive to change. It is no longer enough to be the low cost producer; it is necessary to differentiate yourself by other means, such as quality, reliability or responsiveness.

Today's environment has a direct effect on automation efforts. To improve quality, reliability and responsiveness, it is necessary to consider projects which will bring processes closer together. The non-value adding steps in the manufacturing process must be reduced by streamlining project flow, eliminating inventory and cutting out material handling. It is not sufficient to automate material handling just to reduce labor costs. It is now more important to reduce lead time by eliminating material handling altogether and automating the flow of information between processes, between plants, and between customers and suppliers.

This new environment has dramatically changed the approach to automating our plants. It is no longer appropriate to do isolated automation projects at each facility. It is important to look at the overall strategy for the complete plant, between plants and for the whole corporation. To do this successfully, a central group that can coordinate and provide focus for this effort is needed. A corporate automation group can provide this coordination and be a central resource for information on the latest automation technology. This group will need to interact with all areas of the company, not just manufacturing. Areas like design, marketing, purchasing and planning are all crucial to the quality, reliability and responsiveness of the company; therefore, they cannot be left out of the automation picture. Automation has a much broader scope now, encompassing the automation of information flow as well as product flow. As a result, this group must be heavily involved in implementing the latest manufacturing and management techniques including Just In Time (JIT), Computer Integrated Manufacturing (CIM), Total Quality Control (TQC), Electronic Data Interchange (EDI), and Quick Response (QR). I feel very strongly that these programs need to be integrated into a single management philosophy which I would call World Class Manufacturing (WCM). A great deal of synergism can be derived from this integration. If they are implemented separately, however, they fight for everyone's time and resources and can result in people getting turned off to any new program.

Specific automation projects should start with a process flow study. This should identify the product routings, processing time, inventory levels, lead times and any other factors which give an indication of how this process affects the overall responsiveness, quality and reliability of this product. This study is usually quite an 'eye opener' and brings to the surface a lot of potential problems to work on. An overall guideline to adhere to is 'simplify first, automate next, integrate last.' If this is utilized, it will avoid automating a mess and instead will lead to streamlined product flows, reduced material handling and shorter lead times. For example, implementing JIT type techniques can drastically reduce the material handling requirements and thereby significantly change the automation requirements. After these steps are taken, a fairly traditional approach can be followed in drawing up project proposals and implementing them.

This new manufacturing environment has also affected the way we justify automation projects. How well projects meet the overall corporate objectives needs to become just as important as return on investment. If a project will give you a competitive advantage, it may be worth doing even if it has a relatively poor ROI. The equation for determining if projects will be funded needs to include factors for: reductions in lead time, quality improvements, better reliability and quick response in addition to labor savings and other standard calculations.

The new manufacturing environment will not wait for those of us who resist change and are reluctant to take risks on investing in new technology. It is an ever changing environment and once you get behind, it will take quick, bold actions on the part of forward thinking managers to get back that competitive edge.

Electronic Data Interchange: The Business Tool of Quick Response

T. J. Little

College of Textiles, North Carolina State University

INTRODUCTION

The textile, apparel and retail industries and their suppliers are all facing increasingly challenging business decisions as to the optimum approach that will make each company and major segment of the pipeline more competitive. To attain a more competitive position in today's marketplace the hard technologies of automation and the soft technologies of information must become the new manufacturing strategies. The hardware of automation has been developed as prototypes but the commercial versions have taken longer than anticipated to deliver. For example, the MITI project began in 1979 as did the Textile Clothing Technology Corporation's Draper Labs project, and only in 1990 and 1991 will the early commercial versions of Hard Apparel Automation become available. Another example of hard automation development is the Department of Defense funding of apparel automation at North Carolina State University and Ark Inc., from 1987 to 1994 that will rapidly convert from civilian apparel assembly to the assembly of similar military products. In this period of time other significant business environment changes created the need for a more responsive soft goods pipeline to be able to deliver the right product at the right time. In the mid-1980s the consumer was rediscovered and has become the focal point for a complete reversal of business strategies in textiles/apparel as well as in many other manufacturing and service oriented industries.

The new textile/apparel strategies are frequently referred to as Quick Response (QR) and Ernst and Whinney (1988) state that QR typically involves three basic levels of strategy:

- the strategic level where trust and commitment is established between supplier and customer;
- the technology level where the various information issues are addressed; and
- the operations level where Just In Time, Total Quality Management, and Employee Involvement Concepts provide some of the fundamental manufacturing initiatives that make QR possible.

Quick Response therefore represents a major change in the entire soft goods pipeline, and the majority of proactive textile/ apparel management schools consider this business enterprise as an entire unit that must have both an effective mechanism for product flow to the consumer and an efficient information flow to the producers and suppliers. To accomplish all of the goals of QR, each organization and industry segment must have a clearly defined objective and begin an implementation process that is most likely to require a total re-education of all employees. The hard automation that manifests itself as the latest machine on the factory floor is much easier to justify for return on investment, much easier to rate for performance as production rate or down-time, and much easier to dispose of when no longer needed. Today we are embracing Soft Automation, a technology that will take the textile/apparel industry into the new business environment of customer responsive flexible manufacturing and once properly implemented will completely change forever how a company operates. Before describing how a company can change with the implementation of soft automation, it is necessary to study the role of Linkage in the fiber, textile, apparel and retail industries.

LINKAGE BACKGROUND

In May of 1985, Haggar Apparel Company hosted an industry meeting which was attended by some sixty people representing apparel, textile, finishers, suppliers and academia. The discussion of the two-day meeting focused on how textile and apparel companies could work closer together and begin to standardize the labelling of fabric rolls, identification of fabric defects, packaging and put-up of fabrics and the advance communication of fabric information prior to the receipt of piece goods. Following the Haggar meeting, some seven major apparel companies convened in June 1985 and drafted a list of goals that needed to be accomplished to facilitate improved flow of product and information. This Apparel Wish List is published in *Textile World*, November 1985, page 46–48, to illustrate the factors considered to be of importance to apparel producers as expressed by representatives of Arrow, Wrangler, Haggar, Kellwood, Lee, Levi and Oxford.

The major textile companies studied the apparel list. Springs Industries and North Carolina State University jointly hosted a meeting of some twenty textile companies in December 1985 to discuss and respond to the proposals put forward by the apparel producers.

A joint meeting of both textile producers and apparel users was convened at Philadelphia College of Textiles and Science in May of 1986 to reach a consensus on the most expedient approach for voluntary standardization on these issues. At this meeting the Textile Apparel Linkage Council (TALC) was formed with the following objectives to:

- Enhance the efficiency of US textile and apparel industries through the elimination of redundant costs and the improvement of overall response time;
- Develop voluntary standards;
- Facilitate implementation of agreed-upon voluntary standards;
- Encourage resolution of opportunities through committee effort;
- Identify new areas that are consistent with the stated TALC purpose;
- Continue inter-industry dialogue to insure a free exchange of ideas and information;
- Inform apparel and textile industry colleagues about TALC voluntary standards and objectives through seminars, meetings and publication of all conclusions.

The Textile Apparel Linkage Council was established as a volunteer organization guided by a Steering Committee comprised of representatives from the textile (5) and apparel (5) industries, the trade associations (2) and academia (2).

The joint meeting of the textile producers and apparel users discussed eight items as candidate applications for voluntary standardization. These eight items were:

- barcoding
- roll identification
- shade measurement
- width/length
- data transmission (electronic)
- packaging
- inventory information
- defects and flagging of defects

During this first joint meeting producers and users agreed on adopting the American National Standards Institute (ANSI) X12 standard for the electronic exchange of business data. Agreement was also reached that shade information would be communicated electronically as either delta values or the 5-5-5 shade sorting convention based on CIE L.A.B. and the methods to be employed in determining and communicating fabric width and length were also decided. Note: It is of interest to note that voluntary standards have been written on all of the original eight items with the exception of packaging which is currently described in a direction statement.

THE NEED FOR OTHER LINKAGES

It was soon recognized that the concept of Linkage could be made to work between other industry segments. In June 1986 the Voluntary Interindustry Communications Standards (VICS) committee was formed to improve the efficiency of retailers and their suppliers. Previous studies by Kurt Salmon Associates had shown that the retailer could gain significantly by reducing inventory, reducing stock-outs and capturing point-of-sale information electronically. VICS formed both a steering committee and a technical committee to determine the most pragmatic approach to streamlining the flow of textile and apparel products to the retailer and the flow of information back to the apparel or textile suppliers.

The Textile Apparel Linkage Council soon realized that the task of adopting voluntary standards for the industry would require significant effort and that other industry segments should develop suitable organizations to represent their interests in the development of voluntary standards for electronic data interchange. The formation of the Fabric and Suppliers Linkage Council (FASLINC) in January 1987 and the Sundries and Apparel Findings Linkage Council in March 1987 is directly attributable to a TALC decision in November 1986.

The FASLINC organization completed its work on the development of voluntary standards in 1990 and studied the remaining industry needs. It was concluded that education was clearly the most immediate need of the industry and this education need could be better fulfilled by having the American Textile Manufacturers Institute (ATMI) involved. Therefore, FASLINC transformed into the Quick Response Committee of ATMI and has actively persued education of the industry and maintenance of the

FASLINC voluntary standards.

TALC and SAFLINC joined together as one TALC/SAFLINC organization in 1992 and continued with its roles of developing additional voluntary standards and getting more involved in education of the apparel companies and their suppliers. Following an analysis of industry needs, the TALC/SAFLINC organization recommended that the American Apparel Manufacturers Association (AAMA) for a committee to continue the work of both the TALC and SAFLINC organizations. The Quick Response Leadership Committee of AAMA held its inaugural meeting in April of 1994 and at the time of writing is actively defining its Vision and Mission.

THE FORMATION OF TRADING PARTNERSHIPS

The approach taken by all the Linkage organizations was that once the specific business requirements or opportunities are defined, successful execution can be significantly enhanced when two or more competent companies form an partnership based on trust, integrity and communication. Through these partnerships, mutually beneficial solutions can be developed and implemented. The process of continuous dialogue between trading partners is the vital ingredient to sustain a breakthrough in the way business is conducted. Frequently, it is only after the formation of partnerships that trading partners can plan their manufacturing strategies based upon each other's strengths and shortcomings. Furthermore, the formation of partnerships also identifies other areas of opportunity where standardization would assist in improving the competitive position of all industry segments.

LINKAGE BETWEEN TRADING PARTNERS

The objective of electronic data interchange is to transfer information via computer from the application of one partner to the application(s) of the other partner. The direct communication maximizes the ability of both partners to reduce process time, improve accuracy and eliminate redundant costs.

Figure 1 illustrates how partners can communicate their business needs between textile producers and apparel users. Today, very few partners have implemented all of the possible business transactions as shown on Figure 1. It is customary for trading partners to agree on the most important EDI transmissions for the product line being considered and the exact configuration of the EDI documents to be exchanged. To gain the greatest benefit from linkage between textile and apparel partners, fabric rolls should have a standardized barcoded unique roll identifier to facilitate receiving and roll selection for spreading. The Advance Ship Notice (with roll identification) should be transmitted between partners electronically so that the planning necessary to operate in a Just In Time mode can be completed prior to the arrival of the raw material. The model Linkage communication system shown in Figure 1 can also be applied to the interface between other segments of the industry pipeline and between trading partners other than textile and apparel.

A major change found upon Linkage implementation is the fact that business decisions are being made based on the quality of the information provided. For example, when

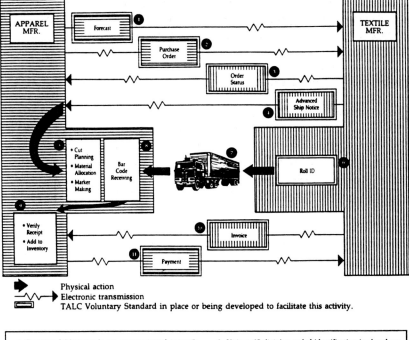

Physical action
Electronic transmission
TALC Voluntary Standard in place or being developed to facilitate this activity.

1. Forecasted fabric needs are communicated to textile manufacturer.

2. Electronic purchase order incorporated into business system of textile manufacturer.

3. Apparel manufacturer notified of order status.

4. Advanced ship notice includes detailed information about each roll.

5. Advanced ship notice information facilitates advanced apparel activities.

6. Unique 15-digit bar coded identification is placed on each roll.

7. Fabric is moved from textile to apparel manufacturer.

8. Fabric receiving process accomplished by scanning bar coded tickets.

9. Information captured at receiving is verified using advanced ship notice. Rolls are added to inventory and made available for cutting.

10. Electronic Invoice received by apparel manufacturer.

11. Electronic payment received by textile manufacturer.

Fig. 1

the textile mill provides the width information on individual rolls of fabric in advance of receipt as needed by the apparel company in planning their cut lots and markers, inaccurate data can eliminate quick response manufacturing and cause additional expenses to be incurred. Conversely, if the apparel company does not provide timely and reliable forecast data to the textile mills it is difficult for the mill to commit to a delivery schedule.

ELECTRONIC DATA INTERCHANGE AND ELECTRONIC COMMERCE

Electronic Data Interchange and Electronic Commerce are Business Tools that can help operate businesses more effectively and efficiently. Electronic Commerce tends to imply doing business over electronic networks with Electronic Data Interchange as a extension beyond Electronic Commerce. To assist in combating competitors, saving money, eliminating redundant costs, responding to shorter product life cycles and responding to fickle customers, businesses need fast and accurate transfer of business documents to their trading partners.

There are three major points that need to be stressed regarding Electronic Data Interchange:

(a) EDI is intercompany ... more than one business is involved, each with its own geography, level of technical sophistication and business priorities.

When a company enters the world of EDI, it can no longer maintain the traditional arm's length relationship with its suppliers, customers, freight carriers and banks. The company will become an integral part of a multi-enterprise system organized to deliver value to the end customer. To succeed in EDI the company must cooperate with the other businesses that compose the value chain that leads from raw material to finished product (Figure 2).

(b) EDI concerns business documents in standard formats. The stuff of EDI is formatted purchase orders, invoices, bills of lading, cash disbursement instructions, etc. The agreement to use a standard format allows each EDI participant to leverage the investment in EDI over many different trading partners. The alternate would be to integrate its business applications with as many formats as it has trading partners.

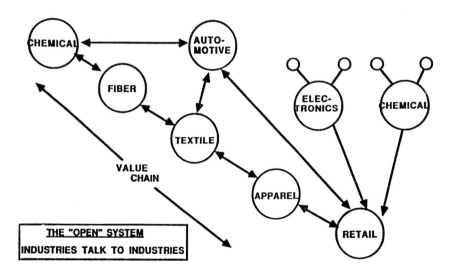

Fig. 2   The 'Open' System

45

(c) EDI is not just between computers but between computer applications. Integrating with the business applications that generate and receive business transactions is the key to the benefits and the costs of doing EDI.

It is application integration that reduces costs by eliminating clerical costs and errors, helps reduce investment by allowing a more aggressive inventory management policy to be implemented and enhances revenues by linking customer ordering with inventory control systems to provide superior customer service.

DEFINITIONS, HARDWARE AND SOFTWARE

The exchange of business information electronically is not new and even within the soft goods pipeline many companies have practised electronic data interchange for almost two decades. The primary difference in today's industry is that the technological tools required to implement EDI have become affordable to virtually every size of supplier, textile, apparel, and retail company. The ability to exchange data electronically requires a computer, a modem, an X12 Translator software package and a vehicle for sending and receiving information.

The software needs are generally recognized to involve three separate functions. The Translation Software is the standardized format for each of the business transactions and must be updated regularly to keep pace with the new versions and releases of the EDI standards. The Communication Software must be able to communicate with the network or trading partner's computer, send comprehensible documents and understand received documents. Communication software packages are available depending on the size of the computer, i.e. whether mainframe, minicomputer or personal computer. Users also need to establish transmission speeds and the type of Communications Controller (synchronous or asynchronous). The Interface Software takes the transmitted information and integrates the information into the company's internal computer or takes internal information and prepares a flat file for the Translation Software. Translation and Communication Software is readily available commercially, but Interface Software is usually written by the company and, at this time, is not widely available as a standard commercial package. Figure 3 illustrates some application integration options with EDI.

PUBLIC DATA NETWORKS

The vehicle is usually a network which can be a computer-to-computer link or a public data network often referred to as a Third Party Network Provider. This should be regarded as different from the many Direct Data Exchange systems that involve direct computer connections between trading partners. Considerable progress in the services available from third party network providers has been accomplished over the last two to three years. This includes the ability of independent networks to electronically transfer and exchange ANSI transactions sets with each other without either user (sender or recipient) being involved in the process. This has allowed access to many more geographic locations. The ability of networks to transfer and exchange information facilitates the task of electronic mailbox collection because a Company can use the services of fewer networks. It should be pointed out that each Trading partner will most likely be using

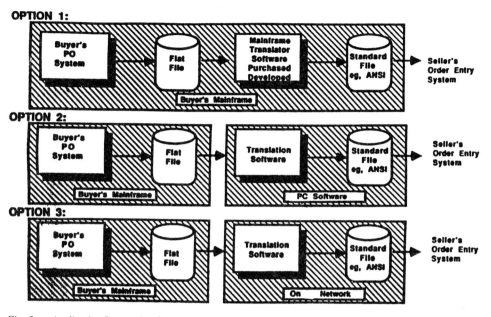

Fig. 3   Application Integration Options with EDI

the services of at least several networks for the foreseeable future.

The desirable characteristics of Public Data Networks include specifications concerning operating characteristics such as availability, confidentiality, security, connectivity, ANSI X12 Transaction support, error reporting, performance reports, audit trail, backup, recovery, archiving, compliance checking, translation, rapid delivery, release procedures, support, billing, etc.

SIZE OF THE ELECTRONIC COMMERCE MARKET

The size of the Electronic Commerce continues to expand in all the major components of this market. Software sales increased 28% from 1992 to a value of US$360 million in 1993, Network Services increased 14% from 1992 to US$925 million in 1993, Electronic Information Services increased 16% from 1992 to a value of US$820 million in 1993 and professional Services increased 25% from 1992 to US$50 million in 1993. [Source: EDI World, Nov., 1993, p. 26].

BENEFITS RESULTING FROM EDI

Although it is possible to justify changing from a mail system to an EDI system on its own merits, the change to a Quick Response and Just In Time manufacturing operation

47

has meant that the manufacturer must order raw material more often and receive shipments more frequently. Exchanging business documents in the traditional manner yields a growth in volume of intercompany paperwork which has been estimated to quadruple if the manufacturer changes from a monthly to a Quick Response or weekly cycle.

Table 1 shows a matrix comparing the benefits of implementing the TALC voluntary standards for the various tasks found in a typical apparel manufacturing operation. It is recommended that each company develop their own benefits matrix and begin implementation so that appropriate benefit/cost outcome can be achieved.

EDI has become a way to gain a competitive advantage, a way to address the needs of the Merchandising Cycle by expediting the purchasing cycle, improving customer service and productivity. EDI has been embraced as an integral part of cost reduction and productivity improvement in many industries.

AMERICAN NATIONAL STANDARDS INSTITUTE (ANSI)

For the textile/apparel pipeline the benefits of having ANSI ASC X12 as the translator include characteristics such as:

- ANSI covers more business requirements
- ANSI has already been adopted by over 40 industries
- ANSI is a non-profit organization
- ANSI is accepted as international standards negotiation body
- ANSI is committed to keeping standards up to date
- ANSI does not favor a particular industry or business segment
- anyone wishing to participate can be part of ANSI

ANSI is working closely with EDIFACT, the most widely recognized European standard for electronic data interchange, with the expectation that business transactions can be exchanged electronically between countries without problems of compatibility or translation.

The implications of using standard business transactions can be better understood by considering The Big Picture as shown schematically in Figure 4. If a company plans to take full advantage of the benefits of EDI, the use of standards as developed by ANSI (and others) allows the company to conduct business with its customers and suppliers as well as the providers of financial, freight, customs and other service suppliers.

TRANSACTION SETS AND TRANSMISSION STRUCTURES

A Transaction Set is that group of standard data segments, in a predefined sequence, needed to provide all of the data required to define a complete transaction such as a purchase order, invoice or freight bill. The Transaction Set is further defined in terms of data segments (or lines of information) and the segment is defined in terms of data elements. The data elements represent the smallest information unit and may be a single character code, a series of characters constituting a literal description or a numeric quantity. The length of a data element may be fixed or variable, but they must be consistent with the data being transmitted. A data segment is composed of a function identifier and one or more functionally related data elements positioned serially in standard

Apparel Tasks	Benefits						TALC Voluntary Standards							
	Inventory & Warehouse Space Reduction	Improved Accuracy, Error Reduction	Labor Savings	Material Savings	Quality of Product	Reduction in Lead Times	Defect ID and Flagging	EDI	Order Status	Roll ID (Bar Coded Ticket)	Shade	Shipment Packaging and Labeling	Vendor Certification	Width-Length
Advanced Cut Planning	●		●	●		●	○	○	○	○	○		○	○
Advanced Marker Making	●		●	●		●	○	○	○	○	○		○	○
Contract Status	●	●				●		○	○					
Elimination of Data Input	●	●	●			●	○	○	○	○	○			○
Faster Spreading			●			●								○
Faster Tracking			●			●		○				○		○
Improved Fabric Utilization Planning				●			○	○		○	○			○
Invoice Verification		●	●					○						
Plant Loading	●	●	●			●		○	○				○	
Production Planning	●	●	●			●		○	○				○	
Reduction/Elimination of Fabric Shading and Inspection	●		●		●	●	○	○			○		○	
Reduced Production of Irregulars			●	●	●		○	○			○		○	
Production of Right Products at Right Time			●	●				○	○		○		○	
Reduced Roll Handling	●		●			●	○	○		○	○	○	○	○

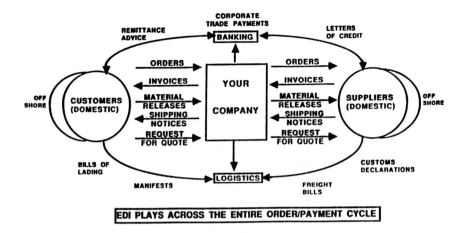

Fig. 4   The Big Picture

manner with a data element delimiter preceding each data element and a segment terminator character immediately following the last data element transmitted.

Each data segment has a unique identifier consisting of two or three alpha/numeric characters and is also terminated by a special character inserted immediately following the last data element to be transmitted.

The Transmission structure is shown graphically in Figure 5 with several Transaction Sets and the Functional Group Header and Trailer segments (GS and GE). The Communication Session refers to the uninterrupted flow of data transferred between two independent computer systems and must include the Header and Trailer segments as shown in Figure 5 (BG and EG).

IMPLEMENTATION OF ELECTRONIC DATA INTERCHANGE

Implementing a new technology and changing the method of conducting business will require a well planned approach that involves all functions within the organization. The first and critical step is to obtain commitment from key management in both the corporate office as well as in each of the departments or functions knowledgeable of the business needs. The next steps include the formation of an EDI project team and the development of a workplan. These stages provide initial estimates of savings by each department, a critical path chart, a responsibility matrix and expected deliverables.

The next steps include designating the business contacts within your company, the technical contacts including those of your trading partners, reviewing the internal systems and business procedures and determining how EDI should be integrated into your present system. A library of appropriate reference documents should be formed and trading partners should be asked to provide information for items such as product identification, tables, files, optional fields, facility locations, etc. A survey of equipment providers should be conducted and data contained in the documents to be exchanged should be

50

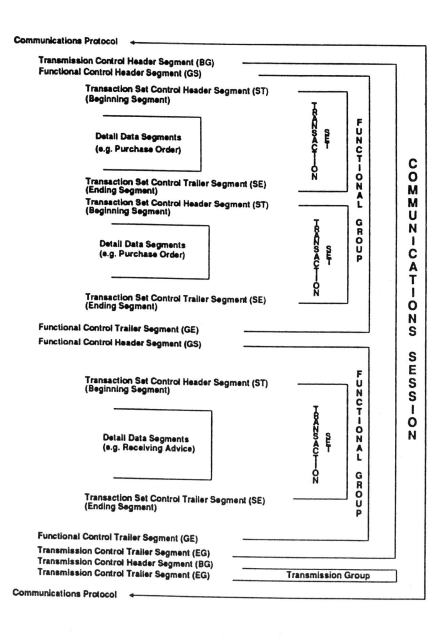

Fig. 5   Transmission Structure

51

thoroughly reviewed. Before sending or receiving transmitted documents from trading partners a company should ensure that the in-house interfaces are functioning properly and decisions have been reached regarding the selection of translation software and network provider including any optional services.

The translation software and network connection should be implemented and a system test conducted with your trading partner. Finally, agreement should be reached regarding the production cut-over date including the signing of all contracts and agreements.

EDI DIRECTIONS

Several recent surveys conducted for different industries clearly show the commitment to EDI and the scanning of product identification on the case, package and product. The National Retail Merchants Association's Second Annual Barcode/EDI Survey Results show that the retail industry is committed to barcoding, scanning and EDI. The survey results showed that 100% of the larger retailers, 88% of the medium-sized and 63% of the smaller retailers were committed to scanning barcode at point-of-sale. The key benefits for the retailer were stated to be the price accuracy at point-of-sale, the productivity at the check-out, improved marketing information and unit inventory accuracy for the smaller and medium sized companies. By the end of 1991, it is projected that all mass merchants, 87% of department stores and 88% of all specialty stores responding indicated that the preferred barcode would be UPC-A.

The key motivators for considering EDI partnerships were cited as competitive advantage (61%), top management (28%) and vendor request (11%). The major benefits of EDI for the retailer were reduced inventory levels, shortened re-order fulfillment cycles, quick response, paperless document processing, improved accuracy of data, reduced costs and streamlined merchandise handling. The majority of the retail industry plans using ANSI X12 (62%) and 58% plan on using a public data network for their implementation approach. The barriers to implementation of EDI at the retailer included the perceived lack of industry standards, the lack of understanding of EDI, incompatibility with vendors and investment costs.

The 1990 EDI survey conducted by the ASC X12D Subcommittee on Education and Implementation of its 375 members yielded a 47% response rate. The ASC X12 survey shows that EDI usage is expected to grow phenomenally over the next five years from an average of 33 trading partners in 1989 to 45 in 1990 and more than double by 1991. Users anticipate that by 1995 they will have over 400 trading partners, an increase of over 800% from 1990. Current EDI users have an average of 7.4 transaction sets in test or production and anticipate having 14 transaction sets by 1995. The budget for EDI within a company is expected to grow at approximately 10% per year over the next five years. The X12 members spent an estimated US$35.2 million on EDI in 1989 and expect to spend US$62.8 million in 1990 and US$71.7 million in 1991. By 1995 the X12 users estimate that expenditures on EDI in 1995 will reach US$102 million on all aspects including internal development, software, hardware, networks and services.

The reasons for using EDI continue to be similar to those of previous years. The most important reason to adopt EDI was to maintain competitiveness. The additional reasons for adopting EDI included competitive advantage, cost savings, trading partner request or requirement, cost of business and cycle time improvement. Consequently, the benefits rated the highest by most companies was maintaining competitiveness and competitive advantage. Improved relations with trading partners and increased quality of service were also cited as benefits of EDI. The cost savings benefits from using EDI were attributable to increased timeliness and flexibility, reduced data error entries, reduced staffing, reduced inventory and reduced cost of money. Companies (78%) that have adopted EDI indicate that EDI has matched or exceeded user expectations, but the two most significant costs were the changes to the existing systems (38%) and the cost of personnel (33%). Other costs included software (13%) systems integration (12%) and maintenance.

SUMMARY

The textile and apparel industries have begun the implementation of Quick Response through the adoption of Electronic Data Interchange and product identification. The fiber, textile, apparel and retail industry segments have no choice but to vigorously pursue full EDI implementation. Continuing to shorten the re-order fulfillment cycle with rapid replenishment techniques coupled with continuous merchandising for new styles will demand the features and benefits that EDI has to offer. Traditional relationships between suppliers and customers will continue to undergo significant changes as the trading partner relationships become established. Information analysis and management of businesses based on information will continue to keep the industry complex focused on the needs of its customers.

Quick Response and Technology

A. Hunter

College of Textiles, North Carolina State University

This chapter is intended to offset the heavy emphasis that has been placed on technology by earlier contributors. Its premise is that, while specific technologies will play a vital role in preserving the textile and apparel industries, they are no more important than several other factors, human and managerial, that make up the total supply system. As to the structure of this chapter, the differences between the traditional supply system and the newer Quick Response (QR) procedures will first be summarized. Then the total content of QR will be examined and finally selected aspects of technology, hard and soft, will be reviewed from a management point of view.

During the last 4–5 years a great deal of effort has been expended by industry analysts in developing a better understanding of how the supply of apparel, from fiber through retail, has worked in the past and how it must work in the future if the manufacturing sectors are to remain internationally viable. The results of these studies are now generally referred to as Quick Response.

The early investigations were devoted to characterizing the supply pipeline in terms of inventories, work-in-process and delivery schedules. For woven goods, they revealed an almost incredible 55 weeks of inventories and a further 11 weeks of work in process. The inventories, with their many duplicate stocks, were clearly a result of each sector: fiber, textile, apparel, and retailing, seeing themselves as separate industries rather than sequential processors of the final article. The long in-process times reflected, at least in part, the heavy emphasis placed by the manufacturers on long runs and unit costs. There is nothing wrong with long runs and low unit costs if the final customer wants a limited range of merchandise at the lowest possible price. Unfortunately, that is generally not the case. A rapidly increasing proportion of apparel and other textiles is falling into 'Fashion' categories with their short shelf lives and diversity of styles and colors.

Further studies of the pipeline showed that the application of well established Industrial Engineering practices could reduce the length of the pipeline to a third of its traditional length; about five months. In doing so, however, the problem of increasing costs because of shorter runs became evident. More flexible manufacturing procedures and rapid change-over techniques would clearly have to be developed if the new system was to work profitably. However, if these problems could be solved, it was apparent that the industry would be in a position to reap enormous benefits — most of them at retail.

Basic goods, i.e. those that are on the shelf all year round, present few problems from either a marketing or a supply point of view. Intelligent inventory and reorder policies should assure a high level of customer satisfaction provided quality and design are satisfactory. The problems become difficult when the merchandise has a finite life and the shorter the shelf life, the greater the problems.

Traditionally, the retail buyer places orders for goods 5–9 months ahead of a season. Most of these are manufactured, and the majority delivered, before the season opens. Several months must be added to this schedule to allow for yarn and fabric design and manufacture and the actual garment design and sampling. Under these conditions, it comes as no surprise that there is a mismatch between the goods being offered and the customer preferences with the result that popular items soon become stocked out and unwanted goods remain unsold. As the season progresses this conflict can only be resolved by price reductions — someone will buy anything at the right price. With the steady growth of fashion apparel, this markdown problem has seriously eroded profits both at retail and upstream and has contributed to the import problem as retailers search for merchandise that will allow a higher markon, thus protecting their final margins. The cost of stockouts, markdowns and excessive inventories under the traditional system has been widely reported and is estimated to be in the tens of billions of dollars each year.

The message of QR is that this need not be. If process cycle times can be reduced to low enough levels it becomes possible to place firm orders for only a part of a season's requirements and to 'reorder' the balance in increments after the season opens and the customer preferences are better known. In this way, the assortment offered can be made to match demand closely. Such a system calls for accurate knowledge of actual Point Of Sale (POS) information at the Stock Keeping Unit (SKU) level of detail and the rapid transmission of such data to the vendors and their suppliers.

The technology required to implement QR is all on the shelf. Further, a growing body of knowledge is proving that, without a shadow of a doubt, the returns on the necessary investments are extremely attractive. Why, then, is the industry not rushing into QR? The answer is far from simple, but centers around the reluctance or inability of managers to implement change even though such change is clearly beneficial.

The very brief account given above made no effort to explore the non-technical aspects of QR. One way of doing this is to give a fairly full definition of QR — something more detailed than the usual, 'Having the products the customer wants, in the right place, at the right time and at the right price'. One such compound definition is:

- QR is an operational philosophy and set of procedures aimed at maximizing the profitability of the apparel supply pipeline.
- QR depends on the integration of all the parts-fiber, textile, apparel and retail-into one consumer responsive whole.
- QR requires the highest standards of product quality at all stages to allow significant reductions in safety stocks and specification testing times.
- QR demands frank and open dialogue between supplier and customer and relies on high levels of trust. Only with such trust are Value Adding Partnerships possible.
- QR is driven by comprehensive and rapid information transfer between the pipeline sectors, from retail point of sale back upstream.
- QR calls for the use of up-to-date hard and soft technologies to minimize work in process, offset the added costs of increased product diversity and maximize responsiveness to the customer.

- QR employs as its principal elements:
  - the pulling back of open-to-buy dates,
  - sharp reductions in firm initial retail orders,
  - point of sale tracking at retail,
  - flexible merchandise planning,
  - frequent buyer reorders,
  - pre-ticketing and drop-shipping of garments,
  - standardised bar-coding of fabrics and garments,
  - electronic transmission of orders, invoices, etc.,
  - highly engineered manufacturing, including such elements as computerized marking, laser cutting, UPS, modular manufacturing and automated sub-assembly sewing,
  - Computer Assisted Design and Manufacture (CAD/CAM),
  - flexible short-run spinning, weaving, dyeing and finishing operations,
  - Just In Time shipping of fiber and fabric,
  - rapid development of sample fabrics and garments.

Even a quick glance at the definition above shows the very broad scope of the QR process and the philosophical and operational changes that must be adopted if everything is to work smoothly. It is worthwhile taking a closer look at several of these factors in order to see how they interlock.

QUALITY

Possibly the most important of the changes needed for the implementation of QR is the industry's attitude to quality. Without very high quality standards, collapsing the pipeline is impossible. Similarly, the necessary levels of trust and cooperation between suppliers and customers referred to above, and the setting up of Partnerships, are impossible without such standards.

In achieving this all-embracing change in corporate culture, no methodology has been more successful than the Quality Management program first developed by Philip Crosby. Several of the leading fiber and textile companies in the US have adopted the program and adapted it to their own environments with outstanding success. Adoption is time and energy consuming but well worth the effort. Crosby estimates that the cost of quality in most corporations amounts to as much as 20% of sales dollars and up to half this amount can be transferred to pre-tax earnings. Extensive industry experience supports these estimates.

At the heart of the program is the corporate commitment. A typical example is that promulgated by Celanese Corporation in the early 1980s:

'Celanese will deliver to its customers products and services that conform exactly to requirements.

This requires that we design our manufacturing, marketing, technical and administrative processes to prevent deviations and that we perform all operating and staff functions right the first time.'

The techniques and mechanics of the Quality Management process cannot be expanded on here, but they include Statistical Quality Control, systematic Error Cause Removal procedures, formal Problem Solving training, Interruption Free Processing and, above all, a Zero Defect mentality at every level in the organization. Once adopted, Quality Management is accompanied by a more participative management style, an increase in employee involvement and a marked improvement in employee morale.

The external objective of the process is to operate with suppliers as customers through partnership programs that set up agreed-on product specifications and allow certification of the product. Certification means the following:

- Quality is the responsibility of the supplier.
- Incoming products meet agreed upon specifications.
- Incoming inspection is eliminated.
- There are no production delays because of substandard materials.
- Cushion inventories are eliminated.
- Buyer/seller production planning is integrated, including free exchange of forecasts as well as consumption and inventory information.

Milliken and Company was an early exponent of Quality Management and it is now the dominant theme in its business style. The company has quantified the savings to its customers of implementing product certification. They are shown in Table I below. To a customer using 1 million yards of fabric per year, certification can cut costs by US$200,000 and at the same time contribute to short production cycles, i.e., contraction of the pipeline.

Table I
Cost Reduction At The Textile/Apparel Interface
(US$ Per Yard Of Fabric)

	US$/Yd.
Greater width utilization - 2% of fabric	0.0500
Discontinue fabric inspection at apparel.	0.0400
Discontinue color/shade control testing.	0.0800
Provision of longer roll lengths.	0.0195
Reduced fabric inventory at apparel.	0.0125
TOTAL	0.200

The importance of Quality Management is paramount. In one sense, QR is an offshoot of QM; certainly the latter is impossible without the former. Also, when industry estimates of the financial impact of QR are listed, they do not include the benefits of QR. Such benefits should be added to the list and employed in the assessment of capital expenditures associated with QR. This subject will be discussed further in the chapter.

One final point under the heading of quality. All too rarely does management realise that suitable technology can have an enormous impact on product quality. Properly controlled, a machine duplicates a manufacturing process exactly, or at least to small tolerances. A human operator simply cannot compete in this regard and this is particularly true in the manufacture of garments where operator turnover is high and at any time only a part of the operator force is fully experienced and in control of the process. A second instance of the impact of technology on quality is provided by Unit Production Systems (UPS). Here, after each sewing operation, the partly constructed garment is open to inspection by the next operator in the line and not hidden in a bundle. Further, at inspection following the final sewing operation, the garment is free from wrinkles and improved inspection standards are possible. This improvement in product quality has proved to be one of the strongest attributes of UPS. One of the areas of current research interest is that of producing fabrics with much greater uniformity of color, side to side and along the length. The value of this work is shown in the table above.

ELECTRONIC DATA INTERCHANGE AND LINKAGE

The importance to QR of collecting and transmitting information backwards and forwards in the pipeline speedily and with a high order of accuracy cannot be over-emphasized. It is fundamental to the concept of changing apparel supply from a manufacturing driven to a consumer driven system.

It is convenient to think of EDI as having two main components. The first of these is the electronic transmission of transactional information such as forecasts of requirements, purchase orders, shipping notices and invoices. The second aspect relates to information accompanying the physical transfer of goods, i.e. fiber, fabric and garments, by means of bar coding of the merchandise, as well as the recording of retail sales information at the cash register by means of Point Of Sale (POS) scanning of bar codes.

The main impediment to early implementation of EDI by the apparel industry was that each pipeline sector considered itself a separate entity and developed its own way of doing business, using its own language. The advantages of using electronic communication and product identification had to mark time until the various industry groups could agree on common information formats and protocols to be used across the interfaces.

A number of individual companies had set up varieties of EDI with their own suppliers and customers in the late 70s and early 80s, but it was not until 1984 that the first set of meetings took place between a few progressive textile and apparel companies with a view to establishing industry-wide standards. These led to the formation of TALC — the Textile Apparel Linkage Council — in May of 1986.

TALC is a volunteer organization composed primarily of textile and apparel manufacturers together with other interested parties. Its principal objectives are to develop voluntary standards for use by the industry and to promulgate and encourage the use of these standards by means of seminars, meetings and publications.

TALC has been enormously successful. Virtually all major textile and apparel companies became members in its first year of operation and there has been rapid progress toward establishing standards of communication between the two industry groups. Its activities have the endorsement of both the AAMA and the ATMI.

The following are brief summaries of the voluntary standards adopted in the first two years of the Council's operations.

- EDI Format. TALC has endorsed the use of ANSI X12 standard formats. ANSI X12 are the American National Standards Institute's standards for the electronic transmission of data for such business transactions as purchase orders and invoices and are widely used in many industries. To facilitate their use, TALC has developed an ANSI standards conventions document entitled Textile Apparel Manufacturers Communications Standards (TAMCS). The communications links between trading partners may take the form either of direct connection between their computers or via a third party networking service. The use of the latter service greatly simplifies the task of linking to many suppliers or customers without loss of confidentiality of information.

- Roll Identification. Each roll of fabric shipped by the textile producer will be uniquely identified by means of a 15-character identifier, consisting of a 6-digit producer number followed by a 9-digit alphanumeric producer-assigned number. The roll identification number is to be represented in both human and Universal Product Code (UPC) bar code readable forms on a hang-tag or pressure sensitive label accompanying the roll. A recommendation has also been approved for the layout of the information on the ticket.

  With an industry-unique roll identification, the apparel manufacturer no longer needs to re-ticket each roll for his own inventory identification which is made more accurate and simpler to handle. The other, and major, benefit is that the standardised ticketing opens the door to the transmission of other quantitative and qualitative information by the fabric producer.

- Width/Length Measurement. By obtaining accurate dimensional information in standard form, the apparel manufacturer is in a position to reduce costs and improve efficiency through better fabric utilization, elimination of duplicated measurements and speeding up the marker making and cutting processes. The standards call for widths to be expressed in ¼" increments, rounded down; the length of the roll is to be given to in 0.1 yard increments.

  In a growing number of textile/apparel partnerships, these and other measurements are being transmitted ahead of the actual shipping of the fabric so that the roll can be taken directly to the spreading table, computerization of the cutting process having taken place while the fabric was in transit.

- Shade Measurement. To eliminate duplicate measurements of fabric shade, the standard calls for each roll to be identified with either delta values or the 5-5-5 shade sorting convention agreed to by the trading partners.

- Identification and Flagging of Fabric Defects. Based on buyer/seller agreement, defects to be flagged by the producer have been established for four categories: Critical, Denim, Standard and No Flagging Required. The principal method for flagging defects for automated detection is the use of metallic stick-on devices, but a number of textile companies are now using more sophisticated mappings of defects that record the distance of the fault from the edge of the fabric. Such methods, of course, allow greater fabric utilization by the manufacturer.

- Packaging of Rolls Within Cartons. This standard established sets of packing specifications for individual rolls within a carton, including weight classifications, packing recommendations, and carton and strapping specifications.

- Packaging for Individually Wrapped Rolls. This standard, adopted in May 1988, established a set of packing specifications including: weight classifications, types of packaging, as well as the fit, material, clarity, and end closure specifications for each weight classification.

- Order Status. The items of information necessary for the seller/buyer interface on delivery data relative to order status are provided by this standard.

Communications on delivery non-conformance are also being reviewed.

In addition to the above standards, TALC committees are working on a number of other topics for possible standardization. These include questions of distribution and transportation: sequential loading and unloading of rolls, recommended materials handling equipment, guidelines for determining cost effective roll size and recommendations for core tube size and strength.

A second study area is that of forecasting. A committee is examining ways to define the items of information and their timing, to be transmitted by manufacturers to textile suppliers projecting future demand. This is a subject of great importance to the textile producer because of the long lead times associated with fabric manufacture.

The need to make use of the voluntary standards is widely accepted by TALC members but it will be some time before adherence is wide spread. In the summer of 1987, TALC surveyed AAMA member firms to assess actual or intended use of the standards. Of the 136 respondents, only 25% were linked electronically with their suppliers though others affirmed their intention of moving in that direction within the year. The survey yielded invaluable information on the progress being made in such areas as acceptance of supplier width, length and shade information. The responses showed clearly that testing duplication is still deemed necessary by far too many manufacturers, but that steady progress is being made. Future surveys will allow TALC to focus on those areas where industry acceptance is lagging.

At a meeting held in Chicago on 24 June 1986, major retailers, manufacturers and textile producers formed the Voluntary Inter-Industry Communications Standards (VICS) Committee whose aim it is to provide leadership in the use of standards for the capture and transmission of product related information between manufacturers and retailers. When formed, the Committee identified two areas on which to concentrate its efforts:

- Standard Item Identification. Here the first of the objectives was to gain general agreement among retailers and manufacturers on the use of the UPC system to identify products so that automated point of sale devices can be employed efficiently to capture accurate information on consumer purchases at the SKU level. Currently, retailers use a variety of methods for product ticketing including pen, magnetics, Optical Character Recognition (OCR) Font and, in some cases, UPC. Until such time as UPC is universally implemented, the trade has agreed to use Dual Technology Vendor Marking (DTVM) which involves both UPC and OCR A.

  The second objective was to encourage the establishment of common item identification standards for yarn and fabric products used in the production of consumer goods. Clearly, this was a direct reinforcement of the TALC activities.

- Standard Data Transmission Format. Again, two objectives were identified; to establish a single set of communication formats and protocols for EDI between manufacturers and distributors and to encourage the development of equipment to record and make available to producers information about consumer purchases.

Having made substantial progress in these areas, VICS has moved into a third action area, that of promoting and monitoring implementation by the industry. Focus is on relating to industry trade associations, providing training and educational programs, stimulating equipment and software vendors and providing leadership in identifying and overcoming barriers to progress.

Most recently VICS and the governing body of UPS, the Uniform Code Council, co-sponsored the VICS Retail Cost/Benefit Study to be carried out by Arthur Andersen. This research was designed to quantify the benefits to the retailer of participating in EDI despite the high initial costs of implementation. The Study paralleled a similar investigation by KSA of the cost/benefit relation for apparel manufacturers. The results of both studies were published in March 1989.

As with TALC, the progress made by VICS has been extremely rapid and in one sense it has even greater importance for the future of the pipeline. There is little question that the rate of adoption of EDI by producers will be determined, in large part, by the speed with which the retailer insists on vendor compliance with his needs. It is, therefore, encouraging to note the increasing number of influential retailers who are applying EDI to their basic product lines for automatic restocking of merchandise. Already, one of the most important advantages to be gained from such systems is being reported; that of the sharp reduction in stockouts accompanied by higher sales volumes.

The use of standard formats for product identification has helped speed the implementation of an important aspect of QR. Ticketing of merchandise by the manufacturer rather than the retailer allows substantial reductions in Distribution Center handling. It also reduces the system costs. Ticketing at retail costs 15¢ to 25¢ per item, compared to the 2¢ to 3¢ incurred by the manufacturer.

The challenges facing the retailer are formidable. The grocery industry has used bar coding with point of sale tracking for several years, but the number of SKU's they must handle is small compared with those of the apparel world which measures its offerings in the millions. Further, the apparel industry is becoming more and more fashion-goods oriented, with garments supplied by between 15,000 and 20,000 vendors. In line with this, a variety of third party systems has sprung up and there is increasing interest in 'electronic catalogs' that will allow the buyer to scan rapidly each vendor's offerings and to handle the increasingly difficult task of relating bar coded information to merchandise descriptions. The more progressive buyers are already calling for such catalogs to contain visual displays of the garments, which, in addition to requiring immense amounts of computer memory, increases the need for information security.

Another kind of problem centers around the vast amount of information generated by point of sale tracking at the SKU level. Turning this body of data into information of use to the buyer is one of the next barriers to be overcome by the industry. However, once the basic problems have been overcome, not only will automatic rapid reordering of best selling garments be possible because of real time inventory control, but the whole new field of style trend analysis will be opened up for study.

In the first quarter of 1987, two more linkage organizations were born, making a full set for the apparel industry. The first of these was the Sundries and Apparel Findings Linkage Council (SAFLINC) which, as its name suggests, concerns itself with all the components, other than fabric, that go into the manufacture of apparel-thread, buttons, zippers and the like. The second group, the Fabric and Suppliers Linkage Council (FASLINC), was organized to develop voluntary standards and protocols for transactions between fiber suppliers, dyestuffs and chemicals producers, yarn spinners and textile mills, thus completing the EDI network for the whole apparel pipeline.

Both SAFLINC and FASLINC are close to TALC in terms of objectives and strategies for achieving them, though they each address areas of special concern to them. SAFLINC members have a strong interest in the forecasting aspect of their interface with customers and also a concern over the optimum methods for handling large numbers of small items such as buttons. In the case of FASLINC, fiber and chemicals quality certification is of great interest and, of course, the distribution and varying standards of cotton fiber present many unique problems.

SAFLINC was intended to handle the needs of suppliers of such nonwoven items as linings and interfacings, but members of the industry were slow to participate. However, in the fall of 1987, INDA, the industry organization, set up study groups to determine the EDI needs of its members when linking to both suppliers and customers. The first step being taken by these committees is to make the greatest possible use of the work done by TALC and the other linkage councils.

The linkage organizations described so far have had as their principal focus the interchange of information and goods with customers and suppliers. There is, however, another part of the apparel supply system where linkages are increasingly needed; apparel manufacturing.

Computerized cutting equipment, Unit Production Systems, and programmable sewing machines are all driven electronically and, as the use of technology increases, the progressive apparel manufacturer will rely increasingly on the computer. The problem is that as these islands of automation spring up, there are few linkages allowing the transfer of information among them. Most machinery manufacturers are concerned with optimizing their own equipment and there are no industry accepted guidelines for information transfer to and from other pieces of equipment. There are exceptions to this generalization, the most important being the integration of CAD with marker making and cutting by such companies as Gerber, Investronica and Lectra which manufacture all the units themselves.

The industry is addressing this need. Between August 1987 and February 1988, four meetings were held by an increasing number of interested industry members. Initially, the idea was to adapt the TALC procedures under the acronym of CIM/LINC, but the specialized nature of the project and the extended time frame over which the teams would have to operate led to the work being transferred to a newly formed AAMA CIM Committee.

There are two other CIM related initiatives that show considerable promise. The first of these forms part of the overall AAMA program and involves the University of Louisiana at Lafayette. In September of 1988, representatives of the two organizations initiated a joint effort to create an Apparel Computer Integrated Manufacturing (A-CIM) Laboratory. The initial project has as its objective the definition and establishment of the system(s) and standards required to implement data driven manufacturing and enable optimum utilization of existing and underdevelopment equipment for the apparel industry. Cooperative efforts with (TC)2 and other universities and agencies will be examined once the first project is underway.

The textile and apparel machinery makers have also seen the clear need for standards rationalization. The newly formed Textile and Apparel Machine Modernization Foundation (TAMMF) has been funded by the Trade Adjustment Assistance office of the US Department of Commerce. Its first project will be devoted to computer communication standards to enable 'textile mills to reduce the need for specially designed protocols for each type of machine and each vendor and to tie all machinery together in one plant'.

With this broadening of effort devoted to CIM, there is a clear need for some group to review all activities and ensure that duplication of effort is kept to a minimum.

NON-TRADITIONAL METHODS OF ASSESSING CAPITAL EXPENDITURES

Non-traditional methods of assessing capital expenditures are of increasing importance as the technology content of equipment increases. Such equipment is usually much more expensive than the machinery it replaces. And so it should be; it does more. But its purchase can be difficult to justify if traditional financial techniques are used.

A HBR article in 1982 crystallized the problem when it identified the new CAM equipment as offering value in a 'systematic', rather than the usual 'point', sense. CAM's ability to tie together other processes, to turn isolated pieces of equipment into an operating unit, requires that it be evaluated in new ways.

Since that time, engineering and academic journals have explored the matter very fully. Books have been written on the subject and it has taken root as an Industrial Engineering discipline, though one that is relatively unknown to industry, and certainly to those in industry who assess capital appropriation requests or who sign the cheques. The Defense Logistics Agency, when it funded the three advanced apparel manufacturing demonstration sites in the US, included in its Statement of Work an objective requiring research into the justification of equipment and systems.

The criteria usually employed when assessing new capital expenditures are heavily quantitative and are limited to a handful of well understood concepts; Payback, ROI, LTROI, DCFROI, Net Present Worth, and the like. Frequently, leading-edge equipment, when evaluated in these ways, fails to pass today's high financial hurdle rates.

There are really two groups of concerns. The first, referred to in the HBR article cited above, is that individual pieces of equipment should not be viewed individually, but as part of the total manufacturing capability. In order to optimize a manufacturing facility, matching sets of the new machinery, plus the attendant systems and software are needed. Until they are all in place and linked together in the way they were designed to be linked, their full potential is not realized; to look at each piece separately is meaningless. Further, it is only when the complete system is operational that management sees improvements in the intangibles-moral, absenteeism, competitiveness-which are rarely worked into classic financial analyses.

The second concern is more fundamental. It is the place of capital in the company's strategic plans. Most apparel companies either ignore long-term strategy or assign it a time horizon which is very short compared with industries that are traditionally capital intensive. The substitution of capital for labor is a painful process and only to be undertaken when the long-term objectives of the enterprise are clearly seen-usually as the result of a great deal of effort. Analysis is part of the process, but only part; the rest is mostly qualitative judgement involving the need for such market-oriented factors as quality, flexibility and speed of response. Risk considerations also play a more important role. Greater benefits are usually accompanied by greater risk or uncertainty and it is notoriously difficult to be objective about such matters, because they tend to be qualitative in nature.

Non-Traditional Decision Analysis methods allow these 'soft' attributes to be worked into analyses of capital expenditure proposals alongside the usual financial measures by giving them rankings or weights on numerical scales.

There is a variety of techniques available. Some are very simple and directed at helping the analyst to be logical and objective; others are more rigorous and are designed to handle complex series of alternative investment options. While no attempt is made to go into detail about any one of them, a partial listing of their names is given below. The methods fall into three groups:

Graphical Techniques	• Scorecards
	• Profile charts
	• Polar graphs
Multi-Attribute Methodologies	• Multi-attribute weighted evaluation analysis
	• Analytic Hierarchy Process
	• Multi-attribute utility analysis
	• Goal/multi-objective programming analysis
Risk/Uncertainty Techniques	• Sensitivity analysis
	• Decision trees
	• Monte Carlo simulation

Software developers have made the techniques more accessible in the last few years. There are now around thirty programs for microcomputers, each under US$1000, that facilitate the organization and analysis of data for most of the important methods.

There is limited value to technological invention until people buy it, and one of our industry's greatest failings is that it has traditionally been so on the uptake. But, as Henry Ford said forty or so years ago, 'If you don't invest in new technology, you will pay for it without ever owning it.'

A TECHNOLOGY MODEL

As a broad generalization, it can be claimed that technology intensity has moved downstream in the apparel pipeline over time. The 1950s saw many of the fiber innovations in both process and product. These were followed by developments in very high speed filament yarn texturing and multi-feed circular knitting. In the 1970s it was the turn of the spinner and weaver. Opening rooms were automated, carding speeds were increased, drawing became semi-automated, open-end spinning systems were developed and new breeds of high speed weaving machines became available. The 1980s have seen the same types of breakthrough for apparel — CAD/CAM, UPS, programmable sewing equipment, etc. In the 1990s the focus is likely to be at retail with the main emphasis on soft technology. POS tracking and allied merchandise control systems will be adopted, video marketing will grow in importance as cable networks change to high resolution TV and CAD, style tracking and Style Testing will become parts of the buyers' box of tricks.

As the focus of technology has moved downstream, it has placed increasing demands on the upstream supplier. Very high speed looms require superior yarns, which in turn place greater demands on the fiber producer and spinner. This has led to today's emphasis on process control and quality assurance which encourage employment of voice recognition and imaging technologies and these, in turn, permit greater use of robotics for package doffing, handling and distribution. QR's insistence on short response times and greater product diversity is already beginning to have a similar effect on the upstream industries. As has been noted, the traditional fabric defect and shade variability levels are at odds with inventory reduction, and highly automated spreading and cutting equipment and short runs demand short fabric forming and wet processing down-times.

This model of technology movement is useful for both pulling together what has happened in the past and providing insight into the ways things are likely to develop in the future. The pipeline is not only a marketing and manufacturing pipeline, it is also a technological pipeline-the sectors are connected in all respects.

MANAGING OF AUTOMATION

Making Investment Decisions — The Age of Discontinuity Revisited

R. A. Barnhardt, G. A. Berkstresser and
G. L. Hodge

College of Textiles, North Carolina State University

Over a decade ago when Peter Drucker wrote his book 'The Age of Discontinuity', Drucker not only proposed that the time was soon coming that we would not be able to use old methodologies that had been slightly altered or dusted off to solve our new problems but that there were some fundamental changes in the way we live that would necessitate discontinuous changes in the way we approached our problem solving.

During the past decade there have been some fundamental or secular changes which affect textile machinery payback ratios, and it is certainly true, as Drucker stated, that we cannot just dust off or slightly alter traditional payback methods and expect them to be of great value for us today. The discontinuities have occurred and we have to live with them. Right up through the period of World War II our domestic market was constantly expanding and the influence of imports was very small. Today we live in a global market with little domestic growth, and imports are playing an ever increasing part in our consumption. It does little good to say that we are not playing on a level field or that the Federal Government is prepared to let segments of the textile industry disappear from our shores.

Perhaps one of the most succinct statements about the problem was made by Karl-Heinz/Narjes, EEC Commissioner, in European Report number 1226 – 31 May 1986. He said, 'The nub of the 'textile trade' problem lies not just in the advantage these (textile exporting) countries have where labor costs are concerned, but also the fact that they keep their markets firmly closed. This stance means that they can concentrate their industrialization effort on specific export oriented sectors without having to worry about international competition for the less well developed products of their textile industry. At the same time they also employ practices like subsidies and dumping which are contrary to the principles of competition'.

Of course, the Western developed countries, which by and large utilize MFA type import restrictions, are most frequently criticized for protectionism but are in fact the least protected. Because of this discontinuity, today's textile manager is making decisions about purchasing textile production machinery in a completely different environment from his predecessors. Thus, the differences in cost of capital between the US and other countries becomes very important.

First published in *America's Textiles International*, Volume 18, No. 3, pp.114–120.

When American textile producers serviced a domestic American market with very little import penetration, the relative difference in cost of capital between individual firms was important but the difference between cost of capital in the US versus different areas of the world was, of course, of far less importance.

According to J. Milton Childress II, of Ernst and Whinny, in a presentation to the conference on Automation for the fiber, textile, and apparel industries 7–8 September 1988 in Raleigh, North Carolina, the average weighted cost of capital in the United States is 10.6% while in West Germany it is only 6.4% and in Japan is 5.8%. Thus we see that US textile manufacturers are not only at a comparative disadvantage to the Asian countries which have much lower labor costs, but also to the highly industrialized nations that have lower capital costs.

Dr William Ouchi, in his speech at the 1988 ATMI meeting in San Francisco, showed that part of the problem is that our laws are different from those in other countries. In Japan virtually every company will have 20–50% of its equity shares held by a group of friendly financial institutions; and the pattern also appears in Germany and in many other countries in the world, but in the US by law we prohibit banks from owning the equities of nonbank businesses.

Further, in the US our equity position is about two-thirds of total capitalization with debt as one-third. The exact opposite is true for West Germany and Japan according to figures presented by Mr Childress at the conference previously mentioned.

In the past, traditional payback methods were measured in savings in direct labor and material cost which are easy to quantify. But, during the past decade the textile industry has reduced its labor cost and material cost about as much as is possible. This means that whereas textile managers in former years could make valid investment decisions rapidly using simple formulas with very few variables, the same luxury is not afforded today's textile executives.

According to a survey by the national association of accountants, 94% of the respondents still use a simple payback of two to five year formula concentrating on direct labor, material and waste savings. The key competitive issues of quality, delivery, and strategy get very little attention. Certainly it is much more difficult to quantify areas such as improved quality, manufacturing flexibility, quicker throughput, and customer service than it is to quantify the savings and direct labor and material costs.

A review of ROI decisions related to the purchase of open-end spinning technology might be used to illustrate today's problems.

Open-end spinning was introduced to the textile industry at ITMA '71 as a new spinning technology that would revolutionize the yarn mill by eliminating the roving operation and eventually the winding operation as well. The success of the technology is reflected in data reported in ITS Textile Leader 2/88:

Cumulative world shipments of ring spinning 1978–1987 is 23,273,591 spindles. There were 7,309,066 open-end rotors shipped during the same period.

This represents a ratio of 3.18 ring spindles to every open-end rotor. However, the delivery speed differential favors open-end spinning by a factor of between 5 and 7 to 1 for ring spinning. Thus, sales during 1978 to 1987 indicate a significant displacement of ring spinning technology with open-end technology.

Many of the decisions relative to spinning purchases may have been easier 10–15 years ago based solely on productivity expectations as illustrated in Figure 1.

When the first-generation open-end spinning technology was introduced, its delivery speed was 3–4 times faster than conventional spinning; the roving process was eliminated; and many US manufacturers determined that in some ways it is a 'forgiving' technology and therefore a lower grade or less expensive raw material could be used. The cumulative effect of these three factors made the conventional ROI analysis quite favorable.

With the success of the original technology and the realization that rotor speeds could be increased by a factor of 2–3, the textile machinery companies began extensive research to further develop open-end spinning. During this time which may have included a second and/or a third generation machine, four major developments occurred:

(i) Improvements in yarn quality that eliminated the need for clearing yarns and therefore eliminated the need for winding as well.

(ii) The formation of large packages including conical shapes that eliminated the need for winding.

(iii) The introduction of extensively high rotor speeds (80,000–100,000 RPM potential) through mechanical redesign.

(iv) The automation of the process including package doffing and yarn piecing.

Once again modernization decisions were not difficult to make using a conventional ROI analysis. The winding process which is extremely costly would be eliminated. In addition, the automation resulted in fewer spinners as well. Finally, the speed factor was sufficiently better than prior generations. Although the machines were costly, they improved their competitive position relative to ring spinning as well as earlier generations of open-end spinning. This is illustrated in Figure 1 showing a larger improvement in cost for the second generation machines. It is also during this time period, which really spans several generations of machines, that the technology gained a significant share of the US market.

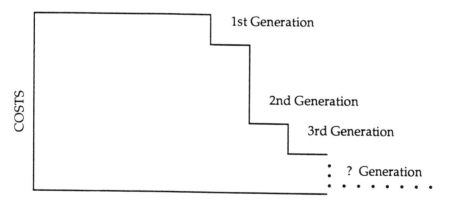

Time or Technology Development (Succeeding Generations,
Using Open-End Spinning as an Example)

Fig. 1   An Illustration of Cost Differentials Through a Series of Open-End Spinning Technology Developments

The succeeding generation machines require a different approach relative to ROI or ROE decisions. The same advantages apply relative to ring spinning, although that process has been automated to a great extent as well. The difficulty arises when comparing the latest open-end generation with the previous generations.

With many of the measurable cost factors being incorporated in previous generation machines, what improvements are left that can be demonstrated for ROI analysis? The latest generation machines include quality monitoring and information gathering not available on previous models. Quality and information are as American as mom and apple pie, but how do you put a value on them when making investment decisions? The quality capability doesn't improve quality directly, it only measures it. The information is just that-information. Management systems must be developed to use the information in a creative and timely manner. This transfers the ROI calculation responsibility from the machinery manufacturers to the machinery user who may not, in fact, know how to use the information in an effective manner. The value of information is difficult to define, especially among a multiplicity of users.

The company that develops an effective statistical process control system using on-line data generated from open-end spinning machines has a mechanism to predict the value of the latest generation OE machines. However, the ROI is likely to be significantly less than similar calculations in the past. The problem is even more difficult for the company that is not as sophisticated in its handling of analytical data.

In most cases, the ROI is predictably less for the current generation of open-end spinning than the previous generation. This means that a company now faces a dilemma; either put off making a modernization decision or develop a non-traditional analysis. The problem is not pressing, but will become so in the future.

Most textile executives state that no company can afford to wait too long before investing in new equipment. The difficulty is in determining the time factor. It may be that if you wait for a favorable conventional ROI analysis, it may be too late-particularly if your major competitors have modernized.

The decision to purchase the next generation of open-end spinning technology may not involve ROI as much as it does the long-term decision to stay in business. Undoubtedly this will be more difficult to sell to executive management and to the Board of Directors. The need for a new approach is evident.

In addition to the large change in the international market situation which US textile firms must now consider, there has also been a discontinuity in the technology area. Entirely new technologies such as open-end spinning and shuttleless weaving have created a very real discontinuity in the technological arena. Again referring to Mr Childress' presentation, during the period from 1980 to 1987 in the United States capital spending per employee rose 49% while sales per employee rose only 19%. Unless a firm has a distinct differential advantage in the market(s) it serves, it is not reasonable to expect sales per employee to grow rapidly, but capital spending per employee will continue to increase as the trend toward increased use of automation and robotics continues. At last year's ATMI conference in San Francisco, Mr Raoul Verret, President of Warner International, informed the industry that 'of the total spinning positions installed in the cotton sector, ring and open end, the percentage that is less than 10 years old is estimated to be 6.5% in the US versus 24% in Germany, 43% in Italy, and 20% in France. In

South Korea it is 39.8%, and in Taiwan nearly 27%.' Further Mr Verret said that 'the situation is similar in the weaving sector. The percentage of shuttleless looms to total looms in the cotton type weaving sector is estimated to be 40% in the US, 55% in Germany, 55% in Italy, and 61% in France. Of the total looms installed, it is estimated that the percentage less than 10 years old is 28% in the US, 49% in Germany, 45% in Italy, 35% in France, and in South Korea 37%, and in Taiwan 35%.'

Another discontinuity of major proportions is the fact that in the past couple of decades major changes have been made in the global textile machinery area. With so much of the spinning and weaving equipment coming from overseas, the changes in the value of the dollar against currencies such as the German mark and Japanese yen introduce a whole new series of considerations which textile managers in a previous era did not have to contend with.

When American firms purchase American machinery there is of course no problem about the value of the dollar, but when American firms purchase Japanese, German, or other foreign machinery, exchange rates are of major importance. We have also gone through some periods of fairly broad swings in the inflation rates during the last couple of decades, and these fluctuations add to the uncertainty for the decision maker as far investing in new equipment.

From a technology side, not only are we moving more and more towards more automated equipment and much more expensive equipment than our predecessors in previous years had to contend with, we are also faced with choices of either buying complete systems and capitalizing the entire investment or in some cases making decisions to buy equipment which does not have all of the possible attachments and capitalizing only that portion of the investment while adding other elements from year to year and trying to claim them as expense items in order to reduce taxes.

One thing is certain and that is that we need to learn which variables to consider in investment decisions, how to qualify them, and how they interact; this is a major problem. We have come up against a discontinuity because we never had to do this before. The simple payback formulas of our parents' and grandparents' generations based on the simple variables of direct labor and materials are inadequate for us, but we have no experience with anything else. However, we are not the only industry to be faced with this problem of justification of new technology. In a review of the Flexible Manufacturing Systems Industry by the Department of Commerce (July 1985), inadequate justification techniques are identified as one of the barriers to implementing flexible manufacturing systems. Automotive, aerospace, and electronics are but a few of the industries considering investments in new automated systems and have had to contend with the problem of how to justify their new investments.

While there isn't one magic formula for evaluating automated systems in the textile industry, there are many techniques which have been shown to be useful in other industries. Some of these techniques include more sophisticated economic analyses, such as net present worth and rate of return. Techniques referred to as Multi-Attribute Decision Analysis (MADA) allow for the consideration of both quantitative and qualitative factors of new technology. MADA techniques include linear scoring/weighted evaluation, Analytic Hierarchy Process, and multi-attribute utility analysis.

Graphical methods like scorecards, profile charts, and polar graphs may be help in presenting the many variables to be considered. Factors used in evaluations may include manufacturing flexibility, setup time, throughput time, quality, labor skill level, scrap rate, floor space, process monitoring, labor cost, work-in-process, etc.

Dr John Canada and Robert Edwards of North Carolina State University have written a handbook entitled 'Should We Automate Now?' (1985, NCSU Industrial Extension Service) which explores both economic and MADA techniques for evaluating Computer Integrated Manufacturing Systems. George Hodge of the College of Textiles has developed a listing of computer software packages which facilitate the calculations for these non-traditional decision analysis techniques (Engineering Economist, Winter 1988).

Accounting firms such as Ernst and Whinny, consulting firms such as Kurt Salmon and Werner Associates, and industrial engineering consultants such as Prof John Canada of North Carolina State University have developed commercially available packages for use in making investment decisions, and they have in common the use of many variables, schemes to try to qualify them, and recognition that one of the major if not the preeminent goal in investment decisions must be the survival of the firm.

The College of Textiles is working on developing decision models for the textile industry. Those firms interested in joining a research consortium with the purpose of developing these decision models are invited to contact the authors. It is not our purpose to propose or suggest any specific formula for use by all firms in all situations. There just isn't any such major formula.

As Henry Ford once said, '*if you need a machine and don't buy it you pay for it and don't get it*'. It is also not the intention of this paper to discourage people from making any decisions simple because those decisions are more complicated than they used to be. We live in a more complicated world. If there is any consolation it is that every manufacturer in the United States is going through the same process of having to learn new ways to make investment decisions.

Multiple Attributes/Criteria for Evaluating Manufacturing Systems —

A non-traditional approach to justifying equipment or systems purchases in the apparel industry, particularly when large capital outlays are involved.

G. L. Hodge[1] and J. R. Canada[2]

College of Textiles[1] and Industrial Engineering[2],
North Carolina State University

As automated equipment is continually being developed and refined for use in the apparel industry, the need for better ways to evaluate and justify such equipment is becoming increasingly important.

Traditional economic analyses often do not adequately include all important considerations in evaluating automated equipment. This is particularly true of before-the-fact investment decisions, which is the focus of this paper, but is also true of operational performance (after-the-fact) evaluations. Traditional economic analysis methods consider only factors which can be reduced to monetary terms-such as investment required, project useful life, direct labor and material usage. These methods can vary from simplistic (payback period or accounting cost-per-unit produced) to more elaborate and defensible (net present worth or return on investment over project life).

For simple decisions, such as replacement of identical equipment, traditional economic analyses methods combined with good intuitive judgement may well be sufficient. However, as alternatives become more complex and far-reaching, analyses beyond traditional economics are recommended. Such analyses are commonly described as multiple attribute (or criteria, or objective, or factor) analyses, because they specifically include all relevant attributes.

Here, we will introduce only a few, simple multi-attribute methodologies which can be helpful in deciding between alternatives for apparel manufacturing.

SELECTING A SEWING WORKSTATION

To illustrate, suppose a decision maker must select one of three types of sewing workstations. Alternative A includes only mechanized workaids. Alternative B is semi-automated and requires an operator. Alternative C is fully-automated and requires only a utility operator to load/unload parts. The attributes selected as being most important

First published in *Apparel Manufacturer* Volume 1, No. 12, pp. 53–57.

are: Net present worth, manufacturing flexibility, quality and serviceability. A full decision model doubtlessly would include additional attributes and much more elaborate analysis than illustrated.

Figures 1 and 2 demonstrate two graphical techniques for presenting simple multi-attribute information. The 'scorecard' (Figure 1) gives descriptions (ratings) of projected results for each alternative, with respect to each attribute. These descriptions may be either quantifiable (US$, or other measures) or verbal (poor-to-excellent, or other measures). The best and worst alternative with respect to each attribute can be highlighted as shown or through use of colors or other symbols.

	Alternatives (Workstations)		
	A mechanized	B semi-automated	C fully-automated
ATTRIBUTES			
Net Present Worth (in $1000)	$200	$300	$250
Manufacturing Flexibility	HIGH	MEDIUM	LOW
Quality (% seconds)	FAIR 15%	GOOD 5%	VERY GOOD 2%
Serviceability	GOOD	FAIR	FAIR

☐ Best Alternative for Attribute

☐ Worst Alternative for Attribute

Fig. 1   *Example Scorecard*

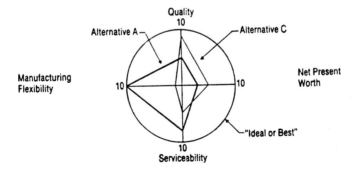

Fig. 2   *Example Polar Graph*

76

Figure 2 is a polar graph showing much the same information for Alternatives A and C only. With this graphical technique, each attribute outcome is rated on a common 10-point scale (10 points being best). The outer circle represents the 'ideal' or 'best' possible alternative; i.e., one that would receive 10 points on each attribute.

Neither one of these graphical techniques requires the decision maker to explicitly state the relative importance of each attribute. A good quantitative methodology, the Analytic Hierarchy Process (AHP) does ask the decision maker for the relative importance of each factor and then uses this information to calculate overall weighted evaluation (priority rating) for each alternative. We will briefly demonstrate this process.

AHP begins with organizing the decision problem into a hierarchy as shown in Figure 3. In our simplified example, we have shown only one level of factors/attributes; however, each attribute may be further divided into sub-attributes. For example, flexibility could be divided into:

(a) process flexibility (ability to adapt to changes induced by the manufacturing process),
(b) part flexibility (ability to adapt to changes in the size or shape of the part), and
(c) product flexibility (ability to adapt to different types of parts).

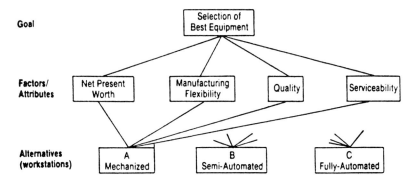

Fig. 3   Decision Hierarchy

Next, the decision maker must answer a set of pairwise comparison questions to determine the relative importance of each attribute. Figure 4 illustrates how the factors may be compared on a verbal scale suggested for use in the AHP. For example, the first line in the body of the table shows that 'Net Present Worth' is moderately to strongly more important than 'Flexibility.' The mathematics of AHP will not be presented, but can be found in many articles and books noted in our references. Attribute weights resulting from the preferences indicated in Figure 4 are shown in the top part of Figure 5. For example, the attribute 'Present Worth' has 0.51 (out of total 1.00) weight.

In a similar manner, alternatives can be compared against one another with respect to how well they meet each attribute. Example results are in the lower left block of Figure 5. Finally, one can calculate a total weighted evaluation (priority rating) for each alternative, the results of which are shown in the right hand side of Figure 5. This

Importance of one attribute over another

With Respect to Selection of Best Equipment Factor/Attribute	Extreme 9	8	Very Strong 7	6	Strong 5	4	Moderate 3	2	Equal 1	Moderate 2	3	Strong 4	5	6	Very Strong 7	8	Extreme 9	
Net Present Worth						X												Flexibility
Net Present Worth							X											Quality
Net Present Worth							X											Serviceability
Flexibility									X									Quality
Flexibility									X									Serviceability
Quality							X											Serviceability

Fig. 4   Pairwise Comparison of Attributes

shows that Alternative B (the semi-automated work station) is the best with a weighted evaluation of 0.40 (out of total 1.00). Figure 6 is a graphical portrayal of this information.

Of course, such multi-attribute results should be given credence and should aid the decision maker according to how well the methodology application incorporates the actual problem and preferences of the decision maker. Attributes/factors relevant to the apparel industry need to be further identified and defined so that these methodologies will be more readily useful to apparel manufacturing decision makers. Such analyses are not limited only to the evaluation of equipment, but can be used for other important decisions, such as business strategies, vendor appraisal, facility location, and employee selection.

BIBLIOGRAPHY

J.R. Canada and W.G. Sullivan. 'Economic and Multi-Attribute Evaluation of Advanced Manufacturing Systems', Prentice-Hall, Englewood Cliffs, NJ, USA. 1989.
T. Saaty. 'The Analytic Hierarchy Process', McGraw-Hill Company, New York, USA. 1980.
T. Saaty. 'Decision Making for Leaders', Wadsworth Publishing, Belmont, CA, USA. 1982.

Low Cost Microcomputer Software for Non-Traditional Economic Decision Analysis

G. L. Hodge[1] and J. R. Canada[2]

College of Textiles[1] and Industrial Engineering[2],
North Carolina State University

This contains extensive summary information on commercial microcomputer software packages which were found to facilitate various types of economic decision analyses. Most include the use of one or more 'non-traditional' approaches such as decision trees, simulation, decision support systems, and/or multi-attribute decision analysis methodologies.

Table 1 is a compilation of 35 microcomputer software packages which facilitate non-traditional economic decision analyses. 24 of the programs were included in a survey conducted in summer 1987 [1]. The survey focused on software packages costing less than US$1,000. Since the original survey, 12 additional programs have been identified. Several of these programs are included with textbooks on management science. Brief descriptions of these additional programs are provided at the end of this paper. Descriptions of the programs listed in the original survey can be found in reference [1].

Some programs are easy-to-use menu-driven packages which contain specific economic models, but lack flexibility. General purpose spreadsheet programs which offer more flexibility are readily available, but require programming by the user and are not included herein. Morse and Whitehouse [7,8] provide a review of some spreadsheet programs. Several of the microcomputer decision support systems included in this listing are based on mainframe versions of DSS4 for financial modelling. These programs require the user to program the financial models to be used.

Many other sources of mostly specialized software for decision analysis are available but not included herein [2,3,5,6,9]. Program listings for these may be available from the authors or sponsoring agencies; however, older programs were written to be run on large computer systems and may require some modification.

The authors believe this compilation to be fairly complete as of summer 1988. The product descriptions are based on vendor literature and sample uses of some programs. Inclusion of a program is not meant to be an endorsement of the product. As we continue to update this compilation we would appreciate from the readers comments and suggestions of additional software.

First published in *The Engineering Economist*, Volume 35, No. 2.

79

Table I
Microcomputer Software to Support Non-Traditional Economic Decision Analysis (Adapted from [1])

Program Name (Company Name)	Multi-Attribute Methods				Financial/Economic Methods					Cost ($)
	Scoring/ weighted evaluation	AHP	Exclusionary Screening	Math. prog.	Traditional economic analysis	Monte Carlo simulation	Decision tree analysis	Goal-seeking ability	Sensitivity analysis	
Arborist (Texas Instruments)							X		X	595.00
BestChoice [i] (Sterling Castle Software)	X									49.00
Cash Flow Analyzer (G.A. Fleischer & Assoc.)					X				X	20.00
Confidence Factor (Simple Software Inc.)	X			X		X	X			389.00
COPE (ANTECH, Inc.)					P			X		395.00
The Deciding Factor [ii] (Channelmark Corp.)				X						95.00
Decision 1-2-Tree [iii] (Fast Decision Systems, Inc.)							X			195.00
Decision Aid II (Kepner-Tregoe)	X		X							250.00
Decision Analyst (Executive Software, Inc.)	X									139.00
Decision Making (N.C. State Univ.)	X									23.00
Decision Map (Softstyle, Inc.)	X									145.00
Decision Pad [iv] (Apian Software)	X									195.00
Decision Support One [v] (Enfin Software Corp.)				X		X		X	X	695.00
Economic Analysis (IIE Microsoftware)					X		X			175.00
ENCORE! (Ferox Microsystems, Inc.)					P	X			P	475.00
Expert Choice (Decision Support Software, Inc.)		X							X	495.00
IFPS/Personal (Execucom)					P			X		895.00
Lightyear	X		X							99.00

Table I (continued)

Program Name (Company Name)	Multi-Attribute Methods			Math. prog.	Financial/Economic Methods			Goal-seeking ability	Sensitivity analysis	Cost ($)
	Scoring/weighted evaluation	AHP	Exclusionary Screening		Traditional economic analysis	Monte Carlo simulation	Decision tree analysis			
MANROB (K.U. Leuven R&D)					X					750.00
MicroFCS [vi] (Thom EMI Computer)					P			X	X	1500.00
Microcomp. Models [x] (West Publishing Co.)				X		X	X			–
Micro Manager [xi] (Wm. C. Brown Publ.)				X			X			–
MicroProphit (VIA Computer, Inc.)					P			X		695.00
MicroSimplan (Simplan Systems Inc.)					P			X	X	850.00
Mindsight (Execucom Systems Corp.)	X				P			X		245.00
Payback+ (MiCAPP, Inc.)					X					99.00
P/G% (Decision Aids, Inc.)	X								X	40.00
Policy Percent (N.C. State Univ.)	X									23.00
Predict! (Unison Technology, Inc.)					P	X				795.00
PRFORM (IIE Microsoftware)	X									600.00
QSB [xii] (Prentice-Hall)				X			X			–
SERIATIM 23.00 (N.C. State Univ.)	X									
Supertree 5.2 [vii, ix] (SDG Decision Systems)							X		X	150.00
Venture Analyst (The Venture Analyst)					X	X			X	365.00
What's Best [viii] (General Optimization, Inc.)				X						695.00

Key: X – Program has this feature; P – Requires programming in model development language; [ ] – Included in 'Description of Packages' section

DESCRIPTIONS OF PACKAGES (IF NOT PREVIOUSLY INCLUDED IN [1])

A. Software with Normal User Information/Manual

(i) BestChoice Sterling Castle Software, 702 Washington St., Suite 174, Marina del Rey, CA 90292. (800)722-7853. Cost: US$49. Hardware Requirements: IBM PC/XT/AT with 128 k. Using a method of paired preferences a ranking of alternatives is determined. Up to thirty alternatives can be evaluated with respect to five attributes by a group of up to five decision makers.

(ii) The Deciding Factor Channelmark Corp., P.O. Box 7600, 2929 Campus Dr., San Mateo, CA 9440. (415)345-5900. Cost: US$95. Hardware Requirements: IBM PC/XT/AT with 256K. Uses a tree structure to develop a decision model. System queries the decision maker for information and then presents recommendations. Program uses an expert system approach to reach conclusions.

(iii) Decision 1-2-Tree FAST Decision Systems, Inc., P.O. Box 264, Cambridge, MA 02238. (617)275-3208. Cost: US$195. Equipment Requirements: IBM PC/XT/AT with 512K, two disk drives. Program performs decision tree analysis.

(iv) Decision Pad Apian Software, P.O. Box 1224, Menlo Park, CA 94026. (800)237-4565. Cost: US$195. Hardware Requirements: IBM PC/XT/AT with 256K. User inputs criteria, alternatives, and weighting. System performs a weighed evaluation and performs a graphical analysis of the data.

(v) Decision Support One Enflin Software Corp., 6920 Miramar Rd., San Diego, CA 92121. (619)549-6606. Cost: US$695. Equipment Requirements: IBM PC/XT/AT with 320 k. This package contains three programs available individually: Goal Solution Plus, Optimal Solutions Plus, and Simulated Solutions Plus. The programs are designed to be used with Lotus 1-2-3. Capabilities include linear optimization, goal seeking, Monte Carlo simulation, and sensitivity analysis.

(vi) MicroFCS Thorn EMI Computer Software, Inc., 285 Mill Rd., Chelmsford, MA 01824. (617)256-3900. Cost: US$1,500. Hardware Requirements: IBM PC/XT/AT with 512 k. This package is a microcomputer version of the mainframe decision support system, FCS. Features include sensitivity analysis and goal seeking.

(vii) Supertree 5.2 SDG Decision Systems, 3000 Sand Hill Road, Building 3 Suite 150, Menlo Park, CA 94025-7127. (800)852-1236. Cost: US$1500. Equipment Requirements: PC with 512K (hard disk suggested). Performs decision tree analysis with up to 8000 endpoints. Sensitivity analysis capability included.

(viii) What's Best! General Optimization, Inc., 2251 N. Geneva Terrace, Chicago, IL 60614. (800)441-2378. Cost: US$695. Hardware Requirements: IBM PC/XT/AT with 512K; also available for the Macintosh. Package is an optimization routine which can be used with most popular spreadsheet programs.

Software Included as Part of Textbooks

(ix) Decision Analysis for the Professional — with Supertree Redwood City, CA: The Scientific Press 1987. Equipment Requirements: Versions of the software are available both for the IBM PC and the Macintosh computers. This program is a student edition of the software program Supertree 5.2 which performs decision tree analysis.

(x) Microcomputer Models for Management Decision-Making: software and text 2nd Edition, by Terry L. Dennis and Laurie B. Dennis. New York, NY: West Publishing Company 1988 (360 pages). Equipment Requirements: IBM PC or compatible with at least 256K memory, one double-sided disk drive, and DOS 2.0. Text and software for many traditional management science methodologies including: Monte Carlo simulation, Bayesian analysis, payoff table analysis, and linear, integer, and goal programming.

(xi) Micro Manager by Sang M. Lee and Jung P. Shim. Dubuque, Iowa: Wm. C. Brown Publishers 1986. Equipment Requirements: IBM PC or compatible. Software package to be used with the text Micro Management Science. The software covers traditional management science methodologies including: decision tree analysis, Bayesian analysis, and linear programming.

(xii) Quantitative Systems for Business by Yih-Long Chang and Robert Sullivan. Englewood Cliffs, New Jersey: Prentice-Hall 1988 (175 pages). Equipment Requirements: IBM PC or compatible with at least 64 k, one disk drive, and DOS 2.0. Text and software for many traditional management science methodologies including: decision tree analysis, Bayesian analysis, payoff table analysis, and linear and integer programming.

ACKNOWLEDGEMENT

Partially adapted from, and updating of Table I, by permission of the publisher.

BIBLIOGRAPHY

J. R. Canada and G. L. Hodge. 'Microcomputer Software Costing Less Than US$1000 for Economic and Multiattribute Decision Analysis', *The Eng. Econ.*, 1988, Winter, 130.

J. Fichefet, J. P. Leclercq, P. H. Beyne, and F. F. Rousselet-Piette. 'Microcomputer-Assisted Identification of Bacteria and Multicriteria Decision Models', *Computers and Operations Res.*, 1984, 11, 4, p.361.

M. S. Jones, C. J. Malmborg, and M. H. Agee. 'Decision Support System Used for Robot Selection', *Ind. Eng.*, 1985, 17, 9, p.66.

D. Kull. 'Decision Support with 20/20 Foresight', *Computer Decisions*, 1986, May 6, 38.

S. R. LeClair and W. G. Sullivan. 'Justification of Advanced Manufacturing Technology Using Expert Systems', 1985 Annual International Industrial Engineering Conference Proceedings, 1985, p.362.

T. W. Morgan and R. L. Thurgood. 'Engineering Tradeoff Problems Viewed as Multiple Objective Optimization and the VODCA Methodology', IEEE Transactions on Engineering Management, EM-31, 2, 1984, p.60.

L. Morse and G. E. Whitehouse. 'Electronic Spreadsheets Evaluated for IE Applications,' *Ind. Eng.*, 1985, 17, 2, p.17.

L. Morse and G. E. Whitehouse. 'IEs Must Look at Equipment Needs in Choosing Spreadsheets', *Ind. Eng.*, 1985, **17**, 3, p.21.

M. Weber. 'A Method of Multiattribute Decision Making with Incomplete Information', *Management Science*, 1985, **31**, 11, p.1365.

Persistent Pitfalls and Applicable Approaches for Justification of Advanced Manufacturing Systems

J. R. Canada[1] and W. G. Sullivan[2]

North Carolina State University[1] and University of Tennessee[2]

ABSTRACT

This article focuses on main pitfalls/errors in application of traditional economic decision models which tend to impede the adoption of advanced manufacturing systems. The three main pitfalls are: arbitrarily high hurdle rates, comparison with the status quo, and insufficient benefits analysis. Several simple models are presented as approaches to overcoming those pitfalls so as to provide for more useful evaluations.

INTRODUCTION

There has been much interest in the past few years regarding why traditional economic decision analysis models and cost accounting practices impede the adoption of advanced manufacturing systems [1–4].

Blind adherence to traditional models such as payback, return on investment (ROI), and discounted cash flow (DCF) is perhaps the greatest single barrier to implementation of new manufacturing technologies. The problems lie with both the models themselves and the way that the models are used. Three errors in application, which will be discussed below, are:

(i)   arbitrarily high hurdle rates;
(ii) comparison with the status quo; and
(3)   insufficient benefits analysis.

Hurdle rates

Surveys have indicated that it is not unusual for US firms to require payback periods of less than two to three years, which roughly correspond to internal rates of return in excess of 30% (after taxes) to justify investment. Firms that gauge a prospective

---

First published in *Engineering Costs and Production Economics*, Volume 18 (1990), pp.247-253.

investment's profitability with DCF techniques often use an after-tax hurdle rate of 20% or more. Such arbitrarily high thresholds force US managers to focus on short-term liquidity/profitability and artificially short planning horizons [5].

High interest rates and abbreviated project lives mean that only certain kinds of investments will be regarded as feasible. Projects having large savings in their early years will tend to dominate the (typically) more strategic investments which are characterized by significant savings in the mid to late part of useful project life.

Comparison with the status quo

The second problem with traditional models is that new investment alternatives are being implicitly compared to 'doing nothing'. The choice of doing nothing is evaluated as if the process that we have today is going to continue performing as it has in the past. To believe that the status quo costs nothing and is without risk in an incremental comparison with an investment in new technology is inconsistent with a competitive marketplace. A firm's competitors that have acquired advanced manufacturing systems will be able
to deliver a wider spectrum of products with lower costs, higher quality, and shorter lead times [6]. This pressures conservative firms to cut costs in existing technology to meet the competition. Consequently these firms find difficulty in justifying investments in new technology, and 'capital decay' created by lost sales due to technological obsolescence in the status quo alternative erodes the competitive position of the firm. The cycle continues until the non-innovative firm no longer has sufficient resources to make the necessary catch-up investments to survive competitive challenges [7].

Incomplete benefits analysis

Many decisions made by manufacturing firms involve technology innovations which cannot be shown in a rigorous, quantitative manner to increase the firm's value (i.e., to produce returns that exceed the hurdle rate). However such innovations may be highly regarded in terms of creating strategic opportunities leading to increased market share for existing products or new markets for future products. Thus, strategic investments have traditionally been analyzed asymmetrically, which means that the front-end costs of the project are relatively well known and quantifiable but the benefits are less subject to quantification in terms of dollars. In a sense, firms appear to be incorporating subjective risk adjustments into the analysis twice, once through the use of a high hurdle rate and then again by omitting many of the 'down-stream' benefits that are difficult to quantify. Remedying this double penalty is a major challenge for any approach to justification of new technology.

JUSTIFICATION STUDIES

Our purpose in this article is to discuss various approaches for overcoming the difficulties mentioned above. Advanced Manufacturing Systems (AMS) are widely credited with creating savings (benefits) due to combinations of increased flexibility, market share, quality and throughput; and/or reduced lead times, labor, inventory, space, scrap, etc. Kaplan has suggested that some of these benefits should be explicitly included in the DCF analysis so that the cost/benefit asymmetry noted previously is reduced [5]. The problem is in quantifying these benefits sufficiently well to make valid and unbiased justification studies. Those benefits which can be quantified in dollar terms are often called 'tangibles', while the remainder may be termed 'intangibles' or 'irreducibles'. We will concentrate on some ways various AMS benefits might be quantified, especially in comparison with 'conventional' alternatives. Then we will present a 'breakeven' approach to deciding whether intangible benefits are sufficient to justify an investment. Finally, a discussion of improved accounting practices for allocating overhead, as they relate to AMS justification, is offered. This is of vital importance in AMS evaluation studies because often a major portion of product cost is allocated overhead which includes the cost of new technology. Several examples herein have been adapted from the authors' recently published book [8].

Quantifying tangible benefits

The following are some common tangible benefits attributed to AMS investments. Brief suggestions for estimating each are offered:

(a) Increased flexibility. The dollar impact might be quantified in terms of increased sales due to flexibility to produce a wide range of products and/or in the dollar savings due to lower setup or product changeover costs. Competitive standing in the marketplace may improve because of ability to introduce new products very quickly.

(b) Increased quality. The dollar impact might be reflected in increased sales and/ or reduced reject, scrap and product warranty costs. Confidence in receiving high quality in a product/service will enhance brand loyalty and promote a company's reputation to potential customers.

(c) Reduced inventory. The dollar savings in working capital due to reduction in raw materials, in-process, and/or finished goods inventories should be readily quantifiable and translatable to savings in finance charges on capital. Certain other 'carrying costs' may also be saved, such as for property taxes, insurance, storage space, and deterioration.

(d) Reduced space. The dollar impact of reduced requirements for manufacturing space can vary according to the 'opportunity cost principle'. While space savings may be 50% or more, that can translate into anything between zero dollars for no alternative use of space saved to many times the historic or standard cost (for very valuable alternative uses of space saved).

Examples of breakeven approach to intangible benefits

Regardless of which tangible benefits are estimated in terms of dollars, almost certainly there are intangible benefits that are significant. Table 1 illustrates a simple example of how one might calculate the 'breakeven' value of intangible benefits, and then decide if the investment should be undertaken assuming revenues are constant. Note from

Table 1 that the net annual worth after taking tangible benefits into account is US$-260M (US$-200M) or US$60M more negative for the AMS alternative than for the conventional alternative. If the intangible benefits of the AMS are judged to be worth more than US$60M, then an investment in AMS can be justified; otherwise not. Note that the final justification decision does not require a specific estimate of the worth of the intangible benefits — only whether they are higher or lower than the breakeven value. Moreover if capital decay had been considered so that additional revenue were attributed to the AMS alternative, the breakeven value of intangible benefits would be much lower.

Table 1
Example calculation of breakeven value for intangible benefits

	Alternative	
	Conventional (status quo)	AMS
Investment	US$300 M	US$1,300
Life	5 yrs	10 yrs
Annual operating costs	US$100 M	US$70 M
Annual tangible benefits (Not included in operating costs)	—	US$120 M

Using zero salvage value and minimum attractive rate of return of 20%, the net annual worth (i.e., tangible benefits minus costs) are:

Annual tangible benefits		US$120M
Less		
Depreciation and interest		
US$300 M (A/P, 20%, 5)[a] =	US$100 M	
US$1,300 M (A/P, 20%, 10)		US$310 M
Annual operating costs	US$100 M	US$70 M
Net annual worth	US$-200 M	US$-260 M
Net annual worth 'deficit' (= Breakeven value for intangible benefits)		US$60 M

[a]Standard functional interest factor for finding annual equivalent, given a present equivalent amount.

Other economic analysis impediments

Estimates of economic lives and residual or salvage values are often conservatively low. This tends to work against realistic justification of AMS alternatives which have greater flexibility and thus longer lives than conventional 'fixed automation' alternatives. Also, the greater flexibility realistically would result in larger residual values, especially if inflation is taken into account.

Summing up the impediments, Allen Seed [9] says:

'What we've got is a kind of combination of factors: conservatism, wrong rates, overlooked savings, underestimated residual values ... (which) ... lead to bad decisions, in many cases, in terms of automation.'

COST ACCOUNTING ANACHRONISMS

It is becoming evident that generally-accepted traditional cost accounting systems are no longer meeting the needs of today's manufacturing firms [10]. Several weaknesses are becoming painfully apparent to managers. First, cost accounting systems place heavy emphasis on the direct labor component of product cost. As the number of information workers increases and as blue collar workers are replaced by AMS, accounting practices that assume direct labor costs are variable with production levels and allocate overhead based on direct labor costs will provide data which are counter-intuitive to good decision making. With higher levels of AMS, direct labor costs are no longer the most important costs to be managed, and labor costs tend to become fixed with respect to production level. Secondly, the investment in hardware and software to operate computer-based systems tends to be essentially irreversible and non-salvageable, even before production begins. Also, the maintenance of this equipment tends to be relatively constant regardless of use, and not a cost that would require much operating management attention.

The costs which need to be measured and managed today are the overhead and material costs. Recent research shows that overhead costs rank behind only (a) quality, and (b) getting new product out on schedule as a primary concern of manufacturing executives [4]. Allocation of overhead must be carefully considered in AMS evaluations to guard against distortions in product cost estimates that can occur when complex versus simple products are common to a cost center. Thus, technology costs (depreciation) should be removed from factory overhead and attached to those products that are technology intensive.

Another weakness in traditional accounting systems is the inability to account for the non-financial or intangible aspects of manufacturing performance [5]. Maintaining a competitive position in today's economy is strongly dependent upon quality, productivity, information management, innovation, and workforce capabilities. A commitment to quality, for instance, requires major changes in the way companies design manufacturing processes, train employees, upgrade and maintain equipment, and deal with suppliers. In traditional cost accounting systems, quality appears as an added cost to direct labor and overhead rather than as part of what would have been allocated to separate cost centers if quality had not been improved.

Cost assignment for AMS

It was recognized in the last section that the nature of manufacturing has changed from labor-paced to technology intensive and machine-paced and that labor costs are now relatively small compared to material and overhead costs. Accordingly, it is becoming increasingly popular to add allocated 'conversion costs' (i.e., labor and factory overhead costs) to materials costs to obtain total product costs in discrete good industries, as has been done in the continuous process industries (e.g., petrochemicals) for many years.

Table 2 shows an example of allocation of conversion costs in a labor-paced versus a machine-paced manufacturing environment. The column headings show a typical division of costs into 'direct' costs which can be directly assigned to cost centers of products and 'indirect' costs which must be allocated or prorated to cost centers or products on some arbitrary basis. The row headings are for the traditional division into 'fixed' and 'variable' costs, according to their behavior with respect to volume of production. For machine-paced production, the division of conversion costs into 'direct' and 'indirect' categories is needed, but the division into 'fixed' and 'variable' categories is not necessary. If the products are relatively homogeneous, the most appropriate measure of production is physically apparent — such as items, pounds or gallons. If the products are of different sizes, shapes, or complexities, then probably the best measure of production is machine hours as was used in the right-hand column of Table 2.

It should be noted that many costs which are typically classified as indirect in conventional manufacturing can be assigned directly to cost centers or products in AMS environments.

Table 2
Example of conversion costs for labor-paced versus machine-paced prodcution (adapted from [9])

Assignment to cost center or product	Labor-paced		Machine-paced	
	Direct	Indirect (Allocated)	Direct	Indirect (Allocated)
Behaviour with respect to production volume:				
Fixed		US$9000	US$15,000	US$6000
(Depreciation, Support Services, etc.)				
Variable	US$20,000		US$3000	
(Energy, Supplies, Labor, etc.)				
Totals	US$20,000	US$9000	US$18,000	US$6000
	US$29,000		US$24,000	
Man-hours	1,000			
Machine-hours			100	
Cost/Man-hour	US$29			
Cost/Machine-hour			US$240	

Equipment rental

One relatively novel way to ensure that users of equipment recognize the full cost (value) of AMS is to charge rental for that equipment much the same as if that equipment were owned by an outside organization. To do so, the equipment is assigned to a cost center, and charges are made based on direct values and costs, including an appropriate return on the capital required. This should result in profitability analyses which reflect equipment or work center profit as well as manufacturing profit.

As an example, consider the product line in Table 3. The column labeled 'normal (without rental)' shows conventional cost accounting results. The 'bottom line' shows a net profit of US$400,000. Because differing amounts of various equipment types are used on the product line, no attempt normally is made to determine how much is the total investment in support of that product line. Hence, the firm lacks a very important measure to judge the profitability of that line (compared, say, to other product lines).

90

	Without rental (normal)	With rental	
		Equipment cost center	Product line
Revenue	US$1,400,000	US$350,000	US$1,400,000
Costs			
Labor	400,000		400,000
Material	300,000		300,000
Depreciation	100,000	100,000	
Equipment rental			350,000
Other overhead	200,000	25,000	175,000
Total costs	US$1,000,000	US$125,000	US$1,225,000
Net profit	US$400,000	US$225,000	US$175,000
		Total = US$400,000	

Suppose on the other hand, the firm sets up an equipment rental system which results in rental charges (to include a return on equipment investment) of US$350,000. The results are shown in the two 'with rental' columns of Table 3. Note that the total net profit with rental is still US$400,000 but now one knows that after all equipment costs are covered the product line itself shows a net profit of only US$175,000.

AMS mortgage model

Another impediment to justification of AMS investments is lack of normal recognition of 'hard' dollar savings from such investments in the accounting system of a firm. One approach for focusing on this issue is to determine the 'mortgage equivalent' of capital investment in AMS and then reduce the operating budget of the organizational unit(s) benefiting from such investments by this amount. The mortgage equivalent is merely the capital recovery amount of investment in automation equipment/systems that is computed at the firm's hurdle rate for such capital appropriations. In theory the equivalent mortgage 'payment is made to the firm's treasury each year through net savings that result from tangible benefits realized by an AMS. If management has the belief and conviction that automation initiatives will pay for themselves over the life of the investment, it will commit to budget reductions in the appropriate organizational units to 'guarantee' that tangible benefits will be captured.

Realistic appraisal of dollar benefits from AMS and the incentive to track such benefits over time are key strengths of this model. Its primary weakness is that the approach places heavy emphasis on being able to dollarize various strategic benefits and defending the validity of such savings in companies where traditional accounting systems are in use.

To illustrate the AMS mortgage model, consider a proposed US$3 million investment in new technology that creates a one-time reduction in inventory of US$4 million. Suppose that the relatively easily-determined financial component of the annual carrying charge on inventory is 15%. (Other non-finance related components of the carrying charge such as reductions in personnel, storage space and functional obsolescence are not included in the 15% rate.) Annual savings in inventory finance charges are thus US$600,000 (US$4 million x 0.15). Suppose other savings in floor space, personnel, etc. are conservatively estimated at US$60,000 per year. Hence, US$660,000 per year can be saved by the AMS. To test the strength of its support for AMS, management must be willing to commit to an annual budget reduction across affected organization units of US$3 million (A/P 15%, 10) = US$597,900, assuming that the hurdle rate is 15% and the life of this investment is 10 years. An actual budget reduction of US$597,000 can be 'covered' by savings in excess of this amount if the accounting system permits reductions in finance charges, etc. to be credited to departments benefiting from investments in advanced technology. This approach to justification forces attention to the true dollar savings from AMS and the ability of the accounting system to recognize formally that such savings exist.

CONCLUSIONS

We have recognized some common difficulties and suggested rational approaches to economic and cost accounting analyses involving AMS. It is desirable that time-tested principles and techniques be adapted to the unique characteristics of AMS to provide decision makers with accurate and relevant information for alternative choices and operating controls.

REFERENCES

[1] J.A. Brimson. 'Bringing Cost Management Up To Date', *Manuf. Eng.* 1988, **100**, 49.
[2] R.H. Kaplan. 'Yesterday's Accounting Undermines Production', *Harv. Bus. Rev.*, 1984, **62**, 95.
[3] D.E. Keys. 'Limitations of Cost Accounting in an Automated Factory', *Comput. Mech. Eng.*, 1987, **6**.
[4] J.G. Miller and T.E. Vollman. 'The Hidden Factory', *Harv. Bus. Rev.*, 1985, **63**, 142.
[5] R.H. Kaplan. 'Must CIM be Justified by Faith Alone?', *Harv. Bus. Rev.*, 1986, **64**, 87.
[6] C. Berliner and J.A. Brimson (eds). 'Cost Management for Today's Advanced Manufacturing', Harvard Business School Press, Boston, MA., USA, 1988.
[7] J.R. Canada and W.G. Sullivan. 'Avoiding Competitive Wipeout — The Tale of Three Manufacturing Firms', *Ind. Manage.*, 1987, **29**, 8.
[8] J.R. Canada and W.G. Sullivan. 'Economic and Multiattribute Evaluation of Advanced Manufacturing Systems', Prentice Hall, Englewood Cliffs, NJ, USA, 1989.
[9] A.H. Seed 3. 'Cost Accounting in the Age of Robotics', *Manage. Acc.*, 1984, **66**, 39.
[10] R.S. Kaplan. 'One Cost System Isn't Enough', *Harv. Bus. Rev.*, 1985, **66**, 87.

Evaluation of Computer-Integrated Manufacturing Systems

J. R. Canada

Industrial Engineering, North Carolina State University

ABSTRACT

A systematic procedure/methodology is illustrated for evaluating prospective computer-integrated manufacturing (CIM) opportunities. The methodology includes strategic and tactical weighted evaluations as well as net present worth or accounting financial projections to facilitate making choices which best meet the firm's strategic and short-term objectives.

INTRODUCTION AND NEED

Much has been, and will continue to be, written regarding the importance of modernizing manufacturing systems to better incorporate high technology — normally characterized by the use of computers/microprocessors for product/process design, manufacturing equipment controls, and/or decision support systems.

We will loosely refer to Computer Integrated Manufacturing (CIM) as any computer-oriented equipment or system which aids in, or achieves, the automation of a manufacturing enterprise; and which is planned to increase, if not eventually complete, integration of the enterprise. CIM regards manufacturing as a continuous flow process. The CIMS acronym is an expression of the ultimate goal and not necessarily the approach to achieving that goal. Integration connotes the typing together of adjacent operations with each other and overall control systems.

A full CIM system very much involves product fabrication and assembly, materials handling, inventory management, and maintenance as well as other important functions such as product design, quality control, cost control, and service; and classically draws upon a common computer data base. Even with non-engineered products, the concept of integration is valid, although it applies to fewer staff functions.

Due to competitive pressures, manufacturers must plan and initiate sound steps toward CIM systems. Some decision makers advocate bold steps, but most recognize the need for phased development of resources (personnel, technological, product, financial, etc.) based on a general master plan.

First published in 'Should We Automate Now?' in 1985 Annual International Engineering Conference Proceedings of the Institute of Industrial Engineers.

93

Computer-based automation equipment and systems require massive capital investments. Many firms have tended to base their investment decisions or traditional discounted cash flow financial justification methodologies best suited to meet profitability criteria rather than long-term strategic goals. These traditional financial justification methodologies, when used in conjunction with high hurdle (minimum attractive) rates prevalent in today's uncertain and capital-scarce environment, often result in rejection of proposed high technology equipment and systems.

The inadequacy of such traditional justification procedures has become apparent. Much of the published literature blames the problem on the inability of traditional justification procedures to quantify and formally consider so-called intangible benefits, and other literature points out the shortcomings of contemporary and allegedly outmoded cost accounting systems, which inhibit the use of relevant, but oftentimes unconventional, measures of performance. Some authors even totally disclaim attempts to justify modern automation through traditional capital budgeting evaluation practices on the grounds that such decisions should be made primarily based on strategic considerations.

Bela Gold, in a landmark article in Harvard Business Review [1], said:

'The real promise of CAM technology lies not in its use as yet another, perhaps fancier than usual machine tool located at a single point in an otherwise unchanged production process. CAM's promise lies, by contrast, in its ability to integrate adjacent operations with each other and with overall control systems. Because it offers a systematic — not a 'point' capability, neither its purchase nor performance should be evaluated in the traditional way.'

METHODOLOGY AND EXAMPLES

Figure 1 diagrams the suggested methodology. The analysis is based on the common procedure of considering investment projects in two categories:

(i)   Opportunities, which are each independent of one another, (i.e., any number of such opportunities can be chosen within whatever constraints without affecting the prospective results of other opportunities), and

(ii) Alternatives, which are mutually exclusive (i.e., at most one of the alternatives within a given opportunity group can be chosen).

For example, opportunities for a firm could be an AS/RS System for a Finished Goods Warehouse or a CIM System for a particular manufacturing plant. Within each such opportunity there probably are numerous alternatives, such as different Vendor Systems. If opportunities happen to be interdependent so that one increases or decreases the desirability of another, then combinations can be considered.

Category (Length of Decision Impact)	Examples
Strategic (long-term)	CIM Systems
	New Product Line
Administrative (medium-term)	Replace General Purpose Equipment
Operational (short-term)	Fixtures and Minor Equipment
	Discretionary Repairs

94

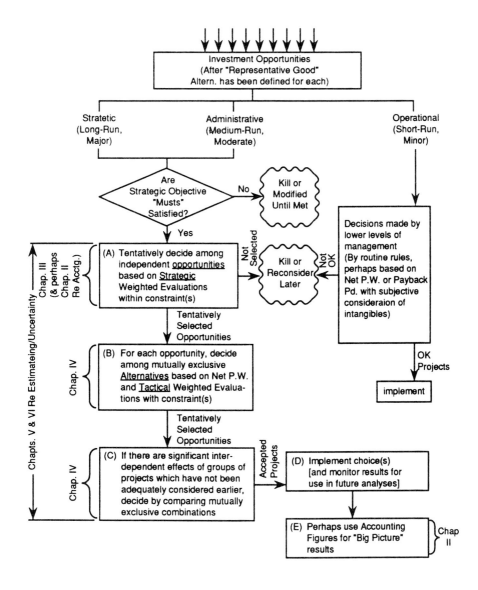

Fig. 1   Recommended Selection Process

Operational decisions are shown as being made by routine decision rules. Investment opportunities in the strategic and administrative categories, because they tend to overlap, are shown to go through the same subsequent steps. They are first screened according to whether strategic objective 'musts' are met. As the name implies, these 'musts' are criteria or questions which must be satisfied before an opportunity would be eligible for further consideration. Examples are: 'Does it maintain or advance the firm's technological capabilities?', and 'Does it keep us concentrated in the _____ business?', and 'Does it risk less than ____% of the firm's worth?'

Opportunity Selection [Figure 1, Block (A)]

Those opportunities which pass the strategic 'musts' test are then ranked and tentatively selected within whatever constraints exist according to a method called 'Strategic Weighted Evaluation.'

Figure 2 lists some eight example strategic attributes together with a description of potential benefits due to CIMS for each. The use of this methodology must determine which of these or any other attributes/criteria are of significant importance to the firm, and those chosen should be as independent [2] of each other as possible.

The calculation of the 'Strategic Weighted Evaluation' is performed in exactly the same manner as for the 'Tactical Weighted Evaluation' (to be explained in the next section) [3] — the only difference is that the chosen strategic attributes and their respective weights will typically differ (significantly) from the chosen tactical attributes and weights.

ATTRIBUTE		POTENTIAL BENEFITS DUE TO CIMS
1. Quality	—	Greater consistency in manufacture and ease in testing
2. Flexibility	—	Increased ability to adapt to changing customer requirements (product or volume) economically
3. Lead times	—	Reduction in time to achieve product/process designs, and to manufacture/ship
4. Capacity	—	Increased manufacturing thruput ability
5. Inventories	—	Reduced size due to flexibility, shorter lead times and precise, fast information systems
6. Controls	—	Tighter due to reliance on computer programs rather than operators for process and shop actions
7. Future options	—	Created through firm's acquisition of new technological capabilities (hardware, software, and people) on which it can build
8. Long Life	—	Maintain capabilities and use rates of facilities due to ability to combine economics of high-volume dedicated automation with the flexibilities of job-shop production

Fig. 2   Example Strategic Attributes/Criteria (Described in Terms of Potential Benefits Which Are a Function of Extent of Implementation of CIMS)

Alternative Selection [Figure 1, Block (B)]

Next, any mutually exclusive alternatives for each tentatively accepted opportunity are considered and tentatively selected by consideration of:
(a) Non-monetary (intangible) factors; i.e., 'Tactical Weighted Evaluation', and
(b) Monetary (quantifiable) factors; i.e., 'Net Present Worth', within whatever constraints.
Each are explained below.

Tactical Weighted Evaluation

Figure 3 is a form illustrating the identification and weighting of attributes. Note that it shows that only four tactical attributes are considered applicable (important). Typically, it is recommended that the most important of these attributes be given a weight of 100, and all other chosen attributes be given less weights according to their perceived importance relative to other attributes. Such weights are often so subjective that it is recommended that one test various combinations for 'consistency of preferences' until one is satisfied the weights are reasonable.

The last column of Figure 3 shows the formula for 'normalizing' the weights to total 100. This is merely a thinking convenience, as people tend to like to refer to quantitative weights as 'parts of 100' or 'percentages.'

Figure 4 is a form illustrating the calculation of 'Tactical Weighted Evaluation' for two alternatives. Note the normalized weights from Figure 3 are used. Note also that an 'evaluation rating' (on a scale of 0–10) is made to reflect how well each alternative meets each attribute. For example, with respect to the first attribute, 'CIMS Tactical Aims,' alternatives P-1 and P-2 scored 7.5 and 9, respectively. These scores could have been based on some quantitative scales, or just subjective judgement with some guides — such as a 0 would be 'very poor' and a 10 would be 'extraordinary.' Alternative P-1 rates a 9 and alternative P-1 rates somewhat less, probably 'very good,' with a 7.5.

The right-hand portion of Figure 4 shows the formula for computations, with the column total for each alternative being the 'Weighted Evaluation' measures — which were 82 and 75, respectively. Note also that the bottom right-hand-side provides a place for entering any Monetary Measure of Merit (separately determined, such as below).

Net Present Worth

Figure 5 shows a good easy-to-use form for calculating the Net Present Worth for an alternative project. The form provides for considering income taxes, after-tax cash flows for up to 10 years, and it also includes discount factors of 10%, 20%, or 40%. The example figures happen to be for Alternative I-B (which was also in Figure 4). For an after-tax discount factor (minimum attractive rate of return) of 20%, the Net Present Worth for that alternative is shown to be US$350M in the right-hand column, next-to-bottom row.

Figure 6 shows a summary of typical study results for all mutually exclusive alternatives for four different opportunity groups in terms of both Tactical Weighted

Evaluation and Net Present Worth. It also provides for information on 'Resources Used' for which there may be constraints (in right-hand columns). In this case, only the investment in year 0 was shown as a constraint, and the total of that resource available was shown at the bottom of the column.

Note in Figure 6 that arrows were used to denote the best alternative for each opportunity group for Tactical Weighted Evaluation and Net Present Worth, respectively. The final choice will depend on the decision maker's preferences for Tactical Weighted

		Pg _____ of _____

	Attributes Identification and Weighting	By _____ Date _____

What: ILLUSTRATION OF WEIGHTING FOR TACTICAL ATTRIBUTES

Check One: _____ Strategic
✓ Tactical

Attribute/Criterion		Check if applicable	Weight	Normalized weight (= Weight/Tot.Weight)
1	Quality			
2	Flexibility – Product			
3	Flexibility – Schedule			
4	Lead Times			
5	Capacity			
6	Inventories			
7	Controls			
8	Future Options			
9	Long life			
10	Scrap/Rework			
11	Employee satisfaction			
12	Riskiness, LACK OF	✓	63	25
13	Serviceability/Maintainability			
14	Mgt./Engr. Effort Req'd.	✓	37	15
15	Other CIMS Aims, How Well Met	✓	100	40
16	Other Profitability, Expected			
17	Other Relations, Empl/Public			
18	Other Producibility			
19	Other Controllability			
20	Other Compatibility			
21	Other Serviceability	✓	50	20
22	Other			
23	Other			
24	Other			
25	Other			
		Total Weight =	250	Total = 100

Comments: _____

_____

Fig. 3

Weighted Evaluation of Opportunities — Alternatives

Check One: _____ Strategic

            ✓ _____ Tactical

What: *ILLUSTRATION OF TACTICAL WEIGHTED*
EVALUATION OF ALTERNATIVES

Project Descriptions:

P-1   *ALT I-A*
P-2   *ALT I-B*
P-3   _____
P-4   _____

Attribute/Criterion (Ref. Fig. IV-4)	Normalized Weight	Evaluation Rating				Weight & Evaluation Rating + 10			
		P-1	P-2	P-3	P-4	P-1	P-2	P-3	P-4
CIMS Tactial Aims	40	7.5	9			30	36		
Riskiness, Lack of	25	8	6			20	15		
Serviceability	20	10	7.5			20	15		
Mgt/Engr's Effort	15	8	6			12	9		
					Total	82	75		
Monetary Measure of Merit ($), Like Net P.W. (If considered separately)						300M	350M		

Comments:

     Other Considerations _____

      _____

     Recommended Decision/Reason(s) _____

      _____

Fig. 4

Evaluation scores versus Net Present Worth. As a typical aid, Figure 7 shows the best alternative for each opportunity ranked by decreasing Tactical Weighted Evaluation. Similar ranking according to decreasing Net Present Worths can be done to facilitate thinking regarding final selections within whatever constraints. If the number of projects and tradeoff possibilities is fairly large, the final choosing can be facilitated by graphical comparisons.

Note in Figure 7 that the choices by decreasing rank are IV-B, IA, IIB, and IIIB. To live within the US$250M total investment constraint, Project IIIB would have to be dropped. Note, however, that Project IIB has a Net Present Worth of -US$10M. One might rationally decide it is worth substituting Project IIIB for Project IIB to include a Net Present Worth of US$200M rather than US$-10M, even though that means having a Tactical Weighted Evaluation of 70 rather than 80. With this substitution, the final choices would be Projects IVA, IA, and IIB with a Total Net Present Worth of US$1,160M, while requiring a total investment of US$225M (within the constraint).

What: ______________________________ Net P.W. @ ________ % = ________

Savings Compared to: (If not obvious in 'What') *No CIM, Keep Status Quo* Payback Pd. = ^*1.7 YRS*

Comments *All Nos. in $M*

Line	How Calc? (Lines)	Year 1986 0	1	2	3	4	5	Each Yr. 6–10	TOTAL
INVESTMENT, CAPITALIZED									
(1) Equipment Cost		130							
(2) Accessories & Tooling Cost		10							
(3) Other ________		—							
(4) Total Capital Inv.	(1)+(2)=(3)	140							
(5) Investment Tax Credit	10% x (4)	14							
INVESTMENT, EXPENDED									
(6) Engineering		30							
(7) Installation		13							
(8) Startup		5							
(9) Other ________		—							
(10) Total Expensed Inv.	(6)+...+(9)	48							
(11) Total All Inv. Aft. Credit	(4)+(10)−(5)	174							
OPERATING SAVINGS (COSTS)									
(12) Direct Labor Savings			50	80	100	— SAME AS YEAR 3 —	— SAME AS YEAR 3 —	150	
(13) Indirect Labor Savings			10	10	10			10	
(14) Material Savings			30	50	60			80	
(15) Maintenance Savings			10	10	10			10	
(16) Other Savings ________			40	50	60			88	
(17) Other Costs			(20)	(20)	(20)			(30)	
(18) Total Operating Savings	(12)+...+(17)		120	180	220			308	
ANALYSIS									
(19) Depreciation	______ x (4)	48	28	28	28			0	
(20) Net Before Tax Savings	(18)−(19)	(48)	92	152	192			308	
(21) Net After-Tax Savings	(20)x(1−.50)	24	46	76	96			154	
(22) Net After-Tax Cash Savings	(21)+(19)	24	74	104	124			154	
(23) Net After-Tax Cash Flow	(22)−(11)	(150)	74	104	124	124	124	154 x 5	1170.0
(24) Discount Factor @ 10%		1.000	0.909	0.826	0.751	0.683	0.621	2.354	
(25) P.W. @ 10%	(23)x(24)	(150)	67.3	85.9	93.1	84.7	77.0	362.5	620.5
(26) Discount Factor @ 20%		1.000	0.833	0.694	0.579	0.482	0.402	1.202	
(27) P.W. @ 20%	(23)x(26)	(150)	61.6	72.1	71.8	59.7	49.8	185.6	350.0
(28) Discount Factor @ 40%		1.000	0.714	0.510	0.364	0.260	0.186	0.379	
(29) P.W. @ 40%	(23)x(28)	(150)	52.8	53.0	45.1	32.2	23.1	58.4	114.6

Fig. 5

ORDERING OF OPPORTUNITIES/ALTERNATIVES

Rank by: Weighted ____ Eval. Net __ P.W. Final __ Recomm. ✓ Other

What: *SUMMARY OF STUDY RESULTS — ALTERNATIVES FOR TOP FOUR*
OPPORTUNITIES (NOTE: TACTICAL WGTD. EVAL. NUMBERS ARE NOT
NECESSARILY THE SAME AS FOR STRATEGIC WGTD. EVAL.)

Ident.	Opportunity/ Alternative/Combin. Description		✓ Tactical __ Strategic Weighted Evaluation	Net P.W. (if applic.) in $M Amt.	Cumul.	Resources Used Invest, Yr 0 in $M Amt.	Cumul.	Amt.	Cumul.
1	IV-AS/RS	ALT. A	85	560		100			
2	WHSE.	ALT. B →	85	660 ∠		75			
3		ALT. C	75	340		50			
4									
5	II-CIM,	ALT. A	72	70 ∠		70			
6	PLT II	ALT. B →	80	–10		70			
7									
8	I-CIM,	ALT. A →	82	300		50			
9	PLT I	ALT. B	75	350 ∠		150			
10									
11	III-CIM,	ALT. A	65	320 ∠		80			
12	PLT III	ALT. B →	70	200		100			
13		ALT. C	68	100		60			
14									
15									

Total Avail. (250) Total Avail. (__)

Comments:
Other Considerations *ARROWS '→' AND '∠' DENOTE BEST ALTERNATIVE FOR EACH OPPORTUNITY (GROUP)*
FOR WGT'D EVAL. AND NET P.W., RESPECTIVELY

Recommended Decision/Reason(s) _____

Fig. 6

Mutually Exclusive Combinations and Interdependent Effects [Figure 1, Block (C)]

The above procedure can be supplemented to consider interdependent effects of opportunity groups. For example, suppose the acceptance of CIM at Plant I would enhance the benefits of CIM at some other plant. Or, possibly the acceptance of an AS/RS Finished Goods Warehouse would decrease the benefits of a computerized Administrative Information System. Such interactive effects can be considered through detailing out all what are called 'mutually exclusive combinations' of projects under

Pg _3_ of _3_

ORDERING OF OPPORTUNITIES/ALTERNATIVES   By _JRC_ Date _3/12/_

Rank by: TACTICAL ✓ Weighted Eval. __ Net P.W. __ Final Recomm. ____ Other

What: *RANK ORDERING BY WEIGHTED EVALUATION FOR BEST ALTERNATIVE WITHIN EACH OF TOP FOUR OPPORTUNITIES*

Ident.	Opportunity/ Alternative/Combin. Description	✓ Tactical __ Strategic Weighted Evaluation	Net P.W. (if applic.) in $M Amt.	Net P.W. Cumul.	Invest, Yr 0 in $M Amt.	Resources Used Cumul.	Amt.	Cumul.
1	IV-B: AS/RS, ALT B	85	660	660	75	75		
2	I-A: CIM at I, ALT A	82	300	960	50	125		
3	II-B: CIM at II, ALT B	80	−10	950	70	195		
4	III-B: CIM at III, ALT B	70	200	1150	100	295		
5								
6								
7								
8								
9								
10								
11								
12								
13								
14								
15								

Total Avail. (250)   Total Avail. (__)

Comments:
Other Considerations _____

Recommended Decision/Reason(s) *INDICATED CHOICES ARE IV-B, I-A, AND II-B*

Fig. 7

Mutually Exclusive Combinations — Illustration of Possible Interdependent Effects for 8 Combinations with Highest Net P.W. in Figure IV-II

PROJ. IDENT – DESCRIPTION   PROJ. INDENT – DESCRIPTION

(See Figure IV-II)

	IV-A	IV-B	IV-C	II-A	II-B	L-A	L-B
Net P.w. $M	560	660	340	70	-10	300	350
Wgtd. Eval.	85	85	75	72	80	82	75
Resource Inv., Yr 0	100	75	50	70	70	50	150
Resource							

Mut. Excl. Comp. No.	IV-A	IV-B	IV-C	II-A	II-B	L-A	L-B	IF OUTCOMES INDEPENDENT — Tot. Net P.W.	IF OUTCOMES INDEPENDENT — Tactical Wgtd. Eval. Per Proj.	IF OUTCOMES INTERDEPENDENT — (adj.)	IF OUTCOMES INTERDEPENDENT — Tot. Net P.W.*	IF OUTCOMES INTERDEPENDENT — Tactical Wgtd. Eval. (adj.)	IF OUTCOMES INTERDEPENDENT — Tactical Wgtd. Eval. Per Proj.*	RESOURCES USED — INV., Yr 0, MF Amt.
21	0	1	0	1	0	1	0	1030	79.7	4200 / -350	$(3) 880	-3 / +5	(4) 81.9	195
34	0	1	0	0	0	0	1	4020	80	-350	$(17) 670	+5 / +5	(1) 85	225
33	0	1	0	0	0	1	0	960	83.5		(1) 960		(2) 83.5	125
23	0	1	0	0	1	1	0	950	82.3		(2) 950		(3) 82.3	195
17	1	0	0	1	0	1	0	930	79.7	+200 / -350	(6) 780	-3 / +5	(5) 81.7	220
32	1	0	0	0	0	0	1	910	80	-350	(8) 560	+5	(1) 85	250
31	1	0	0	0	0	1	0	860	83.5		(4) 860		(2) 83.5	150
19	1	0	0	0	1	1	0	850	79.7		(5) 850		(6) 79.7	220

Total Avail. (250)   Total Avail. ( )

Other Considerations _____ * Numbers in ( ) Indicate Rank Order for the Respective Measures _____

Recommended Decision/Reasons _____

103

consideration and choosing the combination which has the best tradeoff of Tactical Weighted Evaluation scores and Net Present Worth. Figure 8 is an illustrative form which uses a 'binary table' (on left side to enumerate which alternatives are included {if 1} or not included {if 0}). That illustration shows example numbers for some eight mutually exclusive combinations. The assumptions for quantifying the interdependent effects do not warrant discussion here. Note, for example, that mutually exclusive combination No. 33 (i.e., projects IVB and IA) is found to have the highest Tot. Net P.W.

SUMMARY

Basing evaluation and justification of investments in CIMS entirely on financial measures is both inadequate and misleading. This paper has illustrated briefly a simplified system [4] which includes strategic as well as tactical factors together with financial measures. It is hoped this will greatly facilitate rational decisions which properly balance the strategic and short-term considerations which are so important in evaluating advanced manufacturing systems.

NOTES

B. Gold. 'CAM Sets New Rules for Production,' *Harv. Bus. Rev.*, November-December, 1982. 'Independent' attributes or criteria mean that evaluations of the desirability of outcomes for a given attribute is not affected by what the outcomes of any of the other attributes happen to be. The 'weighted evaluation' methodology is known by many names, such as 'simple additive weighting.' For more background and examples, see J. R. Canada and J. A. White, *'Capital Investment Decision Analysis for Management and Engineering'*, Prentice-Hall, 1980, 452–55. Complete system is included in 'Should We Automate Now?, Evaluation of Computer Integrated Manufacturing Systems: An Applications Manual with Handy Forms,' Industrial Extension Service, North Carolina State University, Raleigh, 1985.

Is Investment in Technology a Winning Strategy?

J. M. Childress II
Ernst & Whinney

It is certainly fair to say that the textile industry has undergone revolutionary changes during this decade. Before I directly address the topic of this forum, the cost of automation, let me digress by briefly addressing each force behind this change.

GLOBAL COMPETITION

The first of these major changes is global competition. The US trade deficit as you know is at record levels and almost 15% of that deficit is made up of textile and apparel trade. Nothing has created such a commonality of interest among today's textile executive as imports.

The decline in the value of the dollar is not that much help. In general, growth in the deficit has slowed but by no stretch of the imagination has it reversed. There are some emerging export opportunities, but in basic manufacturing we are often ill equipped to exploit these opportunities. Even the dollar's decline has little impact on imports from those countries where currency is pegged to the dollar. Many of these are the Pacific basin countries which represent the major textile apparel threat.

One of our competitive disadvantages has been the relatively high labor costs in our country. Among our major textile competitors the US has the third highest labor rate. There are other disadvantages, including some basic economic structural differences of our country and our competitors. But it is the labor cost disadvantage of which we have responded most dramatically. And that brings us to the second major change.

TECHNOLOGICAL REVOLUTION

There has been a tremendous move toward capital intensity in response to the increased global competition and the ensuing strategies of quick response. The rapid advancement in manufacturing process technology is surpassed only by that in information technology which itself is today a US$117 billion industry.

As you see in Table 1, the capital intensity of the textile industry is demonstrated by the fact that it takes more assets per sales dollar than it did in 1980. Capital spending per employee is up 49% for the decade, and productivity per employee is up 19%. Yet despite the competitive response of increased capital intensity, there is evidence that our global competitors are likewise making investments in technology and at a rate that outpaces our own. A survey last fall by the ITMF shows that the US lags many of its global competitors in reinvesting in textile technology. The study further suggests that to correct this lag the level of capital reinvestment should be over twice current expenditures, or 216% of the industries' 1987 net earnings. A reasonable challenge? I hardly think so, especially given the third major business change.

Table 1
Technological Revolution

Physical Technology

Information Technology

Textile's Capital Intensity

	1980	1987	Percent Change
Sales per asset dollar	US$ 1.98	US$ 1.66	(16%)
Capital spending per employee	1,816	2,712	49%
Textile's Productivity			
Sales per employee	52,927	63,041	19%

MERGERS AND ACQUISITIONS

Nothing creates headlines today like corporate reorganizations. In the textile industry alone, there have been over 225 corporate reorganizations in this decade. In any given year about 10% of the industry's equity changes hands through mergers and acquisitions.

Figure 1 shows that, while 1986 was a big year in terms of the number of transactions, motivated in part by the elimination of the capital gains exclusion that year, 1987 really saw some mega deals. Wicks' US$1.16 billion acquisition of Collins & Aikman and Burlington's US$2.15 billion leveraged buyout are two examples. Of course, 1988 is continuing along that same trend as exemplified by the breakup of Stevens and the continuing acquisition program of Delta Woodside.

These changes have had a tremendous impact on the textile industry. Let's take a look at the textile industry as a whole. As you can see from Table 2, the textile industry has become more leveraged. While we have added and swapped assets at an overall increase of 22%, we have incurred more debt to accomplish this. During the 1980's the lenders' share of textile companies outgrew the equity investors' share by a ratio of 3.4 to 1. Shareholders equity measured in current dollars has increased by only 10% since 1980.

Table 2
Textile Corporate Reorganizations in Perspective Changing Financial Condition

	1980		1987		
	Amount (US$ Million)	Amount (%)	Percent (US$ Million)	Percent (%)	Change (%)
Assets	US$22,721	100	US$27,738	100	22
Liabilities	11,090	49	14,920	54	34
Equity	11,631	51	12,818	46	10

Number of
Transactions

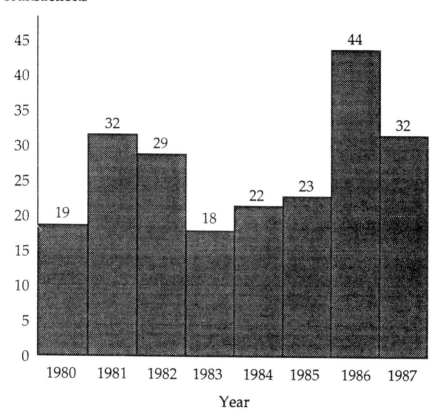

Fig. 1   Textile Corporate Reorganizations in Perspective

To summarize, the scenario we face is this:
• Extremely tough global competition
• A revolution in technology resulting in a more capital intensive industry
• Higher debt on our balance sheets
• Global competitors who out invest us
My objective today is to address the issue of technological investment in view of this
rather perplexing scenario.
• Specifically to see whether there are reasons to explain why the US lags other
  countries in investing in new technology?
• And whether investment in technology itself is a winning and sustainable business
  strategy?
Let's take a look at the first issue.

107

WHY DOES THE US LAG IN REINVESTING IN NEW TECHNOLOGY?

There are two basic sets of circumstances that can help explain our investment lag. The first of these deals with problems we encounter in applying our capital investment decision methodologies. Whether we use discounted cash flow methods, payback periods, cost of capital or return on investment, there are a number of ways in which these capital justification methods consistently get misused.

The second set of circumstances involves structural differences that exist among our global competitors and that impact the capital investment decision.

APPLYING DECISION METHODOLOGIES

Let's take a look now at the first issue-problems in applying decision methodologies. Today's financial literature overflows with examples of these difficulties.

Quantifying Today's Key Business Issues

The first problem arises in how we quantify the returns which will accrue to us from making investments in technology. It used to be very easy when those returns were in the form of savings in direct labor or material costs. But you are an industry that has already reduced your labor and material costs almost as much as you can.

Today's competitive issues have changed greatly. Labor costs and material costs, while still very important, seem to be in control, and our attention has shifted to other issues.

For the last five years, Boston University's Roundtable on Manufacturing has surveyed manufacturing executives concerning current competitive issues.

As you can see from Table 3, today's key competitive issues focus on quality and delivery. Quick Response is very much oriented toward these issues. Yet when it comes to quantifying expected returns from our capital investments, these key factors rank extremely low.

Table 3
Key Competitive Issues Facing
US Manufacturing Executives

- Quality of Conformance
- Delivery Dependability
- Quality of Performance
- Delivery Speed
- Low Price
- Production Flexibility
- Broad Product Line
- Customer Service
- Broad Distribution

Source: BU Manufacturing
Futures Survey

In a recent survey by the National Association of Accountants, executives were asked to rank the factors most frequently used in their investment analyses. As you can see by Figure 2, direct labor, material and waste savings lead the list while the key competitive and strategic issues of quality, delivery, even consistency with business strategy get very little quantitative attention. One of the primary reasons for this is that traditional cost accounting systems do not focus on the emerging strategic issues. This is particularly troublesome for investments like computer integrated manufacturing where

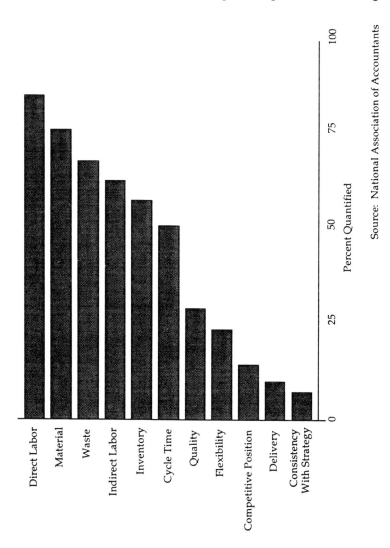

Fig. 2   Capital Investment Decision Criteria

109

the emphasis is on the key issues of improved quality, manufacturing flexibility, quicker throughput, and customer service.

With today's sophisticated financial modeling tools, there is no reason to ignore these key considerations in our quantitative analyses. Robert Kaplan, a noted Harvard accounting professor, suggests using a type of sensitivity analysis to get a firmer grip on factors that are not easily quantified. Without such an approach, we end up penalizing some very worthwhile investment projects. We, in effect, artificially raise the cost of automation.

Internal Hurdle Rates

A second misapplication of capital justification methods involves actually using hurdle rates that are too high, or payback periods that are too short. Referring again to the NAA survey mentioned earlier (Table 4), 94% of those surveyed who use payback justification methods use payback periods of 2–5 years. For those using the discounted cash flow method, 92% used a 13% or greater hurdle rate while 53% used a 15% or greater rate. These rates are well in excess of today's average cost of capital for a US textile company.

Table 4
Payback Periods and Hurdle Rates

	Percent of Survey
Using payback of 2 to 5 years	94
Using hurdle rate greater than 13%	92
Using hurdle rate greater than 15%	53
Source: National Association of Accountants	

Inflation

The third misuse of our decision methodologies results from an inconsistent treatment of inflation. This occurs by not adequately taking into consideration the impact of inflation on expected investment returns, and using discount or hurdle rates that are typically inflation adjusted, which is like comparing apples and oranges. Therefore, unless your expected investment returns are adjusted to reflect future inflation, your actual cost of capital is overstated.

The No-Investment Alternative

I think, in general, we pay very little attention to what happens if we don't make the investment. The typical assumption is status quo, business as usual. Status quo is a myth. The more realistic assumption is that our competitors may make the investment, the competitive environment will change, and our future competitive position, market share, and operating performance may decline. A recent Harvard Business Review article succinctly summarized this situation with a quote by Henry Ford:

'If you need a machine and don't buy it, you pay for it and don't get it'.

110

As a result, by not adequately considering the no-investment alternative, we again artificially increase our cost of capital.

Incremental Investing

The final misapplication I would like to mention should come home to roost to some of you, especially larger companies where capital investment decisions, within defined approval limits, are decentralized. The general response in this environment is to keep the amount of the investment below the authorization limits of the local executive. As you might guess, this situation can lead to a number of small projects whose cumulative benefits when compared to a larger, corporate-wide project could, in fact, be suboptimal. Investments in information technology are prime candidates for this type of misuse.

INTERNATIONAL STRUCTURAL DIFFERENCES

As we have discussed, these five ways in which we potentially misapply our capital justification methods can artificially raise our cost of capital. If this isn't bad enough for our capital investment programs, we also must deal with the uneven playing field of global competition. Generally speaking, because of international structural differences our cost of capital is higher than many of our global competitors, which means we must achieve higher returns to satisfy our lenders and shareholders.

Examples

Let's see by example how these differences interact on a global scale to put the US at a comparative disadvantage with respect to the cost of capital. Table 5 includes three very different types of competitors:
- Europe as illustrated by West Germany,
- The Pacific basin as illustrated by Japan.

Europe

West Germany is one of the more stable of the European economies. Interest rates are relatively low. The corporate tax rate, however, is 56%, which is the highest of our global textile competitors. The US rate is right at the average of 35% for these countries. The rates range from about 15% in Taiwan to 56% in West Germany.

The apparent key to the low cost of capital in West Germany seems to be the very close relationship between capital sources, principally banks, and business. This close relationship serves to reduce the perceived risk on the banks' part in making loans to business. As a result, the average amount of debt for a German textile company is over twice that in our industry. For this reason and as you can see from Table 5, German textile companies enjoy a lower cost of capital than we do, even taking into consideration an assumed same cost of equity. In fact, West Germany probably enjoys a lower cost of equity as well.

Table 5
Comparison of the Cost of Capital

		Pretax Cost	Tax Rate	After Tax Cost	Percent of Total Capitalization		Weighted Average Cost
US							
	Debt	10.4%	38%	6.4%	6.4%	34%	2.2%
	Equity	12.7			12.7	66	8.4
							10.6%
West Germany							
	Debt	6.0%	56%			63%	1.7%
	Equity	12.7				37	4.7
							6.4%
Japan							
	Debt	5.1%	42%			67%	1.6%
	Equity	12.7				33	4.2
							5.8%

Pacific Basin

Since Japan is the economy most Pacific basin countries would like to emulate, let's look at some of the key structural differences in Japan. Inflation and interest rates are lower and tax rates are somewhat higher in Japan than in the US.

The major factor impacting investment in Japan appears to be the Japanese trading company. These very large, diverse conglomerates generally include financial and operating companies. The financial companies help finance the operations of other trading company businesses. This internal funding capability, along with the size and diversity of operations of the trading company, substantially reduces perceived risk and can, therefore, attract external financing as well. For this reason, debt carried by Japanese companies is also much larger than that carried by the US. As a matter of fact, it is not uncommon for Japanese growth companies to have debt 5 to 10 times equity. As you can see from Table 5, these factors again result in a substantially lower cost of capital than we have here in the US.

Government Influence

In addition to the structural differences leading to a lower cost of capital, our global competitors often benefit from the extraordinary role played by government through direct intervention. This can take several different forms. Let's consider three types:

- Export-led growth strategies. These can include:
    - Direct subsidies by the government to businesses involved in export-related activities
    - Tax incentives
    - Loans, and
    - Domestic market protection through import restrictions.

Korea has perhaps the most aggressive export-led growth strategy impacting our industry. The Korean government has announced its intentions to make Korea the world's number one textile exporter by the year 2000.

112

Latin America provides another example of government intervention through exported strategies.

- A second form of direct government intervention includes subsidies for purposes other than stimulating exports. These subsidies usually attempt to facilitate an industrial restructuring, target certain industries or geographic regions for expansion, or help alleviate unemployment. Both Canada and West Germany, to name only two, have tax incentives targeted toward improving industrial expansion in certain geographic areas.
- Finally, governments get involved in regulating output and prices through cartels. OPEC is a prime example, as are the fiber industries in Japan and Taiwan.

IS INVESTMENT IN TECHNOLOGY A WINNING BUSINESS STRATEGY?

We have discussed how our apparent lag in technological investment can partially be explained by our difficulties in applying capital justification methodologies and by international structural differences that help create the uneven playing field of global competition. Given this, is technological investment at a rate suggested by ITMF a winning business strategy? The answer is a resounding maybe.

Why maybe? Let's look at two examples — one from history and one from today. Both examples deal with technological investment. The first in a losing strategy and the second in a winning strategy. At issue are a combination of factors. But in both examples, overall business strategy and market influence play the key roles.

A LESSON FROM HISTORY

Let's first take a look at history. During the early part of this century, the US textile industry, as we all know, moved a significant portion of its resources to the South because of comparative advantages in labor cost. One of the responses to this shift by New England textile manufacturers was to invest in new technology which at that time was the Draper loom. The industry had experienced good times due to pent-up domestic demand created by World War I. But by the mid-twenties, the industry hit the skids due to decreased demand and high cotton prices.

According to MIT's Martha Schary, most of the survivors of this downturn in the New England industry did not make the investment in the Draper loom. As a result, when business declined they were able to successfully cut back production without the high fixed costs associated with capital intensity. Those who did make the investment, however, either:

- Were sold and thus exited the industry early because their assets were easily transferable to other textile companies, or they
- Suffered through poor cash flow during the initial years following investment and exited later because of poor financial performance.

The major factor at work during this period was not whether to invest in technology or even whether to seek lower costs by moving south. The major factor was the significant impact that selling agents in New York and other market centers had over directing the market. The manufacturers, themselves, had very little impact on the market.

As we look back on this lesson from history, there was a definite misreading on the part of certain New England manufacturers of the driving force impacting their businesses. It wasn't technology. It was market influence and control, and that influence was held by the selling agents.

TEXTILE WINNERS AND LOSERS

Today's story is a little different. If one looks at those textile companies that are more successful, several observations emerge.

- First and foremost, these companies are well focused in their market strategy. They, like the selling agents earlier, have influence over their markets.
- Given this market-focused strategy, the successful companies invest 93% more in fixed and working capital per employee.
- The relative age of equipment for these successful companies is 26% newer than the others.
- The growth in investment per employee is 23% for the successful companies compared to 6% for the others.
- Strategic expenditures like research and development for successful companies are 33% above the other companies.

Therefore, the more successful companies capture and fortify their market segments through aggressive investment in equipment, working capital, and strategic expenditures.

Is investment in technology a winning business strategy? The answer can be a resounding yes, if you:

- Apply your investment decision methodologies properly.
- Understand the uneven playing field of global competition.
- Seek to take advantage of your market proximity by looking at Quick Response strategies, especially issues like total quality management, JIT programs, and employee involvement.
- Make your capital investment decisions in the context of your overall market and business strategy, and remember that capital intensity without appropriate market segmentation to provide some element of market influence could result in a road to bankruptcy.

ECONOMIC AND HUMAN FACTORS

Factor Input and Output in the German Textile Industry – An Econometric Approach

F. W. Peren

Forschungsstelle für allgemeine und textile Marktwirtschaft an der Universität Münster

INTRODUCTION

The objective of the study is to analyse the factor input and output in the German textile industry. Therefore the effects of substitution and technical progress of the following textile sectors should be analysed: spinning industry; weaving industry; knitting industry; textile finishing industry; and the textile industry, as a whole [1].

The methodology is based on a model of production treating among inputs and changes in technology symmetrically. The model is based on a production function for each textile sector, giving output as a function of time and of capital, labor, energy and material inputs. Necessary conditions for producer equilibrium in each sector are given by equalities between the distributive shares of the four productive inputs and the corresponding elasticities of output with respect to each of these inputs.

Producer equilibrium under constant returns to scale implies that the value of output is equal to the sum of the values of capital, labor, energy and material inputs into each sector. Given this identity and equalities of output with respect to each of the inputs, we can express the price respectively the unit costs of output as a function of the prices of capital, labor, energy and material inputs, and time. We refer to this function as the sectoral cost function.

Given sectoral cost functions for all textile sectors, we can generate econometric models that determine the rate of technical change and the distributive shares of the four productive inputs endogenously for each sector. The distributive shares and the rate of technical change, like the unit costs of sectoral output, are functions of relative prices and time. We assume that the costs of sectoral outputs are transcendental logarithmic or, more simply, translog functions of the prices of the four inputs and time.

While technical change is endogenous in our models of production and technical change, these models must be carefully distinguished from models of induced technical change [2]. In those models the biases of technical change are endogenous and depend on relative prices. In our models the biases of technical change are fixed, while the rate of technical change is endogenous and depends on relative prices.

117

All of the implications of the theory of production can be described in terms of the sectoral cost functions. The sectoral cost functions must be homogeneous of degree one in prices of the four inputs, symmetric in the input prices and time, and nondecreasing and concave in the input prices. A novel feature of our econometric methodology is to fit econometric models of sectoral production and technical change that incorporate all of these implications of the theory of production.

The translog cost functions that we employ to generate our econometric models cannot be monotone and concave for all possible input prices. However, concavity of these functions can be assured for any input prices that result in nonnegative distributive shares for all four inputs, so that price effects on demands for productive inputs are nonpositive wherever the inputs themselves are nonnegative. This methodology is based on the Cholesky factorization of a matrix of constant parameters in our econometric models associated with price effects. These matrices are fitted subject to the condition that they must be negative semi-definite [3].

Under constant returns to scale the rate of technical change for each sector can be expressed as the negative of the rate of growth of the price of output, plus a weighted average of the rates of growth of the prices of the four inputs. Indexes of the rate of technical change are employed and the four input prices that are exact for translog cost functions. This important innovation assures consistency between the representations of technology that underlie our measures of technical change and input prices and the representations that underlie our econometric models. The econometric models have been fitted to annual data for the period 1976–1986.

ECONOMETRIC MODELS

The development of the econometric model of production and technical change proceeds through two stages. First, a functional form has to be specified for the sectoral cost functions, say c, [4] taking into account restrictions on the parameters implied by the theory of production [5]. Secondly, an error structure for the econometric model must be formulated and procedures for estimation of the unknown parameters should be discussed.

The first step in formulating an econometric model of production and technical change is to consider specific forms for the sectoral cost functions [6].

Up to now the effects of substitution and technical progress in textile industry are analysed by use of Cobb-Douglas- or CES-functions [7]. These functions normally contain just the inputs labor and capital. The following analysis should base on flexible functions. In contrast to the classical models, these kinds of production functions are not valid for all possible combinations of inputs. They only consider a local approximation to the existing production process. This kind of model using a logarithm form is the transcendental logarithmic cost function, or simply called, translog cost function [8]:

118

$$\ln c = a_0 + \sum_i a_i \bullet \ln q_i + a_p \bullet t + \frac{1}{2} \sum_i \sum_j b_{ij} \bullet \ln q_i \bullet \ln q_j$$

$$+ \sum_i b_{ip} \bullet \ln q_i \bullet t + \frac{1}{2} b_{pp} \bullet t^2 \tag{2.1a}$$

where i,j = K,L,E,M

c = unit costs of the production process

q_i = price of the input i

The cost function (2.1a) is homogeneous of degree one in the input prices. The translog cost function is characterized by homogeneity of degree one if and only if the parameters satisfy the following conditions:

$$\sum_i a_i = 1 \tag{2.1b}$$

$$\sum_i b_{ij} = 0 \qquad V_j \tag{2.1c}$$

$$\sum_i b_{ip} = 0 \tag{2.1d}$$

The cost shares of the inputs i, say w_i (i = K,L,E,M), can be expressed in terms of the logarithmic derivatives of the cost function (2.1a) with respect to the logarithms of price of the corresponding input:

$$w_i = \frac{\partial \ln c}{\partial \ln q_i} = a_i + \sum_j b_{ij} \bullet \ln q_j \bullet b_{ip} \bullet t \qquad V_i \tag{2.1e}$$

Finally, for each sector the rate of technical change, say w_p, can be expressed as the negative of the rate of growth of the costs of sectoral output with respect to time, holding the prices of capital, labor, energy and material inputs constant. The negative of the rate of technical change takes the form:

$$-w_p = \frac{\partial \ln c}{\partial t} = a_p + \sum_i b_{ip} \bullet \ln q_i \bullet b_{pp} \bullet t \tag{2.1f}$$

Given the cost function (2.1a), share elasticities can be defined with respect to price [9] as the derivatives of the cost shares with respect to the logarithms of the prices of capital, labor, energy and material inputs. For the translog cost function the share elasticities with respect to price are constant. This form can be characterized as a constant share elasticity cost function [10], indicating the interpretation of the fixed parameters that enter the cost function. The share elasticities with respect to price are symmetric, so that the parameters satisfy the conditions:

$$b_{ij} = b_{ji} \qquad V_{i,j} \qquad (2.1g)$$

Similarly, given the cost function (2.1a), the biases of technical change with respect to price can be defined as derivatives of the cost shares with respect to time [11].

Alternatively, the biases of technical change with respect to price can be defined as derivatives of the rate of technical change with respect to the logarithms of the price of capital, labor, energy and material inputs. Those two definitions of biases of technical change are equivalent. For the translog cost function (2.1a) the biases of technical change with respect to price are constant; these parameters are symmetric and satisfy the conditions:

$$b_{ip} = b_{pi} \qquad V_i \qquad (2.1h)$$

Finally, the rate of change of the negative of the rate of technical change bpp can be defined as the derivative of the negative of the rate of technical change with respect to time. For the translog cost function, these rates of change are constant.

The next step in considering specific forms of the sectoral cost functions is to derive restrictions on the parameters implied by the fact that the cost functions are increasing in all four input prices and the concave in four input prices. First, since the cost function (2.1a) is increasing in each of the four input prices, the cost share are non-negative:

$$w_i \geq 0 \qquad V_i \qquad (2.1i)$$

Under homogeneity these cost shares sum to unity:

$$\sum_i w_i = 1 \qquad (2.1j)$$

The concavity condition for the linear homogeneous cost function (2.1a) is that the Hessian matrix H is negative semi-definite [12]. The Hessian matrix is the matrix of second-order partial derivatives and for the translog cost function (2.1a) H is denoted as follows:

$$H = c \cdot Q^{-1} \cdot (B + w \cdot w' - W) \cdot Q^{-1} \qquad (2.2)$$

where: $\quad$ H $=$ $\quad$ Hessian matrix from c with the elements

$$h_{ij} = h_{ij} = \frac{\partial^2 c}{\partial q_i \partial q_j}$$

B $=$ $\quad$ matrix of constant share elasticities with the elements b_{ij}

$$
Q = \begin{bmatrix} q_K & & \cdots & 0 \\ & q_L & & \vdots \\ \vdots & & q_E & \\ 0 & \cdots & & q_M \end{bmatrix} \quad W = \begin{bmatrix} w_K & & \cdots & 0 \\ & w_L & & \vdots \\ \vdots & & w_E & \\ 0 & \cdots & & w_M \end{bmatrix} \quad w = \begin{bmatrix} w_K \\ w_L \\ w_E \\ w_M \end{bmatrix}
$$

The Hessian matrix H is negative semi-definite when $(B + w \bullet w' - W)$ in equation (2.2) is negative semi-definite. The matrix $(w \bullet w' - W)$ is negative definite, because all of the cost shares are less than unity {nonnegativity restriction (2.1i)}. Therefore if B is negative semi-definite, the Hessian matrix H might be sufficiently negative semi-definite.

On the other hand, when setting the matrix $(w \bullet w' - W)$ to converge to zero as a special case that wi approximately becomes unity, while other shares go to zero, the matrix B must be negative semi-definite as a necessary condition for the negative semi-definiteness of H.

Necessary and sufficient conditions for the negative semi-definiteness of H can be expressed as non-positive conditions for Cholesky values after the Cholesky factorization of matrix B as follows [13]:

$B = U \bullet D \bullet U'$

$$
= \begin{bmatrix} 1 & & \cdots & 0 \\ u_{LK} & 1 & & \vdots \\ u_{KE} & u_{LE} & 1 & \\ u_{KM} & u_{LM} & u_{EM} & 1 \end{bmatrix} \bullet \begin{bmatrix} d_K & & \cdots & 0 \\ & d_L & & \vdots \\ \vdots & & d_E & \\ 0 & \cdots & & d_M \end{bmatrix} \bullet \begin{bmatrix} 1 & u_{LK} & u_{KE} & u_{KM} \\ & 1 & u_{LE} & u_{LM} \\ \vdots & & 1 & u_{EM} \\ 0 & \cdots & & 1 \end{bmatrix}
$$

$$
= \begin{bmatrix} d_K & d_K u_{LK} & d_K u_{KE} & d_K u_{KM} \\ & d_K u_{LK}^2 + d_L & d_K u_{LK} u_{KE} + d_L u_{LE} & d_K u_{KM} u_{LK} + d_L u_{LM} \\ & & d_K u_{KE}^2 + d_L u_{LE}^2 + d_E & d_K u_{KM} u_{KE} + d_L u_{LE} u_{LM} + d_E u_{EM} \\ & & & d_K u_{KM}^2 + d_L u_{LM}^2 + d_E u_{EM}^2 + d_M \end{bmatrix}
$$

$$(2.3)$$

Under constant returns to scale the constant share elasticities satisfy symmetry restrictions implied by homogeneity of degree one of the cost function. These restrictions imply that the parameters of the Cholesky factorization (u_{ij} and d_i; i,j = K,L,E,M) must satisfy the following conditions:

$$1 + u_{LK+} + u_{KE} + u_{KM} = 0$$
$$1 + u_{LE} + u_{LM} = 0$$
$$1 + u_{EM} = 0 \qquad (2.4)$$
$$d_M = 0$$

Under these conditions there is a one-to-one correspondence between the constant share elasticities bij and the parameters of Cholesky factorization. The matrix of share elasticities are negative semi-definite if and only if the diagonal elements d_i of the matrix D are all non-positive.

In order not to make the model too restrictive only the local concavity at the approximation point is demanded. Concavity for a linear homogeneous cost function implies that the matrix $(B + w \bullet w' - W)$ is negative semi-definite. If the concavity restriction only applied for the base year $(q_i = 1, V_i; t = 0)$, the cost shares w_i correspond with the parameters a_i [14]:

$$(B + w \bullet w' - W) = (B + a \bullet a' - A) \qquad (2.5)$$

where

$$A = \begin{bmatrix} a_K & & \cdots & 0 \\ & a_L & & \vdots \\ \vdots & & a_E & \\ 0 & \cdots & & a_M \end{bmatrix} \quad ; \quad a = \begin{bmatrix} a_K \\ a_L \\ a_E \\ a_M \end{bmatrix}$$

Analogue to the equation (2.3) the matrix of the share elasticities B can be Cholesky factorized as follows:

$$B = U \bullet D \bullet U' - a \bullet a' + A \qquad (2.6)$$

$$= \begin{bmatrix} d_K - a_K^2 + a_K & d_K u_{LK} - a_K a_L & d_K u_{KE} - a_K a_E & d_K u_{KM} - a_K a_M \\ & d_K u_{LK}^2 + d_L - a_L^2 + a_L & d_K u_{LK} u_{KE} + d_L u_{LE} - a_L a_E & d_K u_{KM} u_{LK} + d_L u_{LM} - a_L a_M \\ & & d_K u_{KE}^2 + d_L u_{LE}^2 + d_E - a_E^2 + a_E & d_K u_{KM} u_{KE} + d_L u_{LE} u_{LM} + d_E u_{EM} - a_E a_M \\ & & & d_K u_{KM}^2 + d_L u_{LM}^2 + d_E u_{EM}^2 + d_M - a_M^2 + a_M \end{bmatrix}$$

The translog cost function (2.1a) is local concave at the approximation point if and only if the Cholesky values d_i, i = K,L,E,M, are all non-positive. This condition completes the specification of the model of production and technical change.

The equations (2.1) build an interdependence system. To formulate an econometric model of production and technical change a stochastic component to the translog cost function (2.1a), to the equations of the cost shares (2.1e) and to the equation of the rate of technical change (2.1f) has to be added.

It is assumed that the adding random disturbances for all equations are normal distributed and have expected value equal to zero for all observations. It is also assumed that the random disturbances have a covariance matrix that is the same for all observations; since the random disturbances corresponding to the four cost shares sum to zero.

So the estimation model likes a Zellner-system [15] but with an unknown covariance matrix. Since the cost shares sum to unity {adding-up-theorem, restriction (2.1j)} the four cost shares equations are linear dependent. Thus every cost share equation from (2.1e) can be described as a linear combination of the other three. Since the cost shares sum to unity the random disturbances add up to zero:

$$\sum_i \varepsilon_i = 0 \qquad (2.7)$$

So the random disturbances ε_i, i = K,L,E,M, are not distributed independently. This takes effect in the singularity of the covariance matrix. Consequently the model in the existing form cannot be estimated.

This problem can be solved, when we omit one of the cost share equations, for example the restriction for material input [16]. When we consider the restrictions (2.1b,c,d,g,h), we come to the following stochastic system:

$$\ln(c/q_m) = a_0 + \sum_i a_i \cdot \ln(q_i/q_m) + a_p \cdot t$$

$$+ \frac{1}{2} \sum_i \sum_j b_{ij} \cdot \ln(q_i/q_m) \cdot \ln(q_j/q_m)$$

$$+ \sum_i b_{ip} \cdot \ln(q_i/q_m) \cdot t + \frac{1}{2} b_{pp} \cdot t_2 + \varepsilon_c \qquad (2.8a)$$

$$w_i = a_i + \sum_j b_{ij} \cdot \ln(q_j/q_m) + b_{ip} \cdot t + \varepsilon_i \quad V_i \qquad (2.8b)$$

$$-w_p = a_p + \sum_i b_{ip} \cdot \ln(q_i/q_m) + b_{pp} \cdot t + \varepsilon_p \qquad (2.8c)$$

where a_i, a_p, b_{ij}, b_{ip}, b_{pp} are unknown parameters and ε_c, ε_i, ε_p are unobservable random disturbances.

This system can be estimated with the Full-Information-Maximum-Likelihood-procedure or with an iterative Zellner-procedure. We use an iterative Zellner-procedure from the SAS software package, SAS-Institute Inc., Cary, NC, USA.

The negative of the average rates of technical change in any two points of time $\left(-w_p^D\right)$, say t and t + 1, can be expressed as the difference between successive logarithms of the costs of output, less a weighted average of the differences between successive logarithms of the prices of capital, labor, energy and material inputs, with weights given by the average cost shares:

$$-w_p^D = \left[1nc(t+1) - 1nc(t)\right]$$

$$-\sum_i \frac{1}{2}\left[w_i(t+1) + w_i(t)\right] \cdot \left[1nq_i(t+1) - 1nq_i(t)\right] \qquad (2.9)$$

where [17]:

$$-w_p^D = \frac{1}{2}\left[w_p(t+1) + w_p(t)\right] \qquad (2.10)$$

and the average cost shares in the two periods w_i^D are given by:

$$w_i^D = \frac{1}{2}\left[w_i(t+1) + w_i(t)\right] \quad V_i \quad i = K, L, E, M \qquad (2.11)$$

It will be referred to the expressions for the average rates of technical change w_p^D as Törnqvist indexes of the sectoral rates of technical change.

Similarly, we can consider specific forms for prices of capital, labor, energy and material inputs as functions of prices of individual capital, labor, energy and material inputs into each sector. It will be assumed that the price of each input can be expressed as a translog function of the price of its components. Accordingly, the difference between successive logarithms of the price of the input is a weighted average of differences between successive logarithms of prices of its components. The weights are given by the average cost shares of the components. So the input prices of the translog cost model q_i and the unit costs c (as total price of the output) will be calculated and described as Törnqvist indexes [18].

Since we use the average of the cost shares and the rate of technical change, we have to use average disturbances, too:

$$\varepsilon_i^D = \frac{1}{2}\left[\varepsilon_i(t+1) + \varepsilon_i(t)\right] \quad V_i \quad i = K, L, E, M \qquad (2.12)$$

and

$$\varepsilon_p^D = \frac{1}{2}\left[\varepsilon_p(t+1) + \varepsilon_p(t)\right] \qquad (2.13)$$

As before, the average cost shares w_i^D sum to unity, so that the average disturbances ε_i^D sum to zero:

$$\sum_i \varepsilon_i^D = 0 \qquad (2.14)$$

The covariance matrix of the average disturbances corresponding to the equation for the rate of technical change is a Laurent matrix, say Ω, where:

$$\Omega = \begin{bmatrix} \dfrac{1}{2} & \dfrac{1}{4} & 0 & \cdots & 0 \\[2mm] \dfrac{1}{4} & \dfrac{1}{2} & \dfrac{1}{4} & \cdots & 0 \\[2mm] 0 & \dfrac{1}{4} & \dfrac{1}{2} & \cdots & 0 \\[2mm] \vdots & & & & \vdots \\[2mm] 0 & \cdots & 0 & \dfrac{1}{4} & \dfrac{1}{2} \end{bmatrix}$$

The covariance matrix of the average disturbance corresponding to each equation for the cost shares is the same.

Although disturbances in equations for the average rate of technical change and the average cost shares are autocorrelated, the data can be transformed to eliminate the autocorrelation. The matrix Ω is positive definite, so that there is a matrix F such that:

$$F'F = \Omega^{-1} \tag{2.15}$$

To construct the matrix F , first Ω can be inverted to obtain the inverse matrix Ω^{-1}, a positive definite matrix. The Cholesky factorization of the inverse Matrix Ω^{-1},

$$\Omega^{-1} = L D L' \tag{2.16}$$

can be calculated where L is a unit lower triangular matrix and D is a diagonal matrix with positive elements along the main diagonal [19]. Finally, we can write the matrix F in the form:

$$F = D^{1/2} L' \tag{2.17}$$

where $D^{1/2}$ is a diagonal matrix with elements along the main diagonal equal to the square roots of the corresponding elements of D.

Before we estimate the translog cost system, the equations (2.8) are transformed by the matrix F to obtain equations with uncorrelated random disturbances.

EMPIRICAL RESULTS

To implement the econometric models of production and technical change we have assembled a data base for the textile sectors we analyse. For labor input we have compiled the working hours and the hourly earnings from blue- and white-collar workers, from home workers and self-employed persons. The sectoral volumes of employment are given in Figure 1.

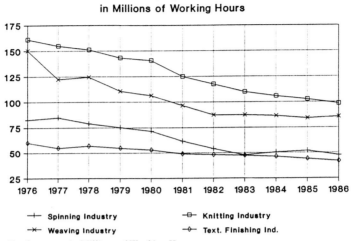

Fig. 1   Employment - in Millions of Working Hours

The costs of capital are calculated by the user costs of capital. It is differed between buildings, equipment and inventories [20]:

$$q_t^{CA} = NA_t^{CA} \cdot r_t + NA_t^{CA} \cdot \delta^{CA} + NA_t^{CA} \cdot \mu_t \qquad (3.1)$$

$\underset{\substack{\text{user costs} \\ \text{of capital}}}{} \qquad \underset{\substack{\text{interest} \\ \text{costs}}}{} \quad \underset{\text{depreciations}}{} \quad \underset{\text{taxation}}{}$

where $\quad q_t^{CA} = \quad$ user costs of capital of CA in t

$\qquad CA = \quad$ buildings, equipment, inventories

$\qquad NA_t^{CA} = \quad$ average net capital stock in

$\qquad r_t = \quad$ internal rate on investment
$\qquad \delta = \quad$ (constant) rate of depreciation
$\qquad \mu_t = \quad$ tax rate of capital using in t

The development of the annual capital input is given in Figure 2.
For material input, the expenditures/prices for the following 20 materials are added:

- raw wool,
- raw cotton,
- cellulose fibres,
- cellulose plies,
- synthetic fibres,
- synthetic plies,
- wool and other hairs of animals,
- combed tops and slub yarns,

126

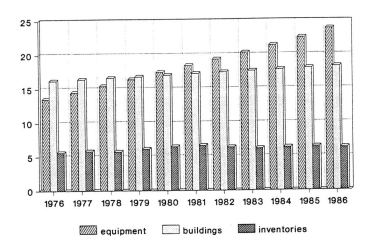

Fig. 2   Net Capital Stocks in the total textile industry - in Billions of DM, in Current Prices

- other worked textured yarns,
- yarn out of cotton,
- yarn out of wool,
- yarn out of bast and durable fibres,
- yarn out of cellulose fibres,
- yarn out of synthetic fibres,
- yarn out of other materials,
- textured yarns out of polyamide,
- sewing threads,
- woven fabric (yard goods),
- warp-knitted and knitted textiles,
- dyestuffs and colours.

The structure of the material inputs is given in Figure 3.

For energy input we have differed between the following kinds of energy:

- coal, coke,
- fuel oil,
- gas,
- electricity,
- district heating and compressed air.

The structure of the energy inputs is given in Figure 4.

Figure 6 shows the development of the real gross output in the textile sectors which were analysed.

To get the input prices q_i and the unit costs c (as total price of the output) we summarize the prices/costs of the special kinds of inputs to the aggregates labor, capital, material, and energy. For this we use the Törnqvist Index [21]:

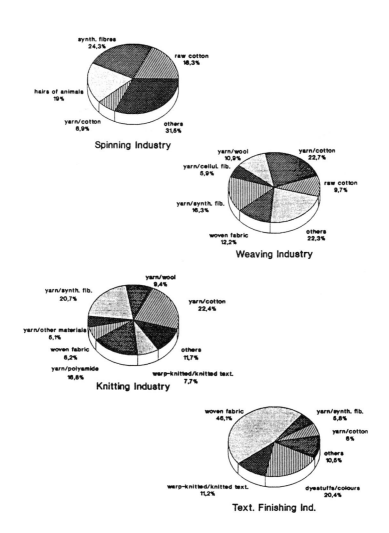

Spinning Industry

Weaving Industry

Knitting Industry

Text. Finishing Ind.

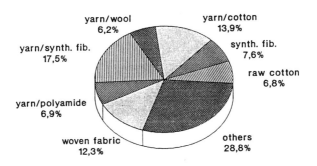

Fig. 3   Structure of Material Inputs

128

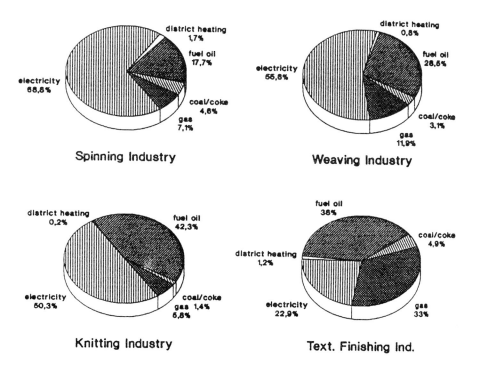

Spinning Industry

Weaving Industry

Knitting Industry

Text. Finishing Ind.

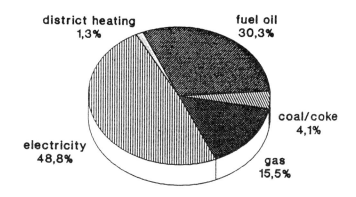

Total Textile Industry

FATM

Fig. 4   Structure of Energy Inputs

$$\frac{q_Q^t \left[q_{Q_i}^t \right]}{q_Q^0 \left[q_{Q_i}^0 \right]} = \pi_{Q_i} \left[\frac{q_{Q_i}^t}{q_{Q_i}^0} \right]^{\frac{1}{2} \left[w_{Q_i}^t + w_{Q_i}^0 \right]}$$

$$V_Q \qquad Q = K, L, E, M$$

(3.2a)

where q_Q = price of the aggregate Q

q_{Q_i} = price of the special input i, i e Q

w_{Q_i} = cost share of the special input i of the total costs of the aggregate Q respectively:

$$\frac{c^t \left[q_i^t \right]}{c^0 \left[q_i^0 \right]} = \pi_{q_i} \left[\frac{q_i^t}{q_i^0} \right]^{\frac{1}{2} \left[w_i^t + w_i^0 \right]}$$

(3.2b)

where c = unit costs of the production progress

q_i = price of the input i, i = K,L,E,M

w_i = cost share of the input i, i = K,L,E,M

For each sector we have compiled Törnqvist indexes of prices of sectoral output and all four sectoral inputs, annually, for the period 1976-1986. We have also compiled data on the cost shares of the inputs and Törnqvist indexes of sectoral rates of technical change [22].

The development of the prices of labor, capital, material and energy inputs and the development of the total input costs per unit in the textile industry as a whole are given in Figs 5 and 7. Figure 8 shows that the unit costs mostly decreased in the knitting industry and the textile finishing industry during the analysed period.

The average structure of the nominal factor inputs in the sectors of the German textile industry is given in Figure 11.

The parameters a_i can be interpreted as average cost shares of capital input, labor input, energy input and material input for the corresponding sector. Similarly, the parameter a_p can be interpreted as averages of the neagtive of rates of technical change. The parameters b_{ij} can be interpreted as constant share elasticities with respect to price for the corresponding sector. Similarly, the parameters b_{ip} can be interpreted as constant biases of technical change with respect to price. Finally, the parameter b_{pp} can be interpreted as constant rate of change of the negative of the rate of technical change. The estimated parameters of our sectoral models of production and technical change are presented in Table 1 [23].

Estimates of the share elasticities with respect to price, b_{ij}, are obtained under the restrictions implied by the necessary and sufficient conditions for concavity of the cost functions presented in section 2. Under these restrictions the matrices of constant share elasticities, B, must be negative semi-definite for all sectors. To impose the concavity

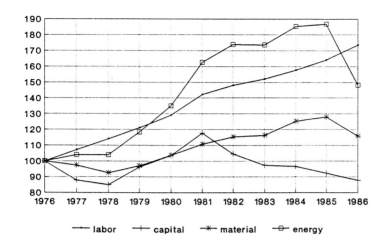

Fig. 5   Price Index of Factor Inputs in the Total Textile Industry

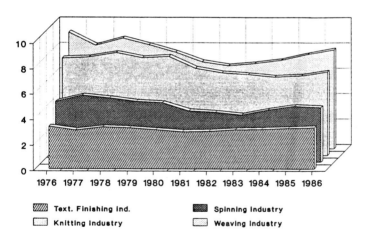

Fig. 6   Real Gross Product - in Billions of DM, in Prices from 1980

restrictions the matrices of constant share elasticities for all sectors are represented in terms of their Cholesky factorizations. The necessary and sufficient conditions are that the diagonal elements d_i of the matrices D that appear in the Cholesky factorizations must be nonpositive.

For the analysed sectors we have to impose the following conditions [24]:

$d_E = d_K = 0$:   weaving industry;

$d_E = d_L = 0$:   knitting industry;

131

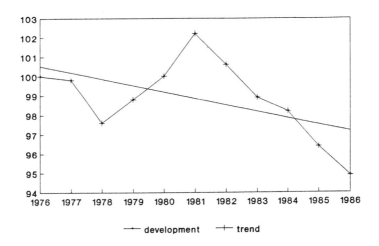

Fig. 7   Unit Costs of Production in the Total Textile Industry

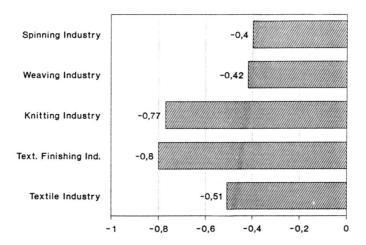

Fig. 8   Change in Unit Costs - average annual rates/in percent

$d_L = d_K = 0$:   spinning industry, textile finishing industry, textile industry (as a whole).

The interpretation of the parameter estimates reported in Table 1 begins with an analysis of the estimates of the parameters a_i (i = K,L,E,M) and a_p. The average cost shares a_i are nonnegative for all textile sectors included in our study. In all analysed sectors the values of the negative of the estimated average rate of technical change a_p are negative.

132

Parameter	Spinning Industry	Weaving Industry	Knitting Industry	Textile Finishing Industry	Textile Industry (Total)
a_0	-0,02574	-0,02835	0,03581	-0,02022	0,00518
	(-1,47)	(-1,97)	(2,54)	(-1,95)	(0,41)
a_L	0,31143	0,32883	0,41186	0,36736	0,34203
	(34,52)	(26,40)	(42,62)	(37,81)	(39,24)
a_K	0,11077	0,11201	0,10834	0,13097	0,12437
	(19,80)	(61,12)	(28,22)	(27,43)	(39,49)
a_E	0,04384	0,03833	0,02213	0,08164	0,03972
	(22,27)	(32,31)	(37,31)	(38,01)	(44,02)
a_M	0,53396	0,52083	0,45767	0,42003	0,49388
a_P	-0,04019	-0,03916	-0,03461	-0,04605	-0,03852
	(-9,02)	(-9,77)	(-9,60)	(-16,05)	(-10,53)
b_{PP}	0,00135	-0,00093	-0,00509	-0,00033	-0,00444
	(0,53)	(-0,47)	(-2,55)	(-0,21)	(-3,44)
b_{LP}	-0,00392	-0,00393	-0,00523	-0,00518	-0,00446
	(-1,60)	(-1,07)	(-1,63)	(-1,79)	(-1,53)
b_{KP}	0,00624	0,00655	0,00792	0,00659	0,00591
	(4,27)	(12,98)	(6,82)	(4,93)	(5,85)
b_{EP}	0,00092	0,00157	-0,00013	0,00579	0,00164
	(1,63)	(3,96)	(-0,71)	(8,14)	(4,90)
b_{MP}	-0,00324	-0,00419	-0,00256	-0,00720	-0,00309
b_{LL}	0,21444	0,22070	0,24221	0,23241	0,22505
b_{LK}	-0,03450	-0,03683	-0,04465	-0,04811	-0,04254
b_{LE}	-0,01365	-0,01280	-0,00977	-0,02999	-0,01359
b_{KK}	0,09850	0,09946	0,09656	0,11382	0,10890
b_{KE}	-0,00486	-0,00429	-0,00318	-0,01069	-0,00494
b_{EE}	-0,01235	-0,01065	0,00511	-0,01172	-0,01368
b_{LM}	-0,16629	-0,17106	-0,18779	-0,15430	-0,16892
b_{KM}	-0,05915	-0,05834	-0,04873	-0,05501	-0,06142
b_{EM}	0,03086	0,02775	0,00784	0,05240	0,03220
b_{MM}	0,19458	0,20166	0,22868	0,15691	0,19814

Source: FATM

The parameter b_{pp} can be interpreted as the rate of change of the negative of the rate of technical change. If the estimated value of this parameter is positive, the rate of technical change is decreasing; if the value is negative, the rate is increasing.

The estimated values of b_{pp} are negative for all analysed sectors with the exception of the spinning industry. The negative parameters b_{pp} directed that the increase of the total productivity accelerated during the analysed period. In contrast to the other sectors, the positive coefficient in the spinning industry implies that the corresponding increase in the total productivity decelerated during the analysed period.

The values of the parameter estimates bpp are all around zero. This implies that the rate of technical change with respect to the productivity of the total factor input developed relatively continuously. Also, Figure 9 shows that the development of the total factor productivity followed approximately a linear trend.

The rate of technical change with respect to the productivity of the total factor input increased with time for all textile sectors included in this study [25]. The average annual rates of the change in total factor productivity in the analysed sectors are given in

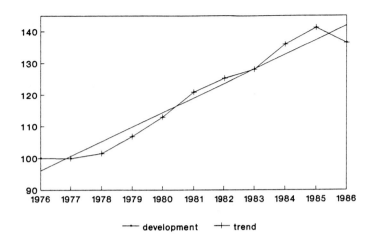

Fig. 9   Total Factor Productivity in the Total Textile Industry

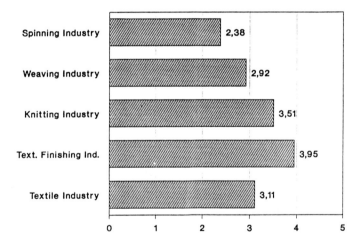

Fig. 10   Change in Total Factor Productivity

Figure 10. The total factor productivity increased mostly in the textile finishing and knitting industries during the considered period.

We continue the interpretation of parameter estimates given in Table 1 with the estimated biases of technical change with respect to the price of each input, b_{ip} (i = K,L,E,M). These parameters can be interpreted as the change in the negative of the rate of technical change with respect to the price of each input or, alternatively, as the change in the share of each input with respect to time. If the estimated value of the parameter b_{ip} is positive, technical change used the input i; alternatively, the rate of technical change decreased with an increase in the price of the input i . If the estimated value is negative, technical change saved the corresponding input and the rate of technical change increased with the input price.

The sum of the four biases of technical change with respect to price is equal to zero, so that we can rule out the possibility that all four biases are either all negative or all positive. Of the fourteen remaining logical possibilities, only two actually occur among the results presented in Table 2.

Table 2
Classification of Textile Sectors by Biases of Technical Change

Pattern of Biases	Textile Sectors
Capital Using Labor Using Energy Using Material Saving	knitting industry
Capital Using Labor Using Energy Using Material Saving	spinning industry, weaving industry, textile finishing industry, textile industry (as a whole)

Source: FATM

Considering the bias of technical change with respect to the prices of capital and labor inputs, we find that technical change was capital using and labor saving for all textile sectors we analyse. Alternatively, the rate of technical change decreased with an increase in the price of capital and increased with the price of labor.

Considering the bias of technical change with respect to the prices of energy and material inputs, we find that technical change was energy using for all textile sectors, with the exception of the knitting industry, and material saving for all sectors we analyse.

Considering the t-values, which are given in brackets under the parameter estimates and the absolute values of the coefficients, we find that the interpretation of a capital using technical change for all analysed sectors is significant. Also, the parameter estimates b_{EP} are significant with the exception of the knitting industry. This implies that technical change was energy using in the spinning industry, the weaving industry, the textile finishing industry and the textile industry as a whole, while the effect of a change in technical progress with respect to the price of energy input was probability neutral in the knitting industry during the analysed period.

The t-values of the parameter estimates b_{LP} imply that the decrease of the (relative) labor input in the German textile industry did not depend mainly on technical change during the considered period. So, probably, the process of reducing the (relative) labor input in the German textile industry during the analysed period depended primarily on direct price effects and/or substitution effects.

The estimated share elasticities with respect to price, b_{ij} (i,j = K,L,E,M), describe the implications of patterns of substitution among capital, labor, energy, and material inputs for the relative distribution of the value of output among these four inputs. Positive share elasticities imply that the corresponding cost shares increased with an increase in price; negative share elasticities imply that the cost shares decreased with an increase in price; share elasticities equal to zero imply that the cost shares were independent of price.

The interpretation of the parameter estimates given in Table 1 continues with the estimated elasticities of the share of each input with respect to the price of the input itself, b_{ii} (i = K,L,E,M). Negative values of the parameters b_{ii} imply that the cost share of the input i decreased with an increase in the price of the input itself; positive values of b_{ii} imply that the cost share of i increased with an increase in price of the input itself. A positive value of b_{ii} is economically explainable if the demand of the factor i reacted unelastically with a change in price of the input itself.

For interpretation of the substitution effects in the German textile industry and its sectors, the Hicks partial elasticities of substitution of the capital, labor, energy and material inputs, say s_{ij} , and the Slutsky partial elasticities, say e_{ij}, as direct price elasticities, are derived. The calculated elasticities are given in Table 3 [26].

The absolute values of the estimated share elasticities bii are usually higher than the parameter estimates of b_{ij}, i = j. This implies that the direct price effects usually dominated the indirect price effects during the analysed period.

The estimates of the parameter b_{LL} are positive for all analysed sectors. Usually the direct price elasticities e_{LL} are negative and the average values of e_{LL} scatter around –1. This implies that the reduction of labor during the analysed period depended in great part on the permanent rise in its own price [27]. In the textile industry as a whole, all annual values of e_{LL} are negative. This illustrates that (relative) labor input was reduced continuously in consequence of the permanent increase in the labor costs.

The reduction of labor input in the German textile industry also happened independently of the trend of production. Especially in the textile finishing and knitting industries, labor input decreased constantly, even in the years of economic growth.

The direct price elasticities of the capital input e_{KK} are tendentiously negative for the years 1977–1978 and 1983–1986; between 1979 and 1982 they are usually positive. The net capital stocks expanded independently of the trend of the user costs of capital. Also, in time of increasing user costs of capital, the net capital stocks, especially the stocks of equipment, expanded [28].

The share elasticities of capital with respect to the price of labor b_{LK} are negative for all analysed sectors. Also, the partial elasticities of substitution s_{LK} imply that the continuous increase in the labor costs effected a substitution of labor input with an intensification of the capital input. Figure 12 illustrates that the capital intensity of the labor input increased continuously during the analysed period [29].

The annual volumes of material and energy inputs depended directly on the trend of production. Therefore an economical interpretation of the direct price elasticities e_{MM} and e_{EE} makes no sense. The level of material and energy inputs did not depend on the trend of the corresponding input prices. There could only be substitution effects among different material or energy inputs, which depended on the corresponding input prices. But the material input respective to energy input as a whole was mainly determined by the trend of the output and not by the factor prices.

There were also no substitution or complementary effects among material and energy inputs during the anlaysed period, even when the estimated share elasticities of energy input with respect to the price of material input b_{EM} are the only parameters of substitution

Table 3
Direct Price Elasticities and Elasticities of Substitution

Year	e_{LL}	e_{KK}	e_{EE}	e_{MM}	s_{LE}	s_{LK}	s_{LM}	s_{KE}	s_{KM}	s_{EM}
Spinning Industry										
1977	0,37	-0,51	3,83	-3,95	1,30	0,07	1,12	-0,54	-3,22	0,87
1978	-0,72	1,32	-7,95	0,61	-0,92	0,62	0,15	4,72	-0,54	1,10
1979	-0,94	0,12	-0,87	-1,15	0,81	-1,38	0,12	-12,4	-1,08	0,70
1980	-0,79	-0,03	-0,88	0,10	1,06	56,3	-2,52	2,34	-0,42	10,1
1981	-1,34	0,30	-0,46	-1,17	-1,99	-12,7	-13,2	3,85	-10,6	-1,54
1982	-3,17	0,10	-1,19	-2,51	-0,96	0,69	3,93	0,30	0,06	1,10
1983	-6,73	0,22	-6,25	-4,86	8,58	1,29	23,4	0,57	0,62	1,65
1984	1,40	-13,1	1,18	1,30	0,29	0,03	-1,13	0,06	-0,62	-1,30
1985	0,57	-1,00	6,79	-14,2	1,79	0,27	1,00	-0,49	-0,52	-0,42
1986	-1,62	-0,26	-0,35	0,01	0,89	0,83	0,44	2,32	-0,44	-0,66
Weaving Industry										
1977	2,50	0,07	-4,12	3,08	1,35	0,90	1,29	0,51	0,39	1,14
1978	0,26	0,32	7,27	-1,41	0,04	-0,26	0,57	3,71	1,26	1,05
1979	-2,80	-0,02	-0,85	-0,72	-0,01	-1,77	-6,75	4,54	-0,65	1,09
1980	-0,62	0,36	-1,53	-0,39	2,75	-6,12	-2,57	5,03	-8,41	4,11
1981	-0,88	0,15	-0,35	-1,95	-0,57	-6,71	-0,80	1,65	-2,36	-0,68
1982	-2,14	0,30	-1,23	-1,23	-0,66	0,51	4,86	0,28	0,05	1,37
1983	-0,10	-0,19	39,7	0,51	8,80	0,19	-0,85	-0,85	-0,01	2,14
1984	-0,30	-1,51	0,62	0,59	-1,68	0,76	-1,16	-0,12	-0,19	-0,48
1985	-0,56	-1,94	7,02	6,71	2,20	0,81	3,03	-2,35	-2,97	-5,67
1986	0,36	-3,94	-0,85	-0,49	0,62	0,18	0,20	0,75	0,20	-1,13
Knitting Industry										
1977	-0,65	-0,16	-0,85	-1,28	0,09	0,37	0,90	0,31	-0,07	1,07
1978	-0,53	-0,13	1,71	-0,32	0,03	0,31	0,45	0,54	-0,47	1,04
1979	-0,70	0,24	-0,75	-0,37	0,80	-1,42	1,59	4,13	-0,63	1,13
1980	-0,28	0,57	-0,56	-0,22	0,84	15,3	1,04	1,52	-30,2	0,96
1981	-1,23	0,07	-1,01	-0,71	0,83	-2,41	2,34	7,11	-0,58	1,48
1982	-2,12	0,06	-0,58	-1,87	-1,79	0,39	1,62	0,10	0,45	30,2
1983	-1,49	0,03	10,0	0,16	1,55	0,51	2,06	0,00	-0,04	-0,42
1984	-1,18	-2,42	-1,04	-0,67	0,93	1,43	0,21	1,08	0,75	114,8
1985	-1,43	-0,20	-13,0	0,50	2,60	0,48	-7,67	-0,11	0,04	0,47
1986	-0,80	-0,06	-0,46	-0,96	0,63	0,47	1,01	0,61	2,67	0,20
Textile Finishing Industry										
1977	-1,14	-0,03	-2,25	-9,39	-1,62	0,51	0,12	0,59	0,53	1,05
1978	0,87	-0,50	-7,55	-4,79	0,74	-0,24	0,79	-2,15	-3,43	1,01
1979	-0,50	0,19	-0,67	0,07	0,84	-1,12	1,26	6,31	-0,25	1,12
1980	-0,50	0,64	-0,84	0,32	1,01	26,0	3,50	1,49	-1,96	1,65
1981	-0,86	0,08	-0,09	-1,74	-0,30	-2,48	-0,29	0,23	-1,31	-0,33
1982	-0,56	-0,07	-0,20	1,52	-0,09	0,21	-16,2	0,11	-0,31	2,12
1983	-1,01	-0,26	-1,77	0,62	1,46	0,45	339,6	-0,40	0,06	0,58
1984	-0,35	0,17	0,81	0,02	-3,93	1,05	2,70	-1,21	0,25	-2,00
1985	-1,81	0,03	8.04	0,01	6,26	0,94	-27,3	-1,77	-0,02	2,81
1986	-1,09	-0,16	-0,30	-0,03	0,51	0,62	0,65	0,38	0,40	0,27
Textile Industry (as a whole)										
1977	-0,91	-0,10	-1,13	-0,77	0,68	0,45	0,98	0,30	-0,06	1,07
1978	-0,49	0,00	-70,8	-0,34	-0,06	0,35	0,46	0,99	0,98	1,05
1979	-0,57	0,19	-0,56	0,16	0,55	-0,92	3,27	17,4	-0,22	1,09
1980	-0,49	0,33	-1,28	-0,22	2,04	-5,79	-10,1	3,18	-4,66	2,92
1981	-1,07	0,10	-0,40	-1,36	-0,35	-4,06	0,50	1,48	-1,68	-0,15
1982	-1,91	0,08	-0,84	-1,20	-0,75	0,49	252,5	0,23	0,22	0,35
1983	-1,49	-0,04	-7,82	1,43	2,09	0,48	3,25	-0,21	-0,13	0,30
1984	-0,42	-3,27	0,04	0,09	-0,60	0,86	-0,56	0,23	0,15	-0,45
1985	-0,64	-0,39	7,38	1,83	2,88	0,55	3,86	-0,76	-0,31	1,43
1986	-0,69	-0,26	-0,45	-0,35	0,60	0,54	0,53	0,54	0,45	0,45

Source: FATM

137

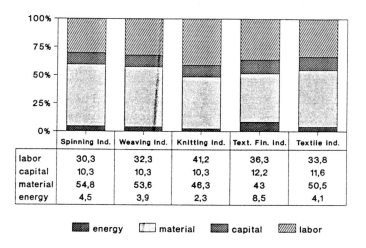

	Spinning Ind.	Weaving Ind.	Knitting Ind.	Text. Fin. Ind.	Textile Ind.
labor	30,3	32,3	41,2	36,3	33,8
capital	10,3	10,3	10,3	12,2	11,6
material	54,8	53,6	46,3	43	50,5
energy	4,5	3,9	2,3	8,5	4,1

■ energy ▨ material ▨ capital ▧ labor

Fig. 11   Average Structure of Nominal Factor Inputs

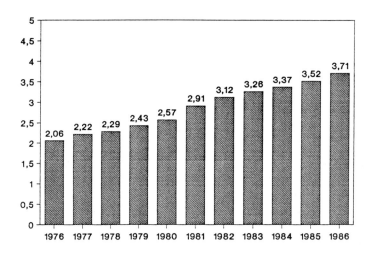

Fig. 12   Capital Intensity of Labor Input in the Total Textile Industry

in the form of b_{ij} , $i = j$, which are positive for all analysed sectors. Per definition, this implies that the cost shares of material input increased with an increase in the price of energy. But in reality there was no economical reason for such a coherence of causality. The volume of both inputs depended mainly on production for all textile sectors during the analysed period.

Finally, there were no substitution or complementary effects among labor with respect to capital input and the inputs of material and energy. The parameter estimates b_{LM}, b_{LE},

b_{KM} and b_{KE} are all negative. Therefore, a clear interpretation, if there were substitution or complementary effects among the corresponding inputs, is not possible [30].

During the analysed period the trends of labor, capital, material and energy inputs were clear: real labor input was reduced strongly by reason of a continuous increase of labor costs, while the net capital stocks, especially the equipment, expanded in all textile sectors. This substitution effect happened independently of the trend of production. Instead, material and energy inputs developed in direct dependence of the trend of the output.

CONCLUSION

The empirical results for sectoral models of production and technical change suggest a considerable degree of similarity across the textile sectors that have been analysed.

During the considered period from 1976–1986 the efficiency of the total factor input increased in all analysed sectors, especially in the textile finishing industry and the knitting industry. The rate of technical change respective to the productivity of the total factor input increased continuously. The unit costs of production decreased in tendency.

Technical change was capital using for all textile sectors. The technical progress induced an intensification of capital input with an increase of material input for all analysed sectors and an increase of energy input in the spinning industry, the weaving industry, the textile finishing industry and the textile industry as a whole.

Labor input decreased continuously. Labor input was reduced independently of the trend of production in all analysed sectors. Especially in the textile finishing and the knitting industries, labor input decreased constantly-also in the years of economic growth.

The reduction of the (relative) labor input depended primarily on a continuous increase in labor costs. The rise in labor costs effected a substitution of the labor input with an intensification of the capital input.

The net capital stocks expanded rapidly in all textile sectors during the analysed period. Independently of the trend of the production and, especially, the user costs of capital, the net stocks of equipment increased.

Finally, we find that annual material and energy inputs were determined mainly by the volumes of production and not by the development of the corresponding input prices. There were no substitutions or complementary effects among both inputs or among labor respective to capital input and the inputs of material and energy.

NOTES

[1]   The theoretical explanations are based on Jorgenson/ Fraumeni (1983).
[2]   Models of induced technical change are analysed by Hicks (1932), Samuelson (1965), von Weizsäcker (1962), and many others.
[3]   Jorgenson/Fraumeni (1981), Lau (1978).
[4]   The different sectors will not be separately indicated.
[5]   Shephard's lemma; Shephard (1953).
[6]   According to the German literature we call this kind of function a cost function. Since we

analyse unit costs it can also be called a price function.

[7] Vaal (1969), Hesse (1969), Heubes (1971).

[8] Recording the adding-up-theorem we will use the duality between production and cost theory. Therefore we will be concerned with the cost function. The translog cost function was introduced by Christensen/Jorgenson/Lau (1971).

[9] The share elasticity with respect to price was introduced by Christensen/Jorgenson/Lau (1971) as a fixed parameter of the translog price function. An analogous concept was employed by Samuelson (1973). The terminology is due to Jorgenson/ Fraumeni (1983).

[10] The terminology 'constant share elasticity price function' is due to Jorgenson/Lau (1982), who have shown that constancy of share elasticities with respect to price, biases of technical change with respect to price, and the rate of change of the negative of the rate of technical change are necessary and sufficient for representation of the cost function in translog form.

[11] The bias of technical change was introduced by Hicks (1932). Binswanger (1974) has introduced a translog cost function with fixed biases of technical change. Alternative definitions of biases of technical change are compared by Binswanger (1978).

[12] The following discussion is due to Lau (1978) and Jorgenson/Lau (1982).

[13] Kuroda/Yoshioka/Jorgenson (1984).

[14] Lau (1978), Unger (1986).

[15] Zellner (1962), (1963); Kmenta/Gilbert (1968).

[16] Barten (1969); Christensen/Green (1976).

[17] The following base on the quadratic approximation lemma by Diewert (1976).

[18] The Törnqvist price index was introduced by Törnqvist (1936) and has been discussed by Theil (1965). This index was first derived from the translog price function by Diewert (1976). The corresponding index of technical change was introduced by Christensen/ Jorgenson (1970). The Törnqvist index, even called translog index, of technical change was first derived from the translog price function by Diewert (1980) and by Jorgenson/Lau (1982). Earlier, Diewert (1976) had interpreted the ratio of Törnqvist indexes of the prices of input and output as an index of productivity under the assumption of Hicks neutrality.

[19] The Cholesky factorisation is calculated by a software package from the Forschungsstelle für allgemeine und textile Marktwirtschaft an der Universität Münster (FATM). Grisar/ Peren (1988).

[20] Christensen/Jorgenson (1969), Jorgenson (1974), Conrad/ Jorgenson (1975).

[21] Look also at section 2. The Törnqvist indexes were calculated by a software package from the FATM. Grisar/Peren (1988).

[22] Look also at section 2.

[23] A test of significance is not possible, because the exact distribution of the estimated parameters of the nonlinear translog model (2.8) is not known. Goldfeld/Quandt (1972).

[24] The econometric evaluation shows that the guaranty of the concavity restrictions is not sufficient to get parameter estimates which are consistent in their economic interpretation all over the observed sectors.

Experience shows that it may be necessary to make different models subject to the same concavity restrictions to get consistent parameter estimates. To assimilate the estimated values, it was sometimes necessary to start with parameter values which are given beforehand; but they are only accepted if the quality of the estimation is not impaired.

[25] Peren (1990).

[26] The Allen partial elasticities of substitution are better than the Hicks partial elasticities of substitution, which imply the restrictions of constant volumes of factor inputs and output. Cf. Uzawa (1962), Berndt/Christensen (1973).

In contrast to the Hicks partial elasticities of substitution, the Allen partial elasticities of substitution, which can be derived directly from the parameter estimates, let the volumes and prices of all inputs variable. The calculation of the Allen 'partial' elasticities of substitution also includes the volumes and prices of all other analysed inputs. Cf., for example, Unger (1986).

But due to the local concavity restrictions the Allen partial elasticities of substitutions, which are derived directly from the parameter estimates, are distorted and thus unrealistic. These elasticities do not represent the real substitutions effects among the analysed factor inputs. Therefore, the Hicks partial elasticities of substitution should be taken. Cf. Peren (1990).

[27] Look also at Figures 1 and 5.
[28] Look at Figure 2.
[29] The capital intensity of labor input is defined as the relation between real capital and labor input.
[30] Unger (1986).

BIBLIOGRAPHY

A. P. Barten. 'Maximum Likelihood Estimation of a Complete System of Demand Equations', Euro. Econ. Rev., 1969, 1, 1, 7.

E. R. Berndt and L. R. Christensen. 'The Internal Structure of Functional Relationships: Separability, Substitution and Aggregation', Rev. Econ. Studies, 1973, 40, 3, 403.

H. P. Binswanger. 'The Measurement of Technical Change Biases with Many Factors of Production', Amer. Econ. Rev., 1974, 64, 5, 964.

H. P. Binswanger. 'Issues in Modeling Induced Technical Change. Induced Innovation', Ed. by H.P. Binswanger and V.W. Ruttan, Baltimore, 1978, 128.

L. R. Christensen and W. H. Green. 'Economies of Scale in U.S. Electric Power Generation', J. Pol. Econ., 1976, 84, 655.

L. R. Christensen and D. W. Jorgenson. 'The Measurement of U.S. Real Capital Input, 1929-1967', Rev. Income and Wealth, 1969, 15, 4, 293.

L. R. Christensen and D. W. Jorgenson. 'U.S. Real Product and Real Factor Input, 1929-1967', Rev. Income and Wealth, 1970, 16, 1, 19.

L. R. Christensen, D. W. Jorgenson, and L.J. Lau. 'Conjugate Duality and the Transcendental Logarithmic Function', Econometrica, 1971, 39, 4, 255.

K. Conrad and D. W. Jorgenson. 'Measuring Performance in the Private Economy of the Federal Republic of Germany, 1950-1973', Tübingen, 1975.

W. E. Diewert. 'Exact and Superlative Index Numbers', J. Econometrics, 1976, 4, 2, 115.

W. E. Diewert. 'Aggregation Problems in the Measurement of Capital', D. Usher (ed.), 'The Measurement of Capital', Chicago, 1980, 433.

S. M. Goldfeld and R. E. Quandt. 'Nonlinear Methods in Econometrics', Amsterdam, London, 1972.

A. Grisar and F. W. Peren. 'Ein PC-gestütztes Zeitreihen-Analyse-Programm-System, Forschungsstelle für allgemeine und textile Marktwirtschaft an der Universität Münster (FATM)', unpublished manuscript, 1988.

H. Hesse. 'Die Mebbarkeit des technischen Forschritts, dargestellt am Beispiel der Textilindustrie', Zeitschrift für Allgemeine und Textile Marktwirtschaft, Sonderheft, Münster, 1971, 7.

J. Heubes. 'Technischer Fortschritt und Substitutionselastizitèt in der westdeutschen Textilindustrie: Ein kritischer Vergleich mehrerer unterschiedlicher Schätzergebnisse', Zeitschrift für Allgemeine und Textile Marktwirtschaft, Münster, 1971, 147.

J. R. Hicks. 'The Theory of Wages', London, 1932.

D. W. Jorgenson. 'The Economic Theory of Replacement and Depreciation', W. Sellekaerts (ed.), 'Econometrics and Economic Theory', London/Basingstoke, 1974, 189.

D. W. Jorgenson and B. M. Fraumeni. 'Relative Prices and Technical Change', W. Eichhorn, . Henn, K. Neumann, and R. W. Shephard, (eds.), 'Quantitative Studies on Production and Prices', Würzburg/Wien, 1983, 241.

Ch. Kennedy. 'Induced Bias in Innovation and the Theory of Distribution', Econ. J., 1964, 295, 541.

J. Kmenta and R. F. Gilbert. 'Small Sample Properties of Alternative Estimators of Seemingly Unrelated Regressions', *J. Amer. Stat. Assoc.*, 1968, **63**, 1180.

M. Kuroda, K. Yoshioka, and D. W. Jorgenson. 'Relative Price Change and Biases of Technical Change in Japan', *Econ. Studies Quarterly*, 1984, **35**, 2, 116.

L. J. Lau. 'Testing and Imposing Monotonicity, Convexity and Quasi-Concavity Constrains', M. Fuss and D. McFadden (eds.), 'Production Economics: A Dual Approach to Theory and Applications', Vol. 1, Amsterdam/New York/Oxford, 1978, 407.

J. Natrop. 'Bestimmung von Translog-Produktions-/Translog-Kostenfunktionen für die Sektoren des Verarbeitenden Gewerbes der Bundesrepublik Deutschland', Frankfurt, 1986.

F. W. Peren. 'Messung und Analyse von Substitutions- und Fortschrittseffekten in den Sektoren der westdeutschen Textilindustrie (1976–1986)', Empirische Untersuchung unter Verwendung von Translog-Kostenmodellen, Münster, 1990.

P. A. Samuelson. 'A Theory of Induced Innovation Along Kennedy-Weizsècker Lines', *Rev. Econ. and Stats.*, 1965, **47**, 4, 343.

P. A. Samuelson. 'Relative Shares and Elasticities Simplified: Comment', *Amer. Econ. Rev.*, 1973, **63**, 4, 770.

R. W. Shephard. 'Cost and Production Functions', Princeton, 1953.

H. Theil. 'The Information Approach to Demand Analysis', *Econometrica*, 1965, **33**, 1, 67.

L. Törnqvist. 'The Bank of Finland's Consumption Price Index', *Bank of Finland Monthly Bulletin*, 1936, **10**, 1.

R. Unger. 'Messung und Analyse der Totalen Faktorproduktivität für 28 Sektoren der Bundesrepublik Deutschland, 1960 bis 1981', Frankfurt/Bern/New York, 1986.

H. Uzawa. 'Production Functions with Constant Elasticities of Substitution', *Rev. Econ. Studies*, 1962, **29**, 291.

J. Vaal. 'Technischer Fortschritt und Faktorsubstitution in der westdeutschen Textilindustrie (1950–1965)', Tübingen, 1969.

C. Ch.v. Weizsäcker. 'A New Technical Progress Function', Massachusetts Institute of Technology, 1962, unpublished manuscript.

A. Zellner. 'An Efficient Method of Estimating Seemingly Unrelated Regressions and Tests for Aggregations Bias', *J. Amer. Stat. Assoc.*, 1962, **57**, 585.

A. Zellner. 'Estimators for Seemingly Unrelated Regression Equations: Some Exact Finite Sample Results', *J. Amer. Stat. Assoc.*, 1963, **58**, 977.

Technology, Trade, and the Future of the US Textile and Apparel Industry

H. C. Kelly

Office of Technology Assessment

THE ARGUMENT

The competitiveness of American manufacturing firms depends as never before on the skill with which firms can manage innovation. US textile and apparel industries are no exception. The technology now entering the marketplace differs in fundamental ways from the kinds of technology which, however spectacular, we have come to expect since the first industrial revolution began with the spinning jennys of the 17th century. The technology allows an unprecedented ability to combine growing productivity with an ability to tailor products to narrowly defined markets — even to individual customers. In effect the flexible manufacturing technology now becoming available has the power to restore the custom design and fitting that were sacrificed in the interest of efficiency three hundred years ago while enjoying all the benefits of highly productive production technology.

In this paper I will argue three basic points: first that the emerging technology has the potential to make production of textiles and apparel in the United States a high-technology enterprise capable of expanding domestic markets and finding significant markets abroad. Instead of being a 'sunset industry' it has the potential to be a major part of the industrial rebirth underway in the US economy. While overall employment is likely to decline because of productivity improvements, the industry can continue to be a major employer and offer an increasingly diverse set of jobs offering opportunities for increased responsibilities and increased pay for much of its work force.

Second, I will argue that none of these potentials can be captured without fundamental changes in the way the industry is managed. This means taking a hard look at internal management techniques based on rigid hierarchical systems, and it means finding more productive ways to link producers and suppliers in production networks that rely on mutual respect and confidence instead of being based entirely on competitive bidding. Making effective use of the new generation of technology will require the industry to rethink the way it manages innovation, the way it pursues new and old market areas, the way it conducts its research, and the way it hires and trains employees at all levels of the organization.

And third I will argue that there is clear evidence that the industry is prepared to make the changes just described. West Germany and other European nations have clearly demonstrated that it is possible for textile and apparel industries to be a part of industrial modernization and offer good jobs for well educated workers. Many American firms are taking up the challenge and finding uniquely American solutions.

While technology has obviously encouraged trade through improved communication and transportation, in the long run it may have the reverse effect. In a world where the textile and apparel industries of many nations are undergoing similar patterns of transformation technology may have the unexpected effect of decreasing trade volume. Systems which depend heavily on sensitive and dynamic response to local markets, and systems that depend on tight links between suppliers place a premium on being physically close to-markets. Technology that reduces economies of scale minimizes the advantage of firms producing for world markets.

HOW TO THINK ABOUT TECHNOLOGY

The background for the theses I've just stated is a major project OTA completed last year that looked broadly at opportunities for real economic growth given the new realities of international trade and emerging technologies [1]. Given its importance in the economy, the textile and apparel industry was a major focus of the research. The discussion that follows draws on this research to show how what we learned about the competitive problems faced by other parts of the economy may be useful to the textile and apparel industries as well as reviewing some of what we learned about the unique experiences of the textile and apparel industries [2].

We found industries throughout the economy facing some starkly contrasting possibilities; there proved to be little deterministic about the new technologies or the dynamics of world trade. An enormous amount depends on the choices made by American management, and the choices made in public policy, during the next few years.

Computers, communication systems, and other 'information technologies' (which now represent 40% of all US orders for producer durables) create some of the most important and least expected choices. They do this in part because they do much more than simply improve the productivity of familiar tasks. They can increase productivity in areas where we never seriously considered productivity changes in the past-productivity in such things as worker training, inventory control, and the processing of orders and invoices. They can increase the productivity of design and the speed with which a design can be converted to a product. It can mean optimizing the use of materials through such things as optimized layouts for cutting.

The new technologies also permit productivity in communication in ways that can facilitate the management of complex production processes. This can mean improved management with a facility using sensors that can optimize the performance of complex equipment or sensors able to detect defects in real-time, thereby reducing waste. Perhaps equally important, however, the communication systems can bring different businesses together in ways never before possible. Tight links can be created that connect retail checkout equipment with transportation systems, warehousing, assembly, and production of basic materials. A well managed network can keep inventories low while greatly increasing sensitivity to changes in the market.

Capturing these changes means doing much more than simply replacing old equipment with more productive models. Efforts to do this have almost universally proved disappointing whether the firm produces automobiles or insurance policies. Exploiting the unique features of the new technologies means asking some tough questions about the nature of growth and competitiveness in today's market and being prepared to make some deep changes in:

- sensitivity to markets (a premium is placed on ability to react quickly to emerging markets and a willingness to serve small, volatile markets efficiently),
- investment strategies (significant capital investments and investment in research are required),
- in management styles (flexible teams involving management and line-employees),
- in the size, scope and location of individual establishments (new systems seem to favor comparatively small establishments but not necessarily small firms),
- in contractual arrangements (production flexibility depends on stable relationships between suppliers and confidence in meeting delivery schedules), and
- in skills required by employees at all levels.

The impact of the changes on the overall skill mix of employees remains a difficult question. It is difficult to prove the point, but anecdotes suggest that real flexibility depends critically on a work force capable of learning to use complex new equipment quickly, and able to work in groups that include many professions. This flexibility is difficult to achieve without significant levels of skill. Moreover, the skills are not necessarily the traditional manual skills, the kind learned primarily by observing and practicing. They are skills that require an ability to read a manual, a blueprint, or a drawing; skills that require the basic mathematics needed to monitor and adjust complex equipment or to make use of constantly changing communication systems.

It seems possible to break the Faustian bargain with technology that was at the core of the first industrial revolution-the need to accept a boring, routine job in order to achieve productivity and high pay. The jobs that survive automation are likely to be dominated by those involving design work, operation and maintenance of new equipment (this means almost continuous process of learning about new equipment and procedures), and working with people. This is clearly true of production but it is even possible that new skills will be required of retail employees and transportation workers operating as a part of a tight production network that places a premium on serving the individual needs of customers.

Figure 1 illustrates the complex relationships that already exist in the textile and apparel industry in the US. It allocates all the money Americans spent on final demand in 1972 and 1984 through from the value added by retail stores to the value added by natural resource industries. The method used corrects for the effect of imports as well as calculating all indirect effects of the purchases (i.e. it estimates the impact of capital spending in the textile and apparel industry on domestic producers of equipment [3]. It can be seen that the industry is deeply involved with virtually all parts of the American economy from business services and other 'transactions businesses' to natural resources. Nearly 40% of consumer spending in these areas ends up as value added in transportation and trade— and the fraction appears to be growing. The textile and apparel industries themselves, which are included in the 'low wage manufacturing industries,' contribute about 18% of all final value added.

Figure 2 takes the calculation a step further and shows how the network of businesses

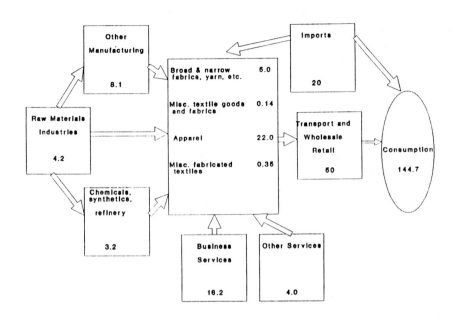

Fig. 1   Tracing Spending for Clothing in 1986 (value added in billions of $1982 dollars)

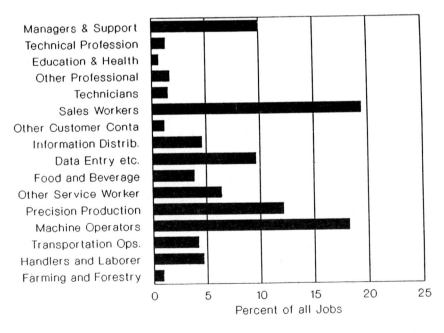

Fig. 2   Jobs Needed to Produce Clothing & Personal Car in 1984 (Percent of 7.5 million jobs)

146

required to produce clothing and personal care in 1984 translated into employment opportunities. Plainly, the activity generates large numbers of jobs for sales clerks and machine operators in textile and apparel facilities. But the industry is also responsible for a growing number of jobs in many other categories: managers, engineers, technicians, and information related jobs. We get a misleading view of the kinds of jobs generated by the industry if we look only at the work done directly in textile or apparel establishments.

SOME RECENT HISTORY

The US textile and apparel industry is clearly aware of the challenges facing it and taking the challenge of restructuring seriously. Textile productivity has increased 300% since 1972, increasing at twice the rate of the average in US manufacturing. The industry is probably the most productive in the world. Because of high labor productivity, real labor costs of US producers are below those of several European nations. The apparel industry has followed the average.

It must be recognized that the textile and apparel industries are making rapid advances but remain far beyond most of US manufacturing in an absolute sense. Capital invested per worker in textiles is still only a third of the average in manufacturing and capital per worker in apparel is 6.5% the manufacturing average. Output per worker in textiles remains half that of the US manufacturing average.

Innovation in the apparel industry has proceeded fitfully, in part because of the fragmented nature of the industry, and in part because of a traditional hesitation to invest in capital equipment. A recent survey found that only 5–20% of sewing machines in large apparel firms were automated. In 1988 only half a dozen of largest firms had as much as 20% automated equipment; investment by smaller firms is very low.

The industry's investment in research and development is far behind that of the 2.5% national average. Most of the productivity gains experienced in the last decade have come because of skillful use of technology developed abroad. Somewhat ironically our textile and apparel industries behave much like Japanese firms in other areas-letting others develop basic concepts and then making good use of them in capturing practical markets. There is little sign that this skill at learning from abroad is diminishing. It is highly likely that advanced apparel assembly equipment developed abroad, for example, will quickly find a home in the US.

The innovation gap is, if anything, likely to widen in the next few years. MITI and the European community are making heavy investments in both textile equipment and apparel assembly. They threaten to overwhelm the modest US investment through such efforts as (TC)2.

There is an obvious danger of relying too heavily on foreign suppliers. Foreign producers may be in a better position to anticipate innovations than US firms. The lack of R&D in domestic firms not only limits the innovations available from US firms, it limits the ability of US firms to learn from others. A good engineering staff is essential for the continuous learning needed in today's environment.

It is painfully obvious that the astonishing technological progress made by the US textile and apparel industry during the past decade has not been enough to pace the competition. Figures 3 and 4 document the painful recent history of trade in textiles and apparel. Because of the tight production linkages described in Figure 1, the damage inflicted by these imports is felt far beyond the textile and apparel industries themselves. Figures 5 and 6 trace the impact of recent trade statistics.

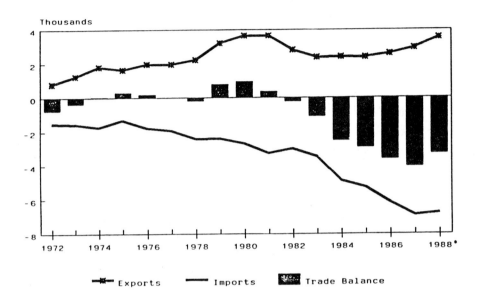

Fig. 3   Trade Balance in Textiles (current dollars)

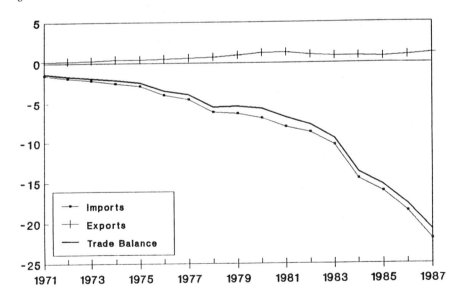

Fig. 4   Trade in Apparel (billions of current dollars)

148

The loss of US technological leadership is painfully evident from Figure 7. In the 1960s the US textile machinery industry held over 90% of the domestic market and enjoyed strong foreign sales. By 1986 the industry held only about 43% of domestic markets and only 5% of world markets. In both cases replacement parts for older equipment accounted for the bulk of sales.

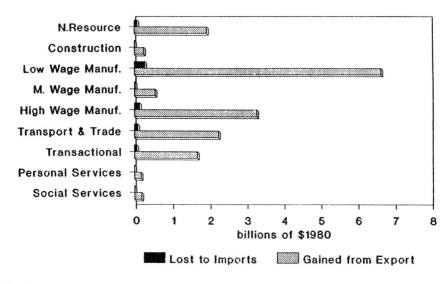

Fig. 5   Impact of Apparel Trade on Value Added in 1986

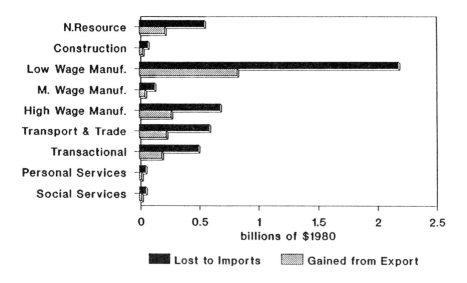

Fig. 6   Impact of Textile Trade on Value Added in 1986

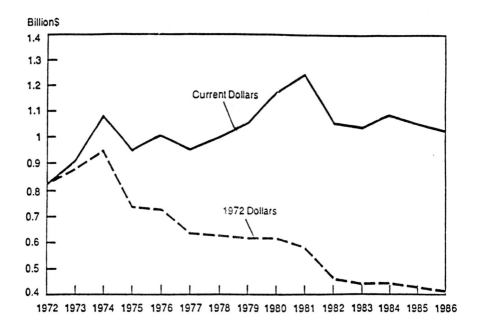

Fig. 7   *Textile Machinery Industry Annual Shipments*

EMERGING TECHNOLOGIES AND THE NATURE OF TRADE

The changes in production systems described earlier have the potential to reshape trade in textile and apparel products in profound ways. They have changed the nature of 'comparative advantage' in international markets by placing a premium on such things as rapid mastery of new production technologies, product quality, and timely delivery. And they have changed our view of the changes in total trade volume.

The factors that have led to an explosion in US imports during the past decade are well understood. While macroeconomic factors and economic development abroad played a dominant role, new technologies contributed to the expansion in several ways. Low cost transportation and communications with the Pacific rim and other areas made it possible to integrate foreign producers into domestic production networks. Advanced communication technologies make it possible to involve foreign producers in tight networks. Once a few pioneering firms were able to establish profitable links with foreign producers, a psychological barrier had been crossed and connections with US markets became irreversible. Rapid flow of technology across international borders, facilitated by multinational firms, reduces the time required for comparatively primitive producers to begin operating at the state of the art.

Declining economies of scale in production has made it possible for foreign producers to enter many niche markets in the US. Complex production networks in the US have been penetrated at many points by alert foreign producers. Producers in Europe and the Far East are able to complete in production runs of a few hundred yards of top grade fabric and US retailers have turned to them because of their flexibility and their ability to guarantee a high quality product-not just because of low production costs. Figure 8 shows that the value of apparel imports increased more slowly than square-yards of imports, suggesting that foreign producers are moving toward more valuable products.

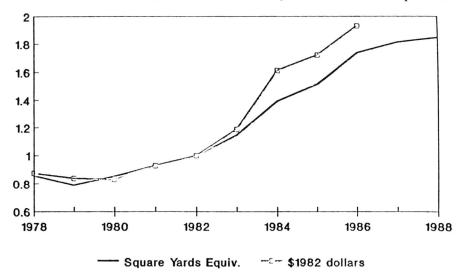

Fig. 8   Apparel Import Index (1982 = 1.0)

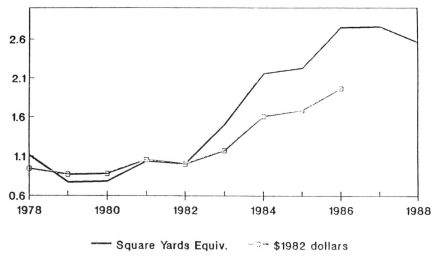

Fig. 9   Textile Import Index (1982 = 1.0)

151

The reverse, however, seems to be true for textile imports (see Figure 9). Considerable caution must be used in these statistics, however, since the techniques used to calculate 'constant dollars' require many difficult assumptions.

There are, however, many reasons to believe that the creation of the tightly knit production networks now emerging in the US textile and apparel industry can actually reverse the growth in trade volume. A system capable of responding flexibly to rapid changes in fashion and seasonal markets while keeping inventories low is clearly difficult to operate over thousands of miles. Tight resupply chains in production networks are also difficult to operate over long distances. Declining economies of scale reduce the advantage of large producers with low production costs.

It is, of course, possible to use air deliveries and rapid communication links to include forcing suppliers in domestic production networks. But there are obvious inconveniences and many hidden costs to such long-distance relationships. The ITC estimates that resupply times from European producers is 50% longer than from domestic producers and supplies from Far Eastern producers take over twice as long as domestic supplies.

The teams needed to operate flexible production systems require mutual confidence and close, continuous personal interactions between suppliers. This can be done by long distance but it is difficult. The production systems require careful integration of marketing, finance, programming assistance, maintenance, and other services with production enterprises. Many of these services are uniquely available in American markets.

There is also a clear need to keep in touch with final markets through sophisticated market analysis and product testing. It is possible that this marketing can be conducted in the US while production moves abroad, but the separation of production from analysis must remain somewhat awkward.

The advantage of domestic production clearly depends on the kinds of products involved. In general it appears that the US has done comparatively well in products with very low labor inputs (industrial fabrics, home-furnishings manufactured in highly-automated textile facilities (towels, sheets, draperies, rugs) and some knit good and men's wear. We have also done comparatively well in the highly volatile fashion and seasonal market with less than a 10-week shelf life. These are markets where the advantage of close links between production and sale are obvious.

What is not clear is how the balance till tip for the 40–50% of the market that falls between these extremes. The outcome of the battle for this market depends heavily on the skill with which domestic producers master the unique capabilities of emerging automation and forge responsive teams that exploit the advantage of domestic production. Price is obviously important, but mastery of markets, quality, and responsiveness are playing a growing role in determining competitiveness.

Paradoxically, shuttleless looms and some of the other technology that has done so much to improve the productivity of textile manufacturing have made the industry less and not more flexible because they require long production runs. There has been significant progress in reducing batch sizes. Lot sizes have been shrinking and it is possible to find firms able to produce denim in lot sizes of 1200–2000 yards and firms able to give competitive prices for dyeing and finishing lots as small as 500 yards with turnaround times of two weeks or less. Firms are running five or six yarn counts and as many as

152

eight different blends in a single establishment. But many problems remain.

The American accomplishments are strongly challenged by European and Asian producers able to manage extremely fast responses to orders and small production runs.

WHERE DO WE GO FROM HERE?

Competition in a growing number of textile and apparel markets depends on mastery of the unique capabilities of new flexible production technologies, communication systems, and the management strategies needed to make such systems work in a growing number of markets. While the US has lost technological leadership in textile and apparel markets during the past decade, it is entirely possible that it can reestablish itself through mastery of this generation of technologies. Domestic producers appear to begin with something of a geographic advantage. Design of flexible marketing, communication, and software systems has become a clear area of American technical excellence. The industry has made astonishing progress in making 'quick response' systems a reality.

Success depends critically on flexibility and imagination of management in the domestic industry. But their role could clearly be made easier with skillfully designed public policy. Such a policy needs to develop a trade policy sensitive to an industry that is both mature and immature as it undergoes a fundamental transformation. It needs to find a way to encourage and reward long-term investment strategies. It needs to find creative ways to mix public and private research money and to focus such effort in directions of practical value to the industry. It needs to find a way to retrain the enormous number of workers whose jobs will be reshaped or eliminated by the changes underway. It needs to find ways to ensure that the benefits of the transformation are not limited to the largest firms.

I am convinced that such policies can, and are, being designed. With them, there is every reason to suppose that the textile and apparel industry has a major place as a 'high-technology' manufacturing enterprise.

NOTES

[1]   OTA 'Technology and the American Economic Transition', (GPO:Washington D.C.) 1988. We examined all parts of the economy and put a significant amount of effort into understanding the future of the nation's textile and apparel industries.

[2]   OTA 'The US Textile and Apparel Industry: A Revolution in Progress' (GPO:Washington D.C.) 1987. This document was prepared as a part of the Technology and the Economic Transition Project.

[3]   The method uses the 1972 and 1982 input output tables available from the Bureau of Economic Analysis. The 1972 calculations use the 1972 benchmark data. The 1984 calculation uses 1984 personal consumption expenditures and government purchases of textile and apparel products. Capital spending is scaled to 1984 using data from the 1977 benchmark (the latest available). 1984 trade patterns are assumed.

Human Resource Management in the Modern Textile and Apparel Industries

T. Bailey

Associate Research Scholar,
Conservation of Human Resources, Columbia University

INTRODUCTION

The fiber/textile/apparel complex is undergoing a profound transformation. Import competition, technological innovation, changing tastes and consumer demands, and the shifting regional patterns of population and economic growth and decline have worked together to create an industrial complex that in many ways bears little resemblance to that complex 15 years ago. Certainly the leaders of the industry have recognized the need to respond to this new environment. Over the last 20 years there have been impressive applications of new technology in at least some of the sectors in the complex. But more recently, the industry's widely-discussed 'quick response' campaign represents a fundamental departure from the traditional management practices. Although quick response is now seen by many in the industry as the key to the competitive position of domestic soft goods production, five years ago, much of the industry was indifferent or even hostile to practices that are now accepted as central components of the quick response strategy.

But while some industry leaders and managers have embraced a new strategic approach, the human resource and especially the educational implications of these changes have received very little attention. Indeed many industry managers continue to be suspicious of innovations in personnel policy and to believe that with the help of advanced communications and production technologies, the industry's traditional human resources strategies can be preserved with little more than cosmetic modifications. But even among those who reject this conservative approach, the discussion is only just beginning and no general consensus has emerged.

This paper examines the changes in the textile/apparel complex from the point of view of human resources, analyzing how human resource strategies should change in the face of the transformation taking place in the industry's environment [1]. I argue that the industry must make changes in its human resources policies that are as dramatic

This paper is based on research funded by the Office of Educational Research and Improvement of the United States Department of Education through the National Center on Education and Employment at Teachers College, Columbia University.

as the technological and communications transformations that are now underway. Indeed, new technology will be much less effective without accompanying redirection of the human resource strategy.

I first briefly characterize the central components of the traditional production system in the textile/apparel complex and describe the human resources strategy that characterizes that system. I then discuss why the traditional production system has broken down and describe the elements of a new strategy that appears to be emerging. The next section draws out the human resource implications of the changes that the industry is experiencing and the paper ends with recommendations.

THE TRADITIONAL PRODUCTION SYSTEM

Many textile and apparel manufacturers will now assert that their industry has shifted from a production to a market orientation. In the past, industry managers did indeed focus their efforts on improving and rationalizing the production process. The success of much of the American textile and apparel industries, like most domestic manufacturing industries, was based on the production of low cost, mass produced goods for a huge domestic market that was large enough to absorb enormous quantities of standardized goods. Moreover, styles changed very slowly [2].

Marketing and product innovation were not primary preoccupations of industry leaders. For example, a 1968 study of the textile industry by the US Department of Labor stated that, 'until recently, little attention was paid to developing new products and markets and little research or advertising was carried out' [3]. Even more telling is the following quote from a book of cases on textile management published in 1978, and presumably used to train textile managers at least through the early 1980's, 'Mr Chandler [the mill superintendent] emphasized the importance of correct mill balance. By properly balancing the process flow in the mill, profits were increased rapidly from US$200,000 to US$1 million. He explained that once the balance had been achieved, it was maintained by accepting orders for only those fabrics that would be appropriate to the balanced flow'[4].

This reflects a passive orientation that assumes that the market will somehow generate orders (that the mill will 'accept') for those fabrics that the mill can produce at lowest cost. There is no hint of consideration for either influencing the demand for the mill's output through marketing or responding to changing market demands.

The production focus was reflected in the inventory practices, the organization of plants, and the industry structure. The overriding goal of the design of the production flow was to isolate each stage of the process. This allowed managers and engineers to examine, engineer, and rationalize each step separately and it prevented, within limits, problems in one step of production from influencing the other steps in the overall process.

One important means for preserving this fragmentation was the accumulation of in-process inventories. The traditional bundle system in apparel manufacturing is a classic example. In this system, cut garment parts were tied into 'bundles' of about 30 pieces. The operator took a bundle and performed one, usually very small, task such as sewing a hem, attaching a pocket, or joining a front panel of a shirt to the back. When the operator had performed her task on the 30 pieces in the bundle, she retied the bundle and began work on another. Although the work of many operators went into the production of each garment, each operator could be paid according to her actual production-piece rates. In effect, the bundle system, linked to piece rates, made each worker independent from other workers.

While the bundle system isolated each worker, the typical organization of garment and textile plants isolated each step within the overall manufacturing process. Factories were set up so that each step in the production flow was carried out in large 'functional' departments. For example, traditionally spinning factories were divided into large departments that carried out particular functions — opening, carding, roving, spinning, winding, and so forth. Orders moved through these factories one at a time and in-process inventories were often accumulated between departments. This guaranteed the continuous use of the equipment in each department, but slowed down the throughput time.

The vertical structure of the textile/apparel complex was also highly fragmented. Although each level of the industry depended on suppliers and customers, there was relatively little communication and interaction among firms at the different levels. Interfirm relationships were at arms length and mediated by the market. Large firms often played smaller suppliers off against each other in order to drive down the price of inputs. Certainly, it was rare that managers of firms in the complex tried to understand the economics and operations of their suppliers or customers, tried to anticipate their needs, or worked together with them jointly. Indeed, even exchange of information between supplier and customer firms was rare [5]. Once again, this reflects the industry's production orientation. Each firm was primarily focussed on their internal operations and production. They accepted orders from their customers but there was little attempt to understand their customers' or suppliers' businesses or to work with them interactively.

Thus isolation and fragmentation permeated all of the interactions in the industry. The bundle system isolated the individual workers, the functional departmental organization isolated the different processes within the plant, and the fragmented vertical structure and arms-length relationships among firms isolated the stages of production within the supply chain.

The Traditional Human Resource Strategy

This traditional production strategy was matched by common human resource practices. Long runs of standard goods allowed the simplification of labor processes in which workers could be employed in standard and predictable tasks. Even the relatively advanced skills could be learned on the job by high-school dropouts. Thus almost all of the jobs up through first level supervisors were filled by employees who had entered as unskilled workers and who had learned the necessary skills for each new position informally on the job. Formal education or training either as a prerequisite for entry level employment or within the firm was not important. Workers learned to do their tasks by observation and trial and error and since their tasks rarely changed, this concrete or experience-based knowledge was adequate. Understanding what they were doing at a deeper conceptual level was not necessary.

The textile and garment industries had an additional characteristic in that they were based in the south where they benefited from a large pool of rural labor that gave the industries an important cost advantage. Given the modest skill needs and the low wages, which were often dependent on the isolation of the factories and industries, management saw little need for education. Indeed, even a high school degree was often seen as a ticket out of the mill town. Mill owners would rather have the bright and energetic young people working their way up through the mills than going off to school and leaving the industry. This tradition has left a residue of mistrust and suspicion of the education system.

Since the overriding goal of the plant organization was to fragment the production so that each step could be rationalized separately, the coordination of the various steps fell completely to management. This led to the development of centralized hierarchies in which there was relatively little scope for individual initiative or responsibility on the part of the production workers.

PRESSURES ON THE TRADITIONAL PRODUCTION SYSTEM

But by the late 1970s, the production-oriented, cost-cutting strategy and consequently, the associated human resource practices, began to unravel. Two reasons stand out.

First, as long as low cost was the primary American comparative advantage, then many segments of the industry were vulnerable to low-cost foreign producers. With the advantage of super low wages, foreign producers could beat US cost-cutting producers at their own game in a growing share of the market. US producers maintained their advantage only in the most standardized commodities such as blue jeans and white underwear or in bulky or heavy garments that were costly to transport such as fleecewear (sweat clothes).

Second, as incomes rose in Europe, Japan, and North America, consumers began to look less at cost and to become more concerned with style and variety. The greater segmentation of markets and the faster changing of styles have shrunk the market for large production runs of identical fabric. Even such a staple mass-produced commodity as denim now comes in dozens of weaves, colors and finishes. Faster changing seasons have also had their effect. In apparel, styles become obsolete much more rapidly, thus apparel makers are less likely to order large quantities of the same material. The changes in styles are reflected in increases in stock-outs and markdowns. Forced markdowns, which are necessary when retailers fail to sell items during the appropriate season, have increased by 50% during the last decade. Industry estimates suggest that losses from stockouts, which occur when retailers run out of hot items, amount to 8% of sales. Now only 20% of the garment output consists of so-called 'commodity' products such as men's underwear and socks that are made in large standardized runs and sold all year [6]. Market analysts consider that the market share of commodity goods will continue to fall.

Thus even as more players joined the cost-cutting game, there was a shrinkage of the share of the market in which cost considerations outweighed style and variety. For example, a survey conducted by the International Trade Commission found that although price was the most important reason why apparel manufacturers imported textiles, many also stated that they imported because some products were not produced in the United States or because foreign producers were more willing to sell in smaller quantities [7].

157

In addition to the profound shift in the markets and in the nature and characteristics of competition, the accelerating rate of technological change has also had a profound effect on the industry. As the cost of both hardware and software continues to drop, new equipment and new applications appear at an increasing rate. And as we shall see below, in addition to the technology, there are also an increasing number of innovations in firm organization and industry structure. Therefore, it is not just that there has been a change in the environment in which textile and apparel firms must do business, but that environment is likely to continue to change. The industry has entered a period of faster change and increasing uncertainty in which the scope for the exploitation of economies of scale and capital intensive production is restricted. As textile and apparel firms attempt to operate in a market that emphasizes innovation, variation and rapid change in style with highly variable lead times, they no longer have the luxury of being able to focus on each stage in the production process, to say nothing of each individual worker, more or less in isolation from the other stages.

THE EMERGING SYSTEM OF PRODUCTION

Some textile and apparel firms have now begun to shift towards more flexible production that is more able to respond quickly to changes in market and technological conditions. Several developments in the industry signal this change.

The shift from a mass production strategy to a more responsive strategy involves a tendency to produce shorter runs of fabric or apparel, and in my own field work in textile and apparel factories increases in styles or stock keeping units (SKUs) are almost universally reported. For example, one spinning mill increased the number of active styles from 3 to 35 in two years, a Burlington plant producing home furnishings had increased the number of styles it produced annually from 100 to 300 in five years. And a Cone Mills denim plant was producing 28 styles while ten years ago it typically produced at most three styles at one time. A sleepwear manufacturer had increased the number of styles he produced from 100 in the mid-1970' to over 300 in 1988. Another producer of men's slacks and shirts said that his average cutting size had fallen from 100–150 ten years ago to 40. He also said that he now sends out orders through United Parcel Service as small as one or two items. For a women's intimate wear maker in the mid-west, SKUs had quadrupled in 10 years.

But industry managers are not simply producing a greater variety of goods, rather they are trying to reduce the time that it takes to design, produce, and deliver those goods. Shorter production times save on inventory carrying costs and allow more immediate responses to changing market demands. Production planners can reduce their reliance on market forecasts, which were never reliable, but which have become even less useful as product changes have accelerated and markets have become more fragmented. And when faster production times are linked to product and style innovations, then the firms do not simply respond to changes but rather take an active role in providing direction to the market.

The quick response movement in the textile and apparel complex is the most obvious manifestation of the attempts to reduce production times. This strategy is only beginning to spread in the domestic industry, but pilot projects have indicated that the manufacturing production time for dress shirts can be cut from 3 days to less than one half of a day, for knit shirts from 4 days to less than one hour, and for cutting tailored clothing from 13 days to 2 days. Early quick response experiments reported by Kurt Salmon Associates indicate that in some cases the overall cycle from fiber production to the retail sale for some items can be cut from over 60 to about 20 weeks [8].

How have some firms been able to increase variety and reduce cycle times? In the following section I examine the contribution of three related responses: technology, internal firm organization, and changes in the industrial structure (the relationships among firms in the supply chain).

Technology

Despite the dramatic growth of textile and apparel imports in the US over the last decade, US manufacturers are still efficient and competitive producers of standardized goods. Textile producers in particular have carried out an impressive modernization campaign over the last 20 years. Although most modern textile and much of the sewing equipment are manufactured abroad, US producers have been among the leaders in using that equipment. Shuttleless looms, open-ended spinning machines, programmable knitting and sewing machines, computerized design and cutting, and a variety of other equipment have transformed the industry in the last 15 years. In 1960, out of 55 manufacturing companies for which the Department of Commerce developed capital stock data, the textile industry had the sixth oldest average equipment age. But by 1980, it had the second newest equipment [9]. In 1987, the International Trade Commission found that textile makers in the United States were more productive than manufacturers in any other country. Labor productivity in Japan and Italy was only about 75% of productivity in the US [10]. Of course, despite being less than half as productive as US producers, most Asian countries, other than Japan, had substantially lower unit labor costs due to lower wages.

As I have pointed out, industry leaders have now begun to turn from a central preoccupation with cost cutting to a greater interest in increasing flexibility and reducing throughput times. To what extent has modern micro-electronic based technology contributed to these goals?

Indeed, computerized inventory tracking and communications were the first components of quick response to be implemented. Computerized design and planning; programmable cutters, looms, sewing machines, and other equipment; and advances in loading and unloading have all enhanced flexibility. But profound barriers remain. Indeed, most of the current modernization of the textile industry started before the onset of the current preoccupation with flexibility and market response. Some of the most dramatic technological advances have been in machines with restricted uses — water jet looms are restricted to continuous filament and open-ended spinning works best with coarse yarn counts. Flexible automation in apparel is still at a primitive stage. All of the equipment is much more expensive and an individual machine now represents a greater proportion of the production capacity. This increases the cost of shutting down the equipment for style changes which in turn creates incentives to restrict the variety of output and increase the length of production runs. Thus the current production technology in textile and apparel falls far short of allowing a continuous flow process with minimal cost differentials between long and short runs [11].

Organizational Change within the Firm

Finding that new technology alone cannot bring about a more flexible quick-turnaround production process, some managers have accompanied their investments in new equipment with major internal reorganizations of production. Generally speaking, these reorganizations have involved a movement away from functionally-oriented organization that characterized the traditional system. Rather than being divided into large departments specializing in one function, increasingly factories are being organized into larger numbers of smaller departments that can carry out larger segments of the production process. These departments are oriented towards particular products, markets, or customers. For example, while functionally organized spinning plants were comprised of separate departments for opening, carding, roving, spinning, and winding each with its own supervisor, product-oriented yarn plants combine a small number of carding, roving, spinning, and winding machines in small departments each under one supervisor. Instead of processing orders sequentially, product-oriented plants can process several orders of different sizes and cycle times simultaneously. This allows more flexibility in handling each order and a more efficient flow of products to the customers. The reduction of in-process inventories that accumulated between functional departments is a central component of product-oriented organization.

The grouping of workers into teams is an extension of the product or market-oriented plant organization. There is a large variety of types of teams, but in most cases, a group of workers is given responsibility for some part of the production process. The group has some autonomy over their production goals and over how they organize themselves to meet those goals.

One team-based strategy used in apparel production for reducing in-process inventory is the 'modular production system'. In modules, operators pass each piece or garment directly to the next operator. Usually there are a small number of pieces between each operator. This eliminates the bundles and the inventory contained in those bundles and saves the time involved in handling the bundles. For most operations it only takes a few hours for a given piece to go through the line. Moreover, without the buffer inventories, presumably operators will help each other out. In this way, the production flow through the unit is balanced. This in turn cuts the need for supervision.

Comprehensive data on the effects of modules or of other types of team-based reorganization are still not available. But in one pilot project using sewing modules, direct labor costs were cut by 5%, throughput time was reduced from three days to less than half a day, the share of second quality shirts dropped from 2% to 0.2%, and space requirements were halved [12].

Industry Structure

Changes in industry structure also reflect the shift from a production to a market-orientation. The traditional fragmentation in the vertical relationships in the industry has begun to break down. Indeed, the attempt to forge stronger and more interactive relationships between producers at different levels in the supply chain and between producers and retailers has so far been the most important accomplishment of the quick response campaign. If a producer is to be able to turn out a variety of goods quickly, without large inventories of supplies, that producer's suppliers must also be able to deliver high quality inputs just as quickly, whether they are manufactured items or services.

Vertical integration is one possible response to this need for greater control over the production and delivery of inputs. Vertical integration allows maximum control over all steps in the supply line. But the central problem with vertical integration is that it makes flexibility much more difficult. Every product does not necessarily require the same mix of inputs, thus it becomes more difficult to balance the capacity of completely integrated operations. Integrated firms often must turn their attention from responding to the demands of the market to concerns about capacity utilization.

One solution to this complex of problems involves the development of networks or loose partnerships among firms in the supply chain. This is indeed a central component of the quick response movement. In only the last three or four years, industry representatives have put together standard communications protocols to allow electronic linkages between retailers and producers and among the various levels of the supply chain. As part of this effort, some firms are beginning to try to develop more interactive relationships with their suppliers.

Thus rather than maintaining arms-length, market-mediated relationships, customer and supplier firms work out partnership arrangements in which they share information on markets and innovations and coordinate their production. In selecting suppliers, manufacturers are beginning to become less concerned with price and more concerned with the long term potential for the two firms to work together. As the executive vice president of Greenwood Mills said, 'If you have a supplier you don't trust enough to sit down with and develop long term strategy with, then for goodness sakes get rid of the supplier and find one you can trust'[13]. As long as each firm can develop this type of relationship with at least a few other firms, each firm can enjoy the advantages of a coordinated and responsive supply pipeline while avoiding the problems of capacity utilization and balance that plague larger more diverse organization [14].

Therefore, whether through backward or forward integration or through the development of subcontracting partnerships, the traditional vertical structure of the textile/apparel complex is blurring. Either as a result of quick response relationships or of the private label movement, large department store chains are becoming more involved with apparel and soft goods production, while garment producers themselves have moved into direct retailing, Benetton being the best-known example. Other large textile firms have restructured by selling off production facilities for related products and buying up supplier or customer firms [15].

In sum, the shift from a production to a market-oriented focus has resulted in what could be referred to as a much denser and more tightly packed production system. Modern technology is crucial, but this only accounts for a part of the change. Lead times, buffer inventories, and other types of slack and margins for error and relaxation are, at least in principle, all being squeezed out of the production system. Workers within firms and firms within the supply chain are now involved in a more integrated network and are therefore much more interdependent. Moreover, the more complicated interactions now extend, more than they did previously, across firms.

HUMAN RESOURCE IMPLICATIONS

The traditional human resource system in these industries was characterized by a preponderance of unskilled and semi-skilled workers engaged in well specified tasks, reliance on informal on-the-job training, low or non-existent educational prerequisites for entry level jobs, and a strong hierarchical and authoritarian management style with little scope for responsibility and initiative on the part of production workers. This section discusses how this system is changing in response to the current transformations in the industry's markets, technology, organization, and structure.

Technology and the Traditional Human Resource System

In many plants, personnel and training practices often first appear inadequate when the firm attempts to install and operate new equipment, thus it is the new technology that is seen as creating pressure on traditional practices. Indeed, over the last 15 years, the impact of modern technology on skills and on the organization of production has been a central issue in the analysis of work and of the general operation of firms. From one point of view, modern technology requires more highly educated workers, but according to the opposing argument, computer-based technology has the potential to simplify or 'deskill' many tasks thus allowing the use of a lower skilled labor force.

This controversy continues today in the textile and apparel industries. Personnel managers and supervisors realize that modern equipment requires some new skills, but some also hope that it can reduce their reliance on skilled workers. For example, an article in the June 1987 edition of *Bobbin* stated that 'Savings in labor costs through the deskilling of sewing operations is becoming a key factor in the apparel manufacturing process'[16]. One men's wear maker in New York was more blunt: 'We have an engineering staff trying to take the labor content out of manufacturing, machines don't get sick and don't need vacations'.

As the south's economic development continues and therefore as the soft goods industries in that region are losing their predominant place in local labor markets, many managers are finding it difficult to attract educated or skilled workers. Furthermore, some managers are still suspicious of educated production workers, believing that they will make excessive demands or expect to earn more than they are worth. And indeed, in the past, the few workers in the traditional mill towns who did get some post secondary training or even finished high school often sought work outside of the mills. Modern technology seems to be a potential means of allowing employers to move into the new era while continuing to rely on high-turnover recruits with low levels of education.

And at least in terms of skills, there are indeed many tasks that can be simplified by automation. New textile machinery, at least in spinning and weaving, requires less demanding operator skills than the machines that they replaced. The machines and the input material is of higher quality and the temperature and humidity of the environment are much more controlled. Knotting broken threads was one of the most difficult tasks performed by textile operators, but now many machines have automatic knotters or splicers. Previously, good operators could have a sense of the quality of the output, for example the weight of material coming out of cards or drawing frames, but now automatic sensors can do that job with more consistency and accuracy. Suction devices have simplified the process of loading bobbins onto winding machines. Advances in programmable sewing machines and other automation in apparel manufacturing also have the potential to reduce the skill requirements on some tasks. As a result of the introduction of semi-automated equipment in one shirt factory I visited, the training required to reach normal efficiency dropped from 16–18 weeks to 10–14 weeks. Pocket setting, traditionally a difficult job, can be done simply by loading a machine.

On the other hand, there are also compelling arguments why employers would not want to put their new technology in the hands of lower skilled workers. For example, to the extent that modern machines are more expensive than previous generation technology, the cost of errors and down-time is higher. Moreover, new technology and accompanying software rarely work as well as expected and workers with a cookbook knowledge of their functions will often be unable to handle the inevitable deviations from the expected norm. This also suggests the need for a greater emphasis on prevention rather than on correcting problems once they arise. Thus the skills required to operate a machine when it is functioning normally may not be an appropriate gauge of the characteristics of the optimal worker.

Moreover, there is a broad consensus that the fixers and technicians in both the garment and textile industries need to be more skilled. Thus in the past, repair technicians were almost always workers who had been promoted from operator positions and had learned their skills informally by watching older workers. Many were semi-literate. Repairing and maintaining modern equipment now usually requires formal training in electronics and literacy is essential. Employers are increasingly trying to hire technicians with two year associate degrees or sending their current workers out to the local community colleges for upgrading [17].

Industry Transformation and the Decline of the Traditional Human Resource System

The argument in the previous section suggests that technology has an ambiguous effect on skills and human resource needs, but new technology is only a part of the current transformation in textiles and apparel. If we add the implications of changes in internal organization and industry structure to the implications of new technology, then the weaknesses of the traditional human resource system become more apparent.

First, when a firm moves from a functional organization to a product-oriented organization and especially if teams are introduced, then it is much more difficult to rely on extreme specialization among workers. Thus more workers will have to be trained to take on multiple tasks. And as styles change more rapidly, workers will have to be more adept at those tasks required to reconfigure their equipment.

Moreover, the efforts to increase throughput speed through the elimination of buffer inventories transform the production process within a factory. It creates an immediate interdependence among the various workers and processes involved in production. Team organization has forced some apparel makers to move away from piece rates, plants using sewing modules, for example, have had to switch to group payments and incentives. Now the planning, execution, and management of each task must take into account the multiple relationships with all of the other tasks in the plant. The tasks of floor supervisors change from the management on an individual basis of particular problems that arise to the management of an integrated system in which actions taken to correct problems in one area have unintended consequences elsewhere.

As a result of the reduction in inventories, the proliferating production variety, the increase in throughput speed and the accelerating pace of product as well as technological change, it is much more difficult, and less efficient, to plan out every contingency that an employee must face, to refer problems to specialized departments, or to await instruction or permission from superiors. More than in the past, workers will have to be able to figure things out for themselves. As one employer said, 'the trouble with my workers was that they couldn't do a damn thing that they had not done before'. He went on to say that his equipment and procedures changed too quickly to allow him to show everyone how to do everything. Increased adaptability involves a switch from a concrete understanding, based on experience and informally acquired on-the-job training, to a more conceptual or theoretical understanding of the work in which employees are engaged. Only if workers understand the deeper logic underlying their work can they adjust to new tasks without having to be shown, step-by-step, what to do.

In product-oriented organization and especially in teams, workers experience more frequent and complex interactions with their coworkers. Indeed, the success of many teamwork experiments depends primarily on how those interactions are managed — how does the group deal with slower members, how do they react when a member is late, and so forth? These dynamics determine whether there is a productive or a hostile atmosphere in the group. And this is a primary reason why the jobs of floor level supervisors have become more difficult.

The changes in industry structure actually amplify many of these new demands. While firm reorganization integrates the worker into broader aspects of the operation of the firm, the increasing interactive links among firms project that integration beyond the boundaries of the firm. More employees in any given firm must have a stronger understanding of the operations, strategies, and needs of supplier and customer firms. There may also be an increase in direct interaction among employees in different firms [18].

There are no definitive data on the relationship between the education of a firm's workforce and the profitability or success of that firm. Nevertheless, in the sample of textile and apparel firms that I have studied, there was a strong relationship between concern about the education and training of the workforce and attempts to implement modern technology or innovative production processes.

ELEMENTS OF A NEW HUMAN RESOURCES STRATEGY

Changing markets for textiles and garments and changing technologies have led to innovations in firm organization and industry structure. These in turn have a potentially wide-ranging impact on human resource strategy. If we consider the new technology in isolation, the implications are ambiguous. Certainly, for some workers, new technology does put a greater premium on basic literacy skills as well as technical skills. On the other hand, many tasks can be simplified. Indeed, some employers look to the technology as a means of preserving traditional human resource strategies, albeit in a slightly updated form.

But when we consider the broad scope of trends taking place in these industries, a different picture emerges. Cross training, broader skills, a stronger conceptual understanding of work processes and business operations, increased ability to interact with other employees, and greater scope of action and responsibility among production workers all play a part in the new human resource strategy. Moreover, management must provide workers with incentives to learn these new skills and must manage their employees in such a way as to exploit these new capabilities.

Below I present some steps that will help strengthen the industry's human resources system. Many firms already have experience with some of these practices, but they will have to spread more widely if the domestic textile and apparel industries are to prosper.

First, just as the industry is moving away from an exclusive focus on cutting the price of its products, it should move beyond a human resource strategy based primarily on cutting labor costs and using labor within a rigid, hierarchical employment system. For years these industries thrived on tapping unskilled pools of labor in the rural south, indeed access to this labor was the primary reason why the industries were concentrated in the south. These unskilled workers were brought into an employment organization characterized by rigid hierarchy, although the effects of this were sometimes tempered by paternalism. But I have argued that this system will be increasingly ineffective as firms try to compete on the basis of flexibility, innovation, and fast turnaround time. Moreover, it is important not to forget that as the general level of education in the population rises it will be more difficult to find pools of workers willing to work in tedious and boring jobs in which they are simply expected to show up and do what they are told.

Second, there must be a genuine rather than a cosmetic change. Past experience with work reorganization is instructive in this regard. Many of the attempts to improve the 'quality of work life' that took place in the 1970s fell apart when workers perceived that these experiments were just sophisticated attempts to increase the pace and intensity of work. As I have argued above, some applications of unit production systems in apparel manufacture have the potential to run into this problem. The use of team-based organization can also be abused. Ideally, a team, for example a football team, is a group of cooperating individuals each of whom brings to the group particular skills, aptitudes, and interests. But one can also strap mules together to make a mule team. There is also a danger that this can happen in the garment and textile industries. For example, many managers who try work group experiments hope that peer pressure will force workers to cut down on absenteeism when threats from the boss do not seem to work. The key here is that team members must have a genuine voice in determining how the work gets done and how team members are treated.

Industry leaders might also rethink their relationship to the industry's unions. One of the most successful and widely discussed work reorganization efforts in the country was carried out at an automobile plant in Fremont, California which is owned jointly by General Motors and Toyota. The reorganization was carried out with the help and cooperation of the United Auto Workers Union. Examples of successful union-management cooperation in work reorganization can also be found in apparel and textile firms. (TC)2 was started with the help of the Amalgamated Clothing and Textile Workers Union and is experimenting with various types of work reorganization and is carrying out an active educational campaign to disseminate the results of its work. And a modular organization was recently introduced, apparently successfully, in the cutting room at Joseph & Feiss, a unionized men's wear maker in Cleveland. The union was reported to welcome the change and cooperate with its introduction [19]. Thus some unions have been willing to cooperate with management when management is engaged in a genuine attempt to restructure work and strengthen the company with the help of the workforce.

Third, textile and garment employers must pay more attention to the basic skill level of their workforce. A firm cannot adapt easily to changes in technology, work processes, and products if a large proportion of its labor force cannot read. In many areas, these industries still dominate local industrial employment. As influential local leaders, large employers or employer associations have a unique opportunity to work with the local schools. Their objective should be to help strengthen the general level of literacy and basic arithmetic skills, but also to see that students gain basic technical skills that will provide the foundation for later technical training in preparation for skilled and supervisory jobs in the plants. Some firms are organizing their own basic skills instruction programs, but an adequate public educational system is clearly more desirable. Moreover, as soft goods employers no longer have the pick of the local labor force, they have a particular interest in raising the general level of literacy and education in their labor market areas.

Fourth, although good secondary education is becoming more important, much of the educational problem of the industry will involve training and retraining experienced workers and current employees. Continuing changes in technology, products, market characteristics, firm organization, and production processes will require more frequent retraining and updating of knowledge. Informal training has always been an integral of workplace education, but informal training is primarily useful for passing on knowledge from one group of employees to another. More explicit and organized means are needed for diffusing more rapidly changing skills.

Institutionally this will involve making use of local junior and senior colleges and technical schools, equipment manufacturers, training vendors, consultants, and internal training departments. In developing a training program, firms should keep in mind several objectives.

- Training efforts should guarantee that workers keep up with the latest technologies, but just as important, they should be organized to facilitate the continuous adaptation to the accelerating pace of technological change. Programs to train or prepare workers for new technologies or procedures should be used as opportunities to strengthen their understanding of the basic principles on which those technologies are based. Since equipment vendors are becoming an important source of training, employers might try to work with these vendors to deepen the content of those training efforts.

- Workers should understand the fundamentals of both the overall production process and the business of the firm. Individual employees should have a clear conceptual understanding of the tasks that they must perform and how they fit into the overall process. As much as possible, they should have some idea about the other processes in the plant. Some workers must also have a better conception than in the past of the problems and needs of suppliers and customers. This broader understanding makes workers more adaptable and strengthens the firm's ability to work with other firms in the supply chain.

- The content and organization of training should promote communication and interaction among workers at different levels of the employment hierarchy and in different departments. (In some cases, it would make sense to conduct joint training or seminars with employees of supplier, subcontractor, and customer firms.) If production is becoming more of a group or joint activity, then training should follow suit. Instruction in new technologies of work procedures should include operators, mechanics, supervisors, sales workers, as well as administrative staff. This not only broadens the understanding of individual workers, but it will improve the direct communications among departments and levels that is more important in a product- or market-oriented production process.

- Training should not only impart new skills and knowledge, but it should be an integral part of the process of innovation. For example, the training program that teaches operators, technicians, and supervisors to work with a new technology should also be used to develop ideas about the most efficient way to use that new technology within the particular context of the firm. And if those receiving the training include sales, marketing or design personnel, then the training process could also be used to promote product innovation. This orientation has many advantages. This process for promoting innovation makes the firm more responsive to the market, and helps workers develop a broader understanding of the firm's operations and promotes communication and interaction within the firm.

The ongoing transformation of markets and technology in textiles and apparel, and indeed in many other industries, is challenging the traditional distinction between work and education or learning. Employees at all levels of the firm should be engaged in a continuous process of learning. Firms must be sure that they provide adequate formal training to keep experienced workers and new recruits current, but work procedures and day-to-day workgroup activities should be designed in such a way as to promote learning and innovation. As the textile and garment industries move into a new and challenging era, firms that can make learning an integral part of work will have a strong advantage in both the product as well as the labor market.

REFERENCES

[1] The arguments presented in this paper are developed in greater detail in two monographs: T. Bailey, 'Education and the Transformation of Markets and Technology in the Textile Industry,' Technical Report, 2. New York: National Center on Education and Employment, Teachers College Columbia University, 1988; and T. Bailey, 'Technology, Skills, and Education in the Apparel Industry,' Technical Report Series. New York: National Center on Education and Employment, Teachers College, Columbia University, January 1989.

[2] This argument is developed for the economy as a whole in M. Piore and C. Sabel, 'The Second Industrial Divide'. Basic Books, NY, USA, 1984. For a more focussed discussion of textiles and apparel see B. Toyne, et al., 'The Global Textile Industry', George Allen and Unwin, London, UK, 1984, and Office of Technology Assessment, 'The US Textile and Apparel Industry: A Revolution in Progress', US Government Printing Office, Washinton, USA, 1987.

[3] US Department of Labor, Bureau of Labor Statistics, 'Technology and Manpower in the Textile Industry of the 1970's', Government Printing Office, Washington, USA, 1968, 1578.

[4] R. D. Olsen. 'The Textile Industry', Lexington Books, MA, USA, 1978.

[5] For a discussion of antagonistic relations up and down the supply chain, see 'Report of the MIT Commission on Industrial Productivity: Textile Sector Study'. Unpublished, Massachusetts Institute of Technology, 1988.

[6] Office of Technology Assessment, 1987.

[7] US International Trade Commission. 'Global Competitiveness: The US Textile Industry' The Commission, Washington, USA, 1987.

[8] Kurt Salmon Associates, 'KSA Perspective', Kurt Salmon Associates, NY, USA, 1986, and 'Quick Response Implementation', Kurt Salmon Associates, NY, USA, 1988.

[9] US Department of Commerce, Bureau of Industrial Economics, Capital Stock Data Base.

[10] US International Trade Commission, 1987.

[11] For a more detailed discussion of the limits of technology in promoting a more flexible production system see Bailey, 1988 and Bailey, 1989.

[12] Kurt Salmon Associates, 1988, p. 13.

[13] 'Retailers Move Into the QR Drivers Seat', *Tex. World*, 1987.

[14] For a more general discussion of the development of these types of partnerships see R. Johnston and P. Lawrence, 'Beyond Vertical Integration-the Rise of the Value Adding Partnership', *Harv. Bus. Rev.*, p. 94, 1988.

[15] For a discussion of this see P. Harding. 'Vertical Integration Creates New Breed of Consumer Products Companies', *KSA Perspective*, 1988.

[16] J. Shepherd. 'Mechanizing the Sewing Room', *Bobbin*, p.93, May 1987. See also 'What's Ahead for Weaving Technology', *Tex. World*, p.86, November 1984; S. Smarr. 'Riding their own Coat Tails', *Bobbin*, p.106, June 1984.

[17] See Bailey, 1988 for a more detailed discussion of the changing skills of textile technicians.

[18] Researchers from the Office of Technology Assessment of the US Congress described an interesting example of interaction among firms: 'Individual looms in Dan River's mill are marked for production for specified customers. A Dan River representative was on the floor [so often] at one shirtmaker's plant that he was mistaken for a new employee'. Office of Technology Assessment, 'Technology and the Textile-Apparel Industry,' unpublished case study, October 1988.

[19] J. Abend. 'Modular Cutting', *App. Ind.*, p.60, June 1988.

Educating Managers for Advanced Manufacturing Environments

R. A. Barnhardt

College of Textiles, North Carolina State University

Universities serve many functions and play a central role in society — not because they are the hub of some huge wheel, but because they interact with so many aspects of society. Just as there are large varieties of corporations in the world, there is a large variety of universities as well. The thoughts presented in this chapter represent what is known in the United States as a Research I university which requires a commitment to both teaching and research. By definition, Research I universities offer a full range of baccalaureate programs and give high priority to research. They award 50 or more doctoral degrees each year, and, in addition, they receive annually US$40 million or more in federal support. In addition, the observations are based on the land grant tradition in the United States which further dictates that such a university is responsible for 'transferring' its knowledge to the general public. Thus, the mission of a Land Grant University includes three aspects: education, research, and extension or information transfer.

Many of the thoughts presented in this chapter are related to discussions held between representatives of the College of Textiles and industry executives who occupy various levels and functions within their corporations. When you ask open ended questions, you must be prepared to receive a wide variety of answers which may conflict with each other. In addition, you must recognize that various levels of responsibility within the same company have differing needs relative to the talents and abilities of people they supervise. Thus, these comments are related to graduates in general but from widely different viewpoints.

In general, the comments about the graduates of the College of Textiles were as follows:

(i)   Today's graduates are not as technically competent as graduates of 'X' years ago. From many perspectives this is true. For example, a few years ago the only significant short staple spinning technology was ring spinning. Therefore, the student in a college environment could acquire an in-depth knowledge and understanding of the various aspects of ring spinning. Today, although ring spinning is still very important, additional technologies such as open-end spinning, air-jet spinning, and friction spinning, etc., have been developed. It stands to reason, therefore, that a student will be less competent in any specific technology, but he/she will have a greater breadth of understanding and competency in related technologies. Another example that could be used is that of weaving. A few years ago the predominant weft insertion technology found in the industry was shuttle weaving. Therefore, students could be given a comprehensive understanding and background in this technology. Today one must consider insertion technologies such as grippers, air-jet, water jet, flexible rapier, rigid rapier, plus multi-phase shedding. Other examples could be cited for various types of knitting technologies, dyeing and finishing procedures, etc.

(ii) The more recent graduates are not as 'dedicated' as they were 10 or 15 years ago. They want everything now!! In fact, young people today are often described as the now generation. This is a valid concern, and many psychologists believe the source of the problem is parental actions during child raising. The observation, although valid, can be made for many young people. While industry representatives are willing to accept this explanation, they seem to think that in four or five years college can exert a greater influence on young people than parents have other the child's entire lifetime. This is unrealistic.

Faculty have a similar observation and concern as they interact with today's students. Although the students are extremely talented and academically gifted when compared by conventional means, they tend to be less mature, wanting to do only that which is absolutely necessary. This does not represent the majority of students, but it is a significant number of students. In fact, from my own observations in the classroom, I believe today's students are often structured in a tri-modal distribution with two 'tails' that may be different from previous generations.

This distribution is based on motivation, not on ability. If one couples the highly motivated student with the highly capable student, then some graduates — a growing number — enter industry with outstanding abilities to contribute quickly and substantially to the profitability of their corporations. Many cases can be cited to show the contributions that can be made when proper employment decisions are made. Included in these analyses are talented, mature, and ambitious young people who are eager to assume greater responsibilities quickly. A second key is managers who are willing to give responsibilities to young employees while realizing the risks and employing techniques to monitor decisions and progress without playing a 'big brother' role or second guessing.

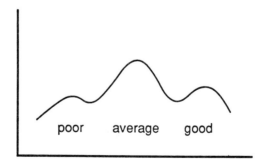

Fig. 1   *Student Motivation*

(iii) Another observation is that young college graduates do not want to work in a difficult manufacturing environment such as the second or third shifts for any length of time. This is the single greatest factor that discourages qualified young men and women from seeking positions in the manufacturing segments of the industry. In the past, there were few alternatives to spending time in off-shift assignments. If you wanted to work in industry, you accepted this as a necessity for career development. The third shift is often a maturing opportunity where tough decisions must be made. Unfortunately, many young people are not told of this; they do not appreciate the valuable experience that is gained through this assignment. I once heard a young alumnus extol the virtues of his third shift experiences. 'I had to make tough decisions. There were employees who tried my managerial capabilities when I wasn't even sure I had any! There were situations where I had to make technical decisions because there was no technical staff present to provide recommendations. I only called the plant manager once during the night. It was obvious that this was not expected except in emergency situations, and I couldn't conceive of such a situation short of having to turn the lights out and shut the door'. As an alternative to off-shifts, many college graduates realize that there are opportunities in the industry that do not require them to spend significant time working shifts, and as long as there are alternatives, many graduates will seek these out. If new people coming into the industry had an idea of the length of service required in some of these assignments, they would be more agreeable to working in the manufacturing environment.

(iv) The graduates of textile colleges today want too many dollars to start; they aren't worth the money. This could be said about any young people beginning a new job. It is a factor of the economy in which we operate. If we want to entice the most capable minds to the textile industry, we must be willing to pay competitive wages with what these same young people can acquire in other industries. When we hire young men and women, we are making an investment in what we believe they can contribute to the companies in the future.

As can be seen in Figure 2, the rate of salary increase for both textile hourly associates and professional new textile graduates entering the industry has grown

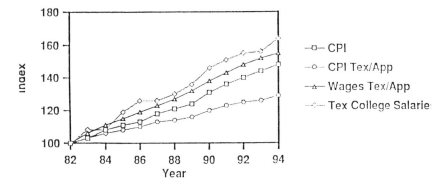

Fig. 2   Indices for Growth

171

at a faster pace and is higher than the Consumer Price Index for textile and apparel products. Thus, the industry is faced with higher wages and suppressed product price growth.

When we look at the graduates of textile programs in the United States, it is evident that alumni of these programs have made major contributions to the textile and allied industries in the United States.

It can be argued that homes and real estate in general are highly overpriced. However, we regard such commodities as an investment in the future which is parallel to the decisions relative to starting salaries for young professionals entering the field as seen in Figure 2.

(v) Young people tend to shy away from manufacturing. This is a valid observation, but the message often sent to young people during the 1960s, 1970s, and 1980s was very clear. The reward system often seemed to favor people with graduate degrees who have worked in marketing, finance, or staff positions. Promotion opportunities through the corporate structure seemed to be less for individuals who had spent a great deal of their time in manufacturing.

(vi) Recent graduates have failed to integrate the college experience. They may have studied a wide variety of subjects, but they have not been able to link concepts together. This problem was identified many times over. It is a failure of the college experience not to have provided opportunities for this. Educators like to think that integration is achieved as it is stated in educational goals and various course outlines. Unfortunately, education seldom achieves this goal or anything near it.

The integration of the college experience is a great challenge. For example, educators have been told for many years that greater emphasis is needed in improving the communication skills of graduates. The response has been to include public speaking and writing courses in curriculums. Unfortunately, this is only a partial solution. In fact, it is an easy response, but not the correct one. Oral and written communications need to be a part of all courses. Without this integration, those subjects will appear to be secondary to many students. Faculty respond that their mission is to teach subject matter or content and that there isn't sufficient time available to cover all of the science, engineering, technology, etc., that is necessary. The truth is that knowledge of these subjects without integration is a disservice to the graduate. On the other hand, knowledge of communications without technology is also a disservice to the graduate. On the other hand, knowledge of communications without technology is also a disservice to the graduate of specialized programs. It is the specialization that differentiates these graduates from traditional college graduates. To use a business example, one might think about value added or differentiated products. Students with specialized knowledge are differentiated graduates.

ATTRIBUTES OF AN IDEAL EMPLOYEE

The second component of these discussions was to ask the manager to describe the characteristics that they would like a young person to have when entering the industry.

In many cases, the terms used to describe individuals were a summation of such attributes as: (a) being technically competent in a wide variety of technologies, with specific in-depth knowledge and experience in one; (b) having great personal skills with particular emphasis on communication; (c) understanding the fundamentals of business with particular emphasis on accounting techniques and financial systems; and (d) acquiring foreign language skills, preferably German or Japanese. When asked to elaborate on these, one manufacturing vice president used the example that whenever his manufacturing or technical managers made presentations to the Board of Directors relative to program or capital needs, his presentations often lacked the professionalism of those presentations made by graduates who had more experience in communication skills.

One of the newest topics to surface when discussing graduate attributes is that of team building and team playing. In this respect, many universities are inadequate. The concept of a 'team' has been an enigma to the university. Team in the past could easily be associated with individual cheating. University education has historically been an individual challenge and accomplishment, and in many disciplines it continues to be so. However, in specialized disciplines teams are often important aspects of the corporate environment. In fact, they may be the most important factor. Having said that we are inadequate, we are taking steps to improve. Many curriculums have a capstone course, which by definition exists to emphasize the integration of the students' experiences in the university. Many graduates indicate that these courses, which often feature team projects, are the highlight to their academic experiences in the university.

From a research perspective, many faculty teams have been created within the past years through the establishment of the National Textile Center. The need for teamwork is understood by faculty who are searching for ways to integrate this into the curriculum. However, at the same time university degrees are awarded to individuals and not to teams. It is a complicated subject matter, but one that deserves a great deal of attention.

Another personality characteristic that is often discussed today is leadership. The art and science of being a good leader is the first requirement of today's C.E.O. Good definitions of leadership abound-everybody recognizes one when they see one. Some people believe they know how to make a leader while others cling to the belief that leaders are born. The truth is probably a mixture of both. Universities have generally taken a passive role, believing that leadership skills are experienced on the athletic playing field or in other extra curricular activities. In fact, many of society's leaders point with pride to their time as student leaders. Unfortunately, not all students have the time or inclination to be involved in campus programs. Therefore, some universities are searching for active curriculum programs that develop leadership skills in students.

In summary, some industry spokespersons are asking, without realizing the far ranging implications, for highly competent young people who are willing to work for 'X'% less than the average starting salary for other graduates, and to spend two to three years in detailed training preparing for an exciting career in the textile and allied industries. Fortunately, this scenario is happening less frequently. The truth is that young people graduating from textile curriculums are first getting jobs. For the College of Textiles, during the 1990s the job placement rates for BS degree students has never been below 90% and has approached 100%. The jobs also have excellent starting salaries. Companies have excellent training programs that are designed to be flexible enough to meet the challenges necessary to keep new employees excited about their future.

There is no doubt that today's managers experience frustrations, and the problems identified are real, but on the other hand, the desired employee attributes may not be realistic. Therefore, one major conclusion that can be drawn is that if we are going to respond better to industry's needs, a better balance is needed between expectations and reality. The universities can and must improve, but we can not change the backgrounds and experiences of students entering the university.

PREPARING BETTER GRADUATES

What can a college of textiles or any specialized educational unit do to respond in a positive manner to the problems identified?

Initially we decided to look at various aspects of this problem, beginning with identifying the major functions of today's managers, and how these might differ from the managers of 10–15 years ago. It is a fact that today's textile and related industries produce a greater number of units with fewer people than in previous years. One might attempt to put these responsibilities into a simple equation:

$$\text{Management} = \text{Produce} > \text{Number Units with} < \text{Resources}$$

The statement could be broken into units of responsibilities: the first component is to produce and the second component is number of units, which are related to manufacturing, productivity, and efficiency; the third component is with fewer resources which has great financial implications. In effect, managers are dealing with products, manufacturing environments, technologies, efficiencies, people, etc. With the number of middle managers being reduced, the managers who remain find that they have a greater number of people to interact with and have a greater amount of capital to be responsible for as well. This is being accomplished at a much faster rate than in the past, and the environment is changing so rapidly, that it is more difficult to manage the information necessary to control all of these parameters. One must only look at the rate of change in the growth of technology and the globalization of the industry to understand what is occurring.

The key item that is truly different and that keeps surfacing is related to computer skills and data acquisition. It is assumed that because we have access to tremendous amounts of data through monitoring capabilities and computer analysis, we can manage more effectively. However, much of these data do not provide any assistance to the manager in making effective decisions. Therefore, although today's manager has more quantitative data to help with decisions, he/she may not have the needed data in a usable form necessary to make important decisions. Or, he/she may be too inexperienced with little or no hands-on experience to make the intuitive decisions that are often the trademarks of a great manager.

Integration of information is the key! Suppliers to the industry have featured 'process information' packages in their equipment, but in many ways we have experienced what it is like to introduce a product that is not quite ready into the market. We have hyped what is needed as if it is what exists. This is a collective 'we'. Computer companies have sold us hardware; software companies have touted the benefits of their programs, and yet the pieces have not come together. In addition, educators describe new programs without clearly indicating that it will take four years or more to introduce their products into the marketplace.

With this scenario's background, those of us in the college environment must educate the young men and women for professional careers in industry and, at the same time, prepare them for leadership positions in the community. Most importantly, today's students must be motivated for continued education which will become more important in a rapidly changing technological environment.

CHARACTERISTICS OF TEXTILE EDUCATION

Textile education is referred to as if it were a single educational process, yet, in fact, curriculum majors include a wide range of programs such as textile and apparel management, textile design, textile chemistry, textile engineering, textile science, and textile technology. Educators have taken a broad subject and compartmentalized it into many individual components. Textile programs by design imply specialization in areas as varied as the textile, fiber, or apparel industries. But, there are many sub specializations within these broad areas that are important. Forty years ago the relationship was simple: a student specialized in textile technology, (i) either spinning or fabric forming, or (ii) wet processing-dyeing and finishing. Synthetic fiber manufacturing followed with its intellectual emphasis on fiber formation including polymer chemistry and extrusion technology. Thus, new curriculums were developed for this segment of the industry. Subsequent programs in textile and apparel management were designed to pay attention to the business and marketing/merchandising aspects of the industry.

For many industrialists, the differentiation among textile majors is difficult to understand with the exception of textile technology and textile chemistry. All employers should carefully quiz potential employees to determine the specific and unique attributes that each discipline has to offer. For example, textile design students should understand both the technical and aesthetic aspects of fabric design. They should have CAD experience and confidence that they can adapt to any computer environment which exists today or will be developed in the future. Good people are hard to find. Good people with particular backgrounds are even more difficult to find.

Given this background, one must carefully construct a curriculum that is committed to educating young people in the broadest perspectives relative to a universal education, and, at the same time, concentrate on a specific career capability such as we have in textiles. In attempting to do so, the curriculum becomes fragmented and it may, in fact, be difficult for a young college student to integrate his/her college experiences.

A general textile/apparel education should have many of the following components:

General Studies	English and Communications
Mathematics & Physical Sciences	Chemistry, Physics, Biotechnologies, Computer Skills
Humanities & Social Sciences	Literature, Psychology, Ethics, Foreign Languages
Business Skills	Economics, Accounting, Financial Analysis, Marketing, Management, Merchandising of Soft Goods, etc.

175

Speciality Technical Subjects	Textile Chemistry, Textile Design, Textile Engineering, Textile Management, Technology, Textile Sciences, TQM, Just In Time, Quick Response, etc.

Unfortunately, given the status of secondary education in the United States, it is often necessary to include some remedial activities at the college level, particularly in the areas of mathematics and English skills, into already broad and demanding curriculums. The task is difficult but achievable, usually through an extension of what is commonly thought to be a four-year program, but which has become five years-often because students choose to make it so as a function of their part-time jobs and a lifestyle they choose to live. This creates a problem since the State has been willing to supplement the cost of higher education for the good of society for four years, but is growing impatient at extending this to five and even six years.

The key to educating managers for advanced manufacturing environments, which is a term that most appropriately describes the future of the textile and allied industries, is that of integration. To the extent possible, all college experiences must be integrated across disciplines. There are lower level courses in all fields that are used for developing an understanding of principles and concepts. These courses may not have an integrating component. However, at the upper levels it is important that students be exposed to the economic aspects of technology in the technical classes themselves. It is also important that communication skills not be overlooked in the technical classes. We simply cannot graduate students who do not understand how the parts are connected and interdependent. Unfortunately, it is believed that this will happen in some magical way in a senior level seminar, which is highly unlikely. Faculty must integrate across disciplines at all levels.

The question that needs to be addressed with the greatest intellectual input is 'Is it possible to expect such a degree of integration and understanding for an average student as opposed to an exceptional student?' In the traditional academic environment, it-may not be a reasonable goal. However, if the academic environment can be modified to include a greater emphasis on teamwork and sharing of knowledge, experience, capabilities, etc., then it is a goal that can be attacked.

In the traditional academic environment, sharing is often equated to cheating. It is feared that students might grow too dependent on the one or two academically gifted who would 'carry the team'. This is possible, but sharing can also be an equal contribution from all members of the team. The team has ways to 'recognize' those who do not contribute. Discussing this with students in the past and trying to implement the concept at the graduate level, one of the problems encountered was that most students find it difficult to depend upon the performance of someone else. In other words, they would rather do it themselves. Thus, the concept is not only a new concept but one that is contradictory to the normal mode of thinking for students and faculty. In addition, there are few models in universities for these types of activities, although most recently it has become apparent that faculty teams are necessary to interact and undertake some of the extensive research activities being funded through research centers. Interestingly enough, private organizations have long recognized the value of this approach.

An additional problem that is faced in academia is that the university is discipline oriented, that is, chemists, engineers, linguists, economists, etc., with little historical preference for interacting among disciplines. The faculty are committed to their disciplines. This is valuable and worthwhile relative to the development of new knowledge in the field, but it may distract from the willingness to cooperate and work together on multi-disciplinary problems.

Finally, it cannot be overlooked that the reward system for faculty clearly emphasizes individual contributions. It is an individual that is tenured and promoted for his/her individual academic contributions in the areas of teaching, research, and service. It is possible that a team member might be penalized in such a decision-making process because it may be difficult to identify the contribution of that individual to the group. This is particularly true for the young aspiring instructor or assistant professor who is developing his/her professional credentials and who is an unknown to the department head, dean, and university officials.

Given the problem identified, can the structure be changed or incentives be provided to faculty to work within a new structure? The key to that answer is to encourage faculty to work on the type of research projects that require multi-disciplinary effort with contributions from various disciplines that transcend departmental boundaries, college boundaries, and perhaps even university boundaries. This can be achieved when faculty believe that their individual contributions will be seen within the broader context or scheme. If properly monitored and analyzed, the teams can be made aware of the contributions of each member, and proper evaluations for tenure and promotion decisions can be prepared.

Organization is important! Industry has gone through a tremendous flattening of its organizations. Some in the university environment might argue that university structure has been flat for many years with decision making shared among the faculty through the committee structure. In effect, this already exists. However, there may be opportunities to further flatten the organization within universities. For example, much can be done through the structuring of many disciplines within a single department-disciplines that by nature have common interests should have common contributions in a highly specialized technical society. We have done this in the College of Textiles by focusing one department in the area of science and engineering along with a second department that focuses on the management and technology components of the textile and allied industries. The linkage between the two departments, and a linkage is essential, is the general integration of the discipline around a core of technology.

A second way to encourage these types of activities is through sponsorship of research activities that demand such an approach. We have helped to foster this at the College of Textiles by our participation in the National Textile Center, which is a consortium of four universities (Auburn University, Clemson University, Georgia Institute of Technology, and North Carolina State University) that work together in consort to form a single organization dedicated to fundamental research in the university to fulfill the research needs of the textile and allied industries. Currently there are 31 projects with over 100 faculty working in teams on various aspects of the projects. The concept of research team efforts has been proven to be effective within the university community, and much effort is being placed now to extend this concept into the academic component of the university experience as well.

This type of research does not pre-empt the traditional individual faculty with one or two graduate students working on a specific area in his/her discipline, but it does provide a model for a broader research effort in projects that are of great interest to industry and a variety of companies within the industry who are willing to support these efforts.

The validity of the model now has been tested and proven to be effective over time. Now that the model is working in research, it will take a number of years before students who have experienced the total benefits of this working research environment will be graduated. Education is an evolving process. There is no right or wrong answer. The correct answer for 1995 may not be the correct answer for 2000; however, it is important to continually look for new ideas and approaches.

No one believes that a textile education in the 1950's would be adequate or even acceptable today to either students or industry. While we can generally agree about what is not acceptable, it is much more difficult to agree upon what is acceptable! The future is unknown and, therefore, preparation for it is unclear. What is clear, however, is that new approaches must be evaluated — implemented and/or abandoned as necessary — while always looking for the perfect combination of experiences that will satisfy the legitimate needs of students and industry.

Training for an Automated Textile Industry

G. A. Berkstresser III and K. Takeuchi

College of Textiles, North Carolina State University

The technological revolution now underway in the textile industry is forcing changes in the areas of capital investment, management, and labor. Automation and robotization imply lower number of workers, but higher skill levels needed and this of course implies radically different training requirements. One problem some organizations have already found is that of trying to decide whether to train completely new employees on the newer, more automated equipment or to retrain older employees. One of the big problems that has to be addressed here is that 'un-learning' time must be added to the time necessary to learn the new technology, and it appears that the longer people have performed with the old technology, the longer it takes them to unlearn that behavior before they can start learning to perform well in the new behavior. According to several mill managers interviewed as the basic research foundation for this paper, the amount of time it took to unlearn the old technology appeared to be highly correlated with the amount of time the person had been working at the old technology so that older workers were more likely to have much more difficulty in this kind of retraining. On the other hand, older workers who had been running machinery that was not completely different than the new machinery but just perhaps one generation removed rather than three and four generations removed were said to have a much easier time in retraining for the new technology.

One phenomenon noted was that the training conducted by machinery manufacturers appears to be necessary for very complicated new technologies. This is a fairly new (during the last two decades) phenomenon in the textile industry. Automobile manufacturers have, of course, been training mechanics for service operations for a very long period of time. Now that textile machinery has gotten very complicated, very automated, and full of electronic components, it seems that textile machinery manufacturers will also have to provide a good deal of training for their new equipment. Of course, this imposes a financial burden on mills that install this equipment since the workers will have to be transported to the training sites and fed and housed at company expense while undergoing the training. It appears that many textile operations recognize that this kind of training must be undertaken because the workers are not going to be trained on just how to operate the machinery but that quality training is combined with operations. Workers will be asked to evaluate not just 'is it running' but 'is it running well'.

Naturally management wants to run machinery on a full time (seven day – three shift) basis. Workers in America want to work Monday through Friday. Automation has certainly changed the lifestyles of workers in some plants. In some cases this is done with great reluctance on part of the workers and is accompanied by continued resentments. In other cases, especially where employee input is sought and compromises are worked out between management and labor, there has been much better success. For example, in some of the newer jobs where the physical demands on the workers are less severe, they find that they can actually work longer hours without becoming exhausted and thus are not as concerned about working an eight-hour shift as they were in the past. On the other hand, workers with children still in school find that working a few twelve-hour shifts frequently deprives them of being able to see their children at all during those days.

One area where there seems to be no disagreement is that all of the plants that are installing more automated equipment feel that they need to upgrade the reading and mathematics skills of the work force. Local community colleges as well as high schools are being used both for onsite training and for formal courses at the educational institutions. One major area involved is in the area of electronics. In past decades, mill electricians were generally concerned with getting power from one place to another safely, but now the emphasis is on being able to repair the complicated electronics that go with the new equipment. Some mill managers feel that they need to have people who can do more than just replace the circuit boards: they must be able to repair them. Many of the textile mills in the South are in small towns at some distance from large metropolitan areas, and if electronics technicians are not able to repair the circuit boards it can mean delays in getting new boards to make the machinery work once again or it can imply maintaining a large and expensive inventory of replacement boards. Most workers, including supervisors, will publicly state that they are always happy to 'get some more education' or participate in various types of training, but frequently it is difficult for management to decide which workers are worth the investment of retraining and how much time and money it will cost to do it. Although management does try to get employee input into areas such as hours and days of work, it is very difficult to get good employee input into the kinds of training to be used because of the constraints with which management is faced.

Another area where it is very difficult to get good employee input is in the area of new machinery purchase decisions. The lack of knowledge about the new equipment, coupled with fundamental resistance to change, makes it very easy for one or two employees to start an active campaign against a new technology before management has even completed its evaluation of this machinery and certainly before any purchase decision has been made. The resistance to change is not only found in the ranks of the operators and technicians. In the new, more highly capital intensive configuration of the textile industry, supervisors are spending less and less time managing people and more and more time monitoring quality and evaluating machinery. Many of the current cadre of first line supervisors in the textile industry in the United States received a great deal of training on managing large groups of people but have received very little training in the areas of monitoring quality and evaluating machinery.

The managers interviewed indicated that they felt that the future of the industry will see a much wider range of pay rates than in past years. The pay rates for operators are expected to remain quite low as more automation takes over more of the boring and dangerous functions while the upper level maintenance and electronic specialists will receive very high wage rates and in all probability move to annual salary pay packages for this level. Fairly short training times can be expected for the operators, but long-term and expensive training times for the upper level maintenance and electronic specialist are anticipated. The use of interactive video for training as well as for trouble shooting will certainly be needed in this new configuration. It is expensive, but firms that will not pay for training will be at a distinct disadvantage. More and more industry wide facilities such as offered by (TC)2 will have to be used for training in the future industry.

Most managers expect to see the following types of shifts in the area of training for the textile industry employees as we approach the 21st century. In the past, most training was done in the plant and we are moving towards more training being done at machinery manufacturers' facilities and in industry-wide facilities such as (TC)2. In the past, the 'hands-on', on-the-job training was the most important part of the training. Larger mills might have had a fairly small training room with one or two major pieces of equipment used for training, but in the future we will expect to see more formal classroom instruction and interactive video training coming along. One of the things that we all must get used to is the shifts in cost. In the past, the training cost per person was fairly low but the high turnover rate in textile employees made total training cost very high. Management recognizes that the new type of training is going to be much more expensive when you look at it on a per person basis so that there is no choice in the matter of turnover. It must be reduced in order to stay competitive. Finally, in the past, most training was done on the basis of teaching people how to operate machinery whereas in the future, the training must be oriented towards how to produce a high quality product.

Titles from The Textile Institute

Woollen Yarn Manufacture

Richards, R.T.D. and Sykes, A.B.
ISBN 1 870812 18 2
1994 GB£35

Published as part of the *Manual of Textile Technology* series, *Woollen Yarn Manufacture* provides a complete account of the woollen system of yarn production, including valuable practical assistance with particular emphasis placed on principles rather than on details of particular machines.

The first part of the book gives a detailed account of the blending process, the first stage in the operation, together with a general description of the woollen yarn system as far as the production of a single yarn. The second part describes in considerable detail the carding and spinning processes in the production of woollen-spun yarns.

Clothing Sizes: A Study of International Sizing Systems

Winks, J.M.
ISBN 1 870812 72 7
1995 c.GB£20

A definitive study of problems concerning international garment sizing, of the accompanying difficulties encountered in commerce and in personal shopping and of their resolution. There is also an insight into the functioning of the relevant ISO Technical Committee of which the author is the Technical Secretary.

Computer Science and Textile Science (TP Vol 26 No 3)

Jayaraman, S.
ISBN 1 870812 62 X
1995 GB£20

Computers and associated techniques are today being used in all facets of the textile product life-cycle, from product design, (both aesthetic and engineering) through development, production planning, manufacturing, quality control and distribution. The concept of computer integrated enterprise is fast becoming a reality.

The author reviews contributions that have had significant influence on the use of computers in textiles, and then explores the current activity that is developing a synergistic relationship between textile science and computer science. Finally, newly evolving possibilities for even more effective synergy between textile science and computer science are discussed.

Stitches and Seams

Laing, R.
ISBN 1 870812 73 5
1995 c.GB£20

Most textiles require cutting and seaming before becoming an acceptable three-dimensional product. With increasing emphasis on objective measurement and specification for a wide range of products, including apparel, the application of current research, design, technology, and analytical methods to seam structure and properties have become crucial. This new book presents a detailed analysis of stitch and seam structures including their performance, surface characteristics and appearance, and test methods. It will provide essential information for anyone who needs to consider the potential and limitations of stitches and seams.

Characterisation and Evaluation of Sensory and Mechanical Properties of Fabrics (TP Vol 26 No 4)

Cassidy, C. and Bishop, D.
ISBN 1 870812 75 1
1995 GB£20

Starting with a brief historical review of early work on fabric characterisation this review will summarise the reasons why the subject is useful, and why it has been so vigorously pursued in recent years. Subject areas include the 'quality' attributes of individual fabrics within a range which are intended for a particular use , the control of textile processing and finishing operations to produce fabrics with specified quality and/or mechanical attributes, prediction of fabric performance in 'making up', prediction of fabric performance in use (e.g. comfort-in-wear, dimensional stability) and finally designing fabric constructions to meet performance specifications.

The bulk of the review will concentrate on the progress made since the early 1970's, looking at Evaluation Techniques, Sensory Methods,

Objective Measurement, Analysis of Data from Subjective and Objective Measurements, Practical Application of Fabric Characterisation Data and Current and Future Directions.

Weaving: Technology and Operations
Ormerod, A. and Sondhelm, W.S.
ISBN 1 870812 76 X
1995 c.GB£45

Weaving is an advanced text book and reference work which completely revises, updates and enlarges Allan Ormerod's Modern Preparation and Weaving Machinery. The book covers all operations from the winding and preparation of the yarn to cloth inspection as well as machine monitoring, buildings and services. The authors look ahead to the requirements of the weaving industry during the next decade and beyond.

Most of the equipment described has been operated under commercial conditions in factories for which the authors have been responsible either as managers or consultants. They have been in charge of many 'green-field' projects involving evaluation, planning and commissioning necessitating a comprehensive and practical approach to the selection and operation of all types of the most modern machinery. All projects — small and large — were designed to obtain optimum overall results in the highly competitive international textile industry.

Protective Clothing (TP Vol 22 No 2/3/4)
Bajaj, P. and Sengupta, A.K.
ISBN 1870812 44 1
1992 GB£30

Reviews recent developments in clothing offering protection against a wide range of agencies and discusses ways in which protection is achieved and tests used to assess the efficiency of the protection.

Barrier Fabrics for Protection Against Aerosols (TP Vol 26 No 1)
Maini, S.M., Hersh, S.P. and Tucker, P.A.
ISBN 1 870812 74 3
1995 GB£20

This review looks at the behaviour and control of aerosols as they influence penetration through fabrics together with the parameters that influence filter performance, such as porosity,

tortuosity, and pressure drop. Analysed and reviewed in detail are the theories of air filtration; the various mechanisms of particle capture and retention by the filter media, and current standard and experimental test methods for measuring filtration of aerosols. The review also takes a look at the effective protection against toxic aerosols under actual working conditions and although research on aerosol filtration through woven fabrics has not been as extensively studied as other areas, it is reviewed.

Quick Response in Apparel Manufacturing
Hunter, N.A.
ISBN 1 870812 30 1
1990 GB£25

Presents the results of industry-sponsored research in America and progress in implementing hard and soft technologies. Focuses on increasing the competitiveness for apparel production in relation to low cost exporting countries.

Globalization: Technological, Economic and Environmental Imperatives
ISBN 1 870812 70 0
1995 GB£100

36 papers presented at the 1994 World Conference in Atlanta, USA examining the ways in which the international textile industry is responding to the challenging issues of globalization, and to the technological, economic, and environmental imperatives now being faced.

Asia and World Textiles
ISBN 1 870812 54 9
1993 GB£100

Papers presented at the 1993 World Conference in Hong Kong looking at the position of Asia, a market and source for textile products; technology; raw materials; investment; and as an opportunity for challenge and wealth.

To place your order for any of the above books or to receive a FREE copy of The Textile Institute's book catalogue *Textile Titles of the World* please contact The Textile Institute Mail Order Book Service, Austicks Bookshops Ltd, 21 Blenheim Terrace, Woodhouse Lane, Leeds, LS2 9HJ, UK. Tel: +44 (0)113 2432446 Fax: +44 (0)113 2430661

Textile Institute Members receive a 20% discount on all of the above titles.